A Green
and Pagan Land

ALSO BY DAVID HUCKVALE
AND FROM MCFARLAND

Music for the Superman: Nietzsche and the Great Composers (2017)

*A Dark and Stormy Oeuvre: Crime, Magic and Power
in the Novels of Edward Bulwer-Lytton* (2016)

Poe Evermore: The Legacy in Film, Music and Television (2014)

Hammer Films' Psychological Thrillers, 1950–1972 (2014)

*The Occult Arts of Music:
An Esoteric Survey from Pythagoras to Pop Culture* (2013)

*Visconti and the German Dream:
Romanticism, Wagner and the Nazi Catastrophe in Film* (2012)

*Ancient Egypt in the Popular Imagination:
Building a Fantasy in Film, Literature, Music and Art* (2012)

*Touchstones of Gothic Horror:
A Film Genealogy of Eleven Motifs and Images* (2010)

Hammer Film Scores and the Musical Avant-Garde (2008)

*James Bernard, Composer to Count Dracula:
A Critical Biography* (2006; softcover 2012)

A Green and Pagan Land

Myth, Magic and Landscape in British Film and Television

DAVID HUCKVALE

McFarland & Company, Inc., Publishers
Jefferson, North Carolina

LIBRARY OF CONGRESS CATALOGUING-IN-PUBLICATION DATA

Names: Huckvale, David, author.
Title: A green and pagan land : myth, magic and landscape in British film and television / David Huckvale.
Description: Jefferson, North Carolina : McFarland & Company, Inc., Publishers, 2018 | Includes bibliographical references and index.
Identifiers: LCCN 2017051745 | ISBN 9781476670508 (softcover : acid free paper) ∞
Subjects: LCSH: Popular culture—Great Britain—History—20th century. | Myth in art. | Paganism in art. | National characteristics, British, in art. | Geographical perception.
Classification: LCC DA589.4 H83 2018 | DDC 941.085—dc23
LC record available at https://lccn.loc.gov/2017051745

BRITISH LIBRARY CATALOGUING DATA ARE AVAILABLE

ISBN (print) 978-1-4766-7050-8
ISBN (ebook) 978-1-4766-2993-3

© 2018 David Huckvale. All rights reserved

No part of this book may be reproduced or transmitted in any form or by any means, electronic or mechanical, including photocopying or recording, or by any information storage and retrieval system, without permission in writing from the publisher.

Front cover: Poster art for the 1973 film *The Wicker Man* (National General Pictures/Photofest)

Printed in the United States of America

McFarland & Company, Inc., Publishers
 Box 611, Jefferson, North Carolina 28640
 www.mcfarlandpub.com

To Markus Wallasvaara

Bring me my Bow of burning gold;
Bring me my Arrows of desire:
Bring me my Spear: O clouds unfold!
Bring me my Chariot of fire!

I will not cease from Mental Fight,
Nor shall my Sword sleep in my hand:
Till we have built Jerusalem,
In England's green & pleasant Land.

(William Blake, "Jerusalem," 1808)

Table of Contents

Preface	1
Introduction: Into the Woods	5
One. The Return of King Arthur	23
Two. Who Is the Grail?	46
Three. The Green Man Cometh…	64
Four. Tristan and Isolde	74
Five. Celtic Twilight	83
Six. The Garden of Pan	104
Seven. Et in Arcadia Ego	129
Eight. The Golden Bough	145
Nine. Witchcraft in the Village	158
Ten. The Road to *Penda's Fen*	179
Chapter Notes	197
Bibliography	207
Index	211

Preface

My aim in this book is to explore the British literature of pagan fantasy that foreshadowed so many celebrated British films. These are the most recent expression of this particular preoccupation of British culture, but such pagan fantasies have also influenced music and the visual arts, to which I will also be casting a passing glance. The films which seem to me to represent this tradition most imaginatively include stories based on Arthurian legend and Celtic mythology such as *Gawain and the Green Knight* (dir. Stephen Weeks, 1973), *Monty Python and the Holy Grail* (dir. Terry Jones & Terry Gilliam, 1975) and *Excalibur* (dir. John Boorman, 1981) and the acclaimed British TV series, *The Owl Service* (prod. Peter Plummer, 1969–1970) and *Children of the Stones* (dir. Peter Graham Scott, 1977). In 2006, the legend of Tristan and Isolde attracted the attention of director Kevin Reynolds, who cast James Franco and Sophia Myles as the doomed lovers in a rather gritty approach to a subject that Richard Wagner had transformed into the world's most revolutionary and influential Romantic opera in 1865.

There are also stories of sacrificial nature worship and ancient magical practices in *Eye of the Devil* (dir. J. Lee Thompson, 1967), *The Wicker Man* (dir. Robin Hardy, 1973) and the television play, *Robin Redbreast* (dir. James MacTaggart, 1970). A third category concerning witchcraft has been particularly appealing to filmmakers, inspiring such classics as *The City of the Dead* (dir. John Llewellyn Moxey, 1960), *Night of the Eagle* (dir. Sidney Hayers, 1962), *Witchcraft* (dir. Don Sharp, 1964), *The Witches* (dir. Cyril Frankel, 1966), *Theatre of Death* (dir. Sam Gallu, 1967), *Witchfinder General* (dir. Michael Reeves, 1968), *Blood on Satan's Claw.* (dir. Piers Haggard, 1971) and *Wakewood* (dir. David Keating, 2010). Nigel Kneale's television drama, *Murrain* (dir. John Cooper, 1975), is also part of this tradition.

Blood on Satan's Claw echoes Lord Dunsany's *The Blessing of Pan*

Sylvan Sacrifice. David Niven as Philippe de Montfaucon is about to be sacrificed in the woods for the good of his vineyards on this German film poster for *Eye of the Devil* (dir. J. Lee Thompson, 1967).

(1927), one of the most successful of all the novels to have exploited the theme of Pan, which was so popular—indeed, something of a cult—around the turn of the twentieth century. Writers variously treated Pan as a symbol of liberation or of terror, all of them anticipated by the now rather forgotten Victorian author Charles Reade, who described the ancient satyr in his novel, *It's Never Too Late to Mend* (1856), as "a black figure with hoof and horns and tail, eyes like red-hot carbuncles, teeth a *chevaux-de-frise* of white-hot iron, and an appalling grin," adding the explanatory footnote, "The god Pan coloured black by the early Christians."[1]

Hammer Films also tapped into the British public school system's preoccupation with classical mythology in its version of *The Gorgon* (dir. Terence Fisher, 1964). Their Gorgon was, however, rather curiously named after one of the Greek Furies (Megera), rather than the Gorgon proper, Medusa; but Medusa later appeared courtesy of Ray Harryhausen in *Clash of the Titans* (dir. Desmond Davis, 1981). *Clash* featured a cast of celebrated British thespians: Sir Laurence Olivier as Zeus and Dames Maggie Smith as Thetis and Flora Robson as a Stygian Witch. The rich and varied British folklore of fairies reached its cinematic culmination in the appropriately named *Photographing Fairies* (dir. Nick Willing, 1997), while the subversive aspect of pagan culture was used to powerful political effect in David Rudkin's now legendary BBC television play, *Penda's Fen*, directed by the even more legendary Alan Clarke in 1974.

However, my approach is by no means entirely devoted to these films and TV productions. For the remainder, I wish to explore how such entertainments emerged from a broader literary tradition of British pagan fantasy, what those fantasies might signify in reality, and specifically how British landscape has informed both page and screen as their principle means of expression (hence the title of what you are about to read).

Introduction:
Into the Woods

The English woods. It is 5:30 on a summer morning. The dawn chorus is beginning its complex Amen, but the Mass is over. Sunlight dapples the loam. Bluebells cluster beneath the ancient oaks, which must have been growing here for over a hundred years. The trees have outlasted all that has changed and weathered, everything that has grown and died beside them. These giants with their richly rutted bark, which spread their canopies of crimped leaves up to the ancient blue, evoke much that is cultural—more so, perhaps, than what is horticultural. Turning to my left at the top of the winding path, I enter the woods proper, and as I walk through this twittering amphitheater towards an area of heather surrounded by towering trees, I am reminded of a passage in Algernon Blackwood's story, "The Man Whom the Trees Loved": The title character is fascinated to the point of obsession with the trees that surround his home. Eventually, the trees absorb him into their own world and his human identity disappears.

> It was one of the breathing places of the forest. Dead, withered bracken lay in patches of unsightly gray. There were bits of heather too. All around, the trees stood looking on—oak, beech, holly, ash, pine, larch, with here another small groups of juniper.[1]

J. R. R. Tolkien must have experienced a similar space, for he places his hobbits in one:

> The leaves were all thicker and greener about the edges of the glade, enclosing it with an almost solid wall, No tree grew there, only rough grass and many tall plants: stalky and faded hemlocks and wood-parsley, fire-weed seeing into fluffy ashes and rampant nettles and thistles. A dreary place: but it seemed a charming and cheerful garden after the close Forest.[2]

I look around me and feel that, yes, this would be a suitable place for a pagan ceremony—even for the kind of human sacrifice that takes place at the end of *Blood on Satan's Claw*, an eighteenth-century tale of devil worship. To emphasize the importance of this film's rural setting, director Piers Haggard framed the main titles with withered bracken fronds, seed heads and leaf-stripped twigs, often filming the characters through a tangle of woodland verdure to suggest their entrapment by the forces of evil around them. In films of this kind, now labelled "folk horror," the landscape is an integral member of the cast.

My mind is also drawn to Sir James Frazer's immensely influential if now somewhat controversial study of comparative religion in *The Golden Bough*. It was first published in two volumes in 1890, and later expanded to a mighty 12 in 1915. In those eloquently written pages, he explored the origins and equivalents of the resonant tale of the Priests of Nemi, Italy, the prehistoric Kings of the Sacred Oak Grove, who had always to be on their guard against usurpers who would slay them.

> In this sacred grove there grew a certain tree around which at any time of the day, and probably far into the night, a grim figure might be seen to prowl. In his hand he carried a drawn sword, and he kept peering warily about him as if at every instant he expected to be set upon by an enemy. He was a priest and a murderer; and the man he sought was sooner or later to murder him and hold the priesthood in his stead. Such was the rule of the sanctuary. A candidate for the priesthood could only succeed to office by slaying the priest, and having slain him, he retained office until he was himself slain by one stronger or craftier.[3]

Frazer's wish to explain why this was so led him on an journey through the world's magical beliefs, and ultimately demonstrated that the king of the woods was the incarnation of a slain and reborn solar god, married through death to the goddess of the Earth. The harvest slays him, spring revives him; and this fertility rite is the backbone of all the world's religions. It is for this reason that the climax of *Eye of the Devil* takes place in the woods, French woods, admittedly, but as we shall see, locations are interchangeable when it comes to woodland landscape, which is of more significance with regard to what it represents psychologically than to any geographical considerations. In *Eye of the Devil*, David Niven's aristocrat, Philippe de Montfaucon, is slain to ensure the recovery of his vineyards, and the woodland setting in which this takes place is a direct echo of the Nemi legend.

One of the elements that later characterized the approach of Hammer Films was appropriately named the Black Park in Hertfordshire. It lies in close proximity to Bray Studios, where Hammer reigned supreme in the 1960s. (*Blood on Satan's Claw*, made by one of Hammer's rivals, Tigon, also exploited the potential of what is now for many horror fans a place of pilgrimage.) Hammer's use of Black Park magnified it into mythical pro-

WOODLAND SACRIFICE. Christopher Lee's Count Dracula prepares to bite Barbara Ewing's Zena amid the sylvan setting of the Black Park. *Dracula Has Risen from the Grave* (dir. Freddie Francis, 1968).

portions, fully evoking the resonance of woodland's archetypal associations.

Appropriately, many of Hammer's heroines and antiheroes are sacrificed amidst this sylvan splendor. Christopher Lee's Creature in the company's first horror success, *The Curse of Frankenstein* (dir. Terence Fisher, 1957), is shot by his creator (Peter Cushing) amid elegiac autumnal foliage. Hapless British tourists are lost in Black Park (standing in for Transylvania) at the beginning of *Dracula—Prince of Darkness* (dir. Terence Fisher, 1966), prior to the ritual sacrifice of one of their number (Charles Tingwell's Alan Kent) inside Dracula's castle. In the third installment of Hammer's Dracula cycle, *Dracula Has Risen from the Grave* (dir. Freddie Francis, 1968), Barbara Ewing's serving maid Zena is seduced beside a tree by the resurrected count in another part of Black Park. In *Vampire Circus* (dir. Robert Young, 1972), a young couple desperate to escape the plague that infects the village of Stetl are fooled by a sinister clown, believing he is leading them to safety, but the lush brackens and woodland canopy through which he guides them lead only to violent slaughter. Maidens are similarly dispatched by another vampire in *Captain Kronos–Vampire Hunter* (dir. Brian Clemens, 1974). All these woodland deaths are distant echoes of ancient woodland rituals.

The English Oak (*Quercus robur*, to give it its Latin name) also reaches down to the very idea of how the British have thought of themselves, inspiring their ideas of strength and solidity. Oak formed the frames of their cottage homes and manor houses, and was, crucially, the basis of the navy that brought them such power. Without the oak tree, there may have never been a British Empire, and without the galls caused by the oak gall wasp, there would have been no long-lasting ink to have written out the Magna Carta, let alone the plays of Shakespeare. Charles II anointed the oak with political significance when hiding in one to escape the Parliamentarians during the Battle of Worcester in 1651. A descendent of the Royal Oak still stands in the park of Boscobel House in Shropshire. In the realm of fantasy, that celebrated Victorian author of so-called "fairy tales," George MacDonald, wrote in his early novel, *Phantastes—A Faerie Romance* (1858): "Trust the Oak, and the Elm, and the great Beech. Take care of the Birch, for though she is honest, she is too young not to be changeable. But shun the Ash and the Alder; for the Ash is an ogre—you will know him by his thick fingers; and the Alder will smother you with her web of hair, if you let her near you at night."[4]

But there is also something sinister about the oak. Oak, after all, is also the name of the burly Scot who carries Sergeant Howie to his sacrificial death in *The Wicker Man* (dir. Robin Hardy, 1973), a film deeply indebted to Frazer's magnum opus. Ironically, this symbol of England was exploited by the Nazis, who also appropriated the oak, decorating their posters and paraphernalia with its magical leaves. In more civilized times, it was under an oak tree that Goethe was said to have written his famous lyric "Wanderers Nachtlied II":

Über allen Gipfeln	Over all the hilltops
Ist Ruh,	is calm.
In allen Wipfeln	In all the treetops
Spürest du	you feel
Kaum einen Hauch;	hardly a breath of air.
Die Vögelein schweigen im Walde.	The little birds fall silent in the woods.
Warte nur! Balde	Just wait … soon
Ruhest du auch.	you'll also be at rest.[5]

The same oak—"Goethe's Oak"—was later incorporated into the Nazi concentration camp of Buchenwald. Prisoners were hanged on it. The remaining beech wood was flattened to make way for the camp, but the Nazis kept the Oak, which symbolized for them what they were fighting for. For the prisoners, it must have seemed a symbol of what they had lost. Only a concrete replica of its stump, provided by the Federal government after the war, remains. Legend has it that when Goethe's Oak fell, Germany would fall with it, rather like the World Ash in the ancient Norse sagas that inspired Wagner's *Ring of the Nibelung*.

Von der Weltesche	From the world ash-tree
brach da Wotan einen Ast;	Wotan then broke off a branch;
eines Speeres Schaft	a spear-shaft
entschnitt der Starke dem Stamm.	the mighty one cut from the trunk.
In langer Zeiten lauf	In the course of a long time
zehrte die Wunde den Wald;	the wound laid waste the wood;
falb fielen die Blätter,	the foliage decayed and died:
dürr darbte der Baum.	the tree decayed and died.[6]

Wotan later piles logs from the World Ash "Yggdrasil" around Valhalla. When they burn, it will bring an end to the gods. M. R. James' witchcraft story, "The Ash Tree [1904], also echoes the magical association of the ash tree, for it is from within the branches of an ash that the hanged witch, Anne Mothersole, exerts her vengeance, spawning supernatural creatures that kill her accuser, Sir Richard.

Trees, as we can see, are powerful symbols; and where there are reassuring oaks, there are also supernatural forces and danger of death. Sacrificial murder, magic, rituals and fairy folk surround them. (Appropriately, the fairies in the film, *Photographing Fairies*, are "discovered" in the spreading canopy of an immense tree in the middle of a magnificent and "magical" forest.)

As much of this book concerns the power of landscape as a means of evoking the various themes I will be exploring, I would like to take a little more time to wander through my imaginary woodland, and discuss why landscape in general is so significant. What does it signify, and why is the geographical location of woodland relatively unimportant when it comes to its place in myth and ritual? Italian, French, German or British, European or American—no matter where woodland is located, each example may easily substitute the other. (Black Park, after all, successfully suggests Transylvania.) Literary descriptions of landscapes are often far more resonant than the experience of actual places. Woodland imagery, regardless of its nationality, carries similar connotations, as does the vocabulary used to describe it, and it is the connotation that matters most. The following description of landscape by Sheridan Le Fanu helps to explain what I mean:

> Steeper grew the banks, higher and gloomier. Precipitous rocks showed their fronts, overtopped by trees and copse. The hollow which they had entered by the old windmill had deepened into a valley and was now contracted to a dark glen, overgrown with forest, and relieved from utter silence only by the moan and tinkle of the brook that wound its way through stones and brambles in its unseen depths.[7]

When writing this poetic description from *The Wyvern Mystery* (1869), Le Fanu may well have been indebted to his memories of reading the Gothic novels of Ann Radcliffe far more than by any real landscape through which he may have passed. The landscape described is fundamentally a literary construct, designed to summon an emotional effect by the use of a specific vocabulary. Obviously, but significantly, the landscape is constructed from words alone. The rocks are "precipitous." The very word suggests a particularly sublime and therefore appealing kind of danger. "Steep" and "gloomier" suggest more than mere physical attributes, implying a particular set of emotional responses. The words in themselves convey the appropriate feeling, bypassing the need for any real, three-dimensional model in reality. The phrase "a dark glen" summons an entire Gothic-Romantic tradition of the sublime, stretching back past the "Wolf's Glen" scene in Carl Maria von Weber's *Der Freischütz* of 1821 to Radcliffe and ultimately Edmund Burke, who largely defined what we now mean by "sublime" in his treatise on the subject in 1757. The words are not merely descriptive of specific details. This is no naturalist's account: Quite the opposite. Details are superfluous, for the words are signposts to a self-contained cultural landscape that resides wholly in language.

Thus we may speak truly of a landscape constructed entirely out of vocabulary in which a dictionary is all we need to navigate our route. As we have seen, individual words can create worlds of feeling—the feelings that natural landscapes may mirror, but which must be viewed with a particular set of expectations if the cultural and emotional complexity of this vocabulary is to be echoed. A description such as in Le Fanu's example represents a particular way of looking at landscape. (Filmmakers similarly transform landscape by means of a particular esthetic: Black Park was made to look much more mythic than it is to a dog-walker who has none of Hammer's films in mind.) The whole point of a literary landscape is that it comes to life in the mind, and explodes there like fireworks, propelling successive connotations through the cultural layers of the imagination. A single word such as "unseen" opens the way to many routes of meaning. It is not quite the same as "invisible," for whatever is unseen is tangible but hidden, and what is hidden, if we continue the pathetic fallacy of personifying the natural world, might be hiding for a reason. To surprise us? To enchant us? To kill us? What is hidden is *occult*. The whole paraphernalia of spiritual terror lurks in this single word; or there could be buried treasure and the excitement of untold wealth. All these possible consequences radiate from one word, and this is the way in which we travel though the landscape of vocabulary, following the many routes of meaning…

Woodland landscape can easily become a metaphor of the dramatic quest for identity, for we work out *where* we are, before deciding who we are. As Frazer so beautifully writes:

In our own country [Britain], the wealds of Kent, Surrey and Sussex are remnants of the great forest of Anderida, which once clothed the whole of the southeastern portion of the island. Westward it seems to have stretched till it joined another forest that extended from Hampshire to Devon. In the reign of Henry II, the citizens of London still hunted wild boar and the boar in the woods of Hampstead. Even under the later Plantagenets, the royal forests were 68 in number. In the forest of Arden it was said that down to modern times a squirrel might leap from tree to tree for nearly the whole length of Warwickshire.[8]

Already, as I walk through my British woodland landscape, I am aware of the power of its symbolism. There is no one else here at this hour, but it takes only one consciousness to politicize this place. Cultural connotations contaminate it, for what was merely a habitat for squirrels and songbirds before I arrived on the scene, becomes, with the presence of just one human mind, mythic and meaningful. The once-strong connections between Britain and Germany, thanks not least to Britain's largely German Royal family, remind me that in both countries their forests have been symbols of the national psyche. In Germany, at least since the eighteenth century, the "German Forest" had been used as a symbol of identity against the perceived corruption of French urbanity; but long before then, there had been the famous battle of the Teutoberg Forest in which Arminius, or Hermann, as he is also known, defeated Varius' Roman army in AD 9. This forest battle became a symbol of German nationalism, and its memory was often resurrected as a mythical justification for later struggles, particularly the Franco-Prussian war in 1871. Hermann's victory was then commemorated by Ernst von Bandel's Hermann Monument, which was completed in 1875, just one year before the première of Wagner's *Ring* cycle at the Bayreuth.

The German forest plays an important role in that work too—particularly in the third opera of the cycle, *Siegfried,* which largely takes place in a forest, inspiring some of Wagner's most frightening but also most lyrical nature music. Wagner and Hermann went on to be used as symbols of German nationalism, through the First World War and into the years of National Socialism; and the Teutoberg Forest was a constant symbol of the reason for those struggles, representing the soul of Germany, at least for those who formulated or agreed with the Nazis' propaganda. The forest is a central image of national identity in the paintings of Caspar David Friedrich, as well as in seminal German Weber's singspiel, *Der Freischütz,* where the forest is an equivocal place of good and evil. Symbolized by the evocative timber of the Waldhorn, Weber's forest is also articulated through key symbolism to suggest its opposing values: C major for the peasants, who live and work in its midst, F-sharp (a tritone away) for the notorious

FAFNER'S FOREST. Joseph Hoffmann's set design for the forest in which Siegfried slays the dragon Fafner in Wagner's *Siegfried* (1876).

Wolf's Glen deep in the heart of the forest, where the Devil is later summoned.

Emerging from this background, the Wandervögel walking clubs (at the turn of the twentieth century) celebrated nature and forests in particular; but they were corrupted by the Völkish ideologies of the National Socialism. Nazi environmentalism might seem to be an oxymoron, but the Nazis were in fact the first Europeans to plant nature reserves and protect hedgerows, as part of the Third Reich's anti-urban ruralism, which was itself a distorted version of a much older Romantic tradition. In 1938, in a pine forest near Zernikow in Brandenburg, Northeastern Germany, larch trees were planted in the shape of a swastika, their golden needles forming a vivid contrast to the darker pines. The design could, of course, only be seen from the air. The offending trees were not felled until 2000, but it was not the only woodland swastika to have been created.

In England, forests similarly became symbols of the nation. Henry VIII planted the New Forest with the sole aim of providing timber for his navy. In Windsor Forest, Falstaff dresses as Herne the Hunter and waits beneath an oak tree in Shakespeare's *The Merry Wives of Windsor*. The Forest of Arden in *As You Like It* becomes a place of sexual freedom, cross-dressing and social chaos. In both instances, these forests became almost mythical embodiments of England, not to mention Sherwood Forest near Nottingham, where Robin Hood became a symbol of that other British myth, fair-play, as well as echoing darker sacrificial traditions.

The entry to the woods has many contradictions, and in many tales it represents the boundary not just between safety and danger but also between the mundane and the transcendental. The entrance is an ancient gateway to the imagination where anything is possible, as Shakespeare demonstrated in *As You Like It*. George MacDonald, deeply influenced by German Romanticism that he was, has the hero of his *Phantastes—A Faerie Romance* enter the imaginative freedom of fairyland via a forest:

> "This," thought I, "must surely be the path into Fairy Land, which the lady of last night promised I should so soon find." I crossed the rivulet, and accompanied it, keeping the footpath on its right bank, until it led me, as I expected, into the wood. [...]
> The trees, which were far apart where I entered, giving free passage to the level rays of the sun, closed rapidly as I advanced, so that ere long their crowded stems barred the sunlight out, forming as it were a thick grating between me and the East. I seemed to be advancing towards a second midnight. In the midst of the intervening twilight, however, before I entered what appeared to be the darkest portion of the forest, I saw a country maiden coming toward me from its depths.[9]

This maiden is the same who has the advice about trusting the Oak and shunning the Ash.

MacDonald greatly influenced C.S. Lewis, whose *The Lion, the Witch and the Wardrobe* (1950) also uses a forest as the barrier between the mundane and the magical. In the first chapter, Lewis' child heroine, Lucy, steps through the back of a wardrobe and finds herself standing in a snowy forest at night. Appropriately enough, the first creature she encounters is a Pan-like faun with a man's torso but hairy goat legs and hoofs instead of feet. Tolkien was equally impressed by MacDonald's metaphor, and wrote in *The Lord of the Rings*, "[T]he Forest *is* queer. Everything in it is very much more alive, more aware of what is going on, so to speak, than things are in the Shire. And the trees do not like strangers. They watch you."[10] The Forbidden Forest in the grounds of Hogwarts in J.K. Rowling's Harry Potter books continued this lineage. Centaurs and unicorns inhabit it, and there are rumors of werewolves.

Like the jungles of Henri Rousseau's primitive paintings, forests are often depicted as landscapes of the unconscious. It was in a forest that

IN THE MIDWAY OF THIS OUR MORTAL LIFE.... Gustave Doré's illustration for Dante's *Inferno* **(London: Cassell, Petter & Galpin, 1866).**

Dante began his journey to Hell in *The Divine Comedy*, which thence led him to Purgatory and Paradise:

> In the midway of this our mortal life,
> I found me in a gloomy wood, astray

> Gone from the path direct: and e'en to tell
> It were no easy task, how savage wild
> That forest, how robust and rough its growth,
> Which to remember only, my dismay
> Renews, in bitterness not far from death.[11]

I have already mentioned the Wolf's Glen scene in *Der Freischütz*: Such forests are often where treasure is guarded by dragons (one thinks of Fafner in Wagner's *Siegfried*) or the impenetrable vegetation of "The Sleeping Beauty." These treasures represent the treasures of our imaginative world, heaped up and placed far beyond the reach of everyday life, which would tarnish them.

Skirting the woods across the open field (where suddenly I come upon a hill, over the brow of which I almost expect to be confronted by a hoard of warriors), I am drawn into the mysteries of the dark spaces to which a nettle bed seems intent on forbidding access. An open space, just before the speaking mouth of the woods, is strangely desolate, inhabited by poppies in the summer but deserted even by them as the year draws on. A path leads up through the antechambers of the woods. There are many doors through which to pass to reach the throne room of this sylvan citadel, where Pan himself perhaps presides. Towards evening, birds sing here but rarely during the day. Descending the slope, I feel that the forest has now claimed me.

As my path winds on, the trees assume an ecclesiastical character, and it is easy to see how all our ideas of columns with their different orders—indeed, our whole understanding of architecture—evolved form the forests of our ancestors:

> Amongst the Celts the oak-worship of the Druids is familiar to every one, and their old word for a sanctuary seems to be identical in origin and meaning with the Latin *nexus*, a grove or woodland glade, which still survives in the name of Nemi. Sacred groves were common among the ancient Germans, and tree-worship is hardly extinct amongst their descendants at the present day.[12]

Tree trunks originally formed the columns of pagan temples. Later transformed into stone, they were decorated with capitals that also derive from natural foliage: the lotus leaves of Egyptian capitals, the acanthus of Roman Corinthian capitals. Trees have always inspired worship. According to Pliny the Elder, the ancient Druids

> hold nothing more sacred than the mistletoe, and the tree on which it grows, provided it be the oak. They choose groves of that tree, and conduct no sacrifice without a garland of its leaves, so that we may possibly suppose the Druids are so called from its Greek name [*drus*]. Whatever grows on the oak is considered a gift from heaven.[13]

The Celtic historian Alexander MacBain, who quotes this passage in his book on the subject, continues:

> Pliny mentions other plant superstitions of the Gauls, connecting the rites naturally enough with the Druids who presided. The next important *fetish* he mentions is the club-moss (selago); it must be touched by no metal, but plucked by the right hand passed through the tunic under the left with a thievish gesture; the worshipper must be dressed in white, with feet washed and bare; and the plant must be carried in a new cloth. The Druids held that it was a charm against all misfortunes, and the smoke of its burning leaves cured diseases of the eye.[14]

In 1930, Edmund Blyth, wanting to create a memorial for friends who had fallen in the First World War, combined the pagan veneration of the ancient woods with Christianity when he planted a tree cathedral near the Bedfordshire village of Whipsnade in England. Having visited Giles Gilbert Scott's unfinished Anglican Cathedral in Liverpool, Blyth was much taken with

> the beauty of its design and the colouring and craftsmanship of its pink sandstone. As we talked of it, we thought what a wonderful and inspiring thing it must be for the workers to be engaged on. We talked of this as we drove south through the Cotswold Hills on our way home and it was while we were doing this that I saw the evening sun light up a coppice of trees on the side of a hill. It occurred to me then that here was something more beautiful still and the idea formed of building a cathedral with trees.[15]

Now owned and maintained by the National Trust, Blyth's tree cathedral contains specimens of ash, beech, birch, cherry, cedar, cypress, horse chestnut, lime, maple, oak, pine, rowan, white beam, willow and yew, all planted to provide the columns of a floor plan for a cathedral, with cloisters, towers, transepts, lady chapel and nave, etc.

Landscape in general is often regarded as a mere backdrop before which we enact the drama of our lives. In fact, landscape is far more significant than that. The desire to find, and even more to *become*, part of the appropriate landscape is much the same urge as our desire to identify with the work of a particular artist or composer. The purpose of landscape, like art, is self-recognition and the articulation of emotion. In itself, a landscape is meaningless. Landscape has no sense of its value to humanity; but when a country is in danger, it is landscape that is called upon to stimulate the idea of patriotism. Human beings are reluctant to act without the encouragement of a mythology. They may never have visited the White Cliffs of Dover or seen the windswept majesty of the South Downs but these were indeed the landscapes that transmitted the *idea* of England to the population at large during the Second World War. When a Russian thinks of the Motherland, his first thought is of the landscape mythologized by Ivan Shishkin's paintings: oaks in the rye, rain in the forest, snow on the firs.

The deserts of the Wild West symbolize the American Dream. It is the same with nationalistic music—the music supposedly of the folk (or at least inspired by it). Folk music, rooted in the land, was politicized by Chopin and the "fake" folk music of *Finlandia* made Sibelius a national hero. Though landscape itself remains apolitical, as soon as the idea of nationhood is applied to it, it becomes charged with patriotic meaning. Even an essentially dissenting text such as Blake's "Jerusalem" uses landscape in this way. "England's green and pleasant land" is already a political phrase. What was merely green and pleasant has become nationalistic, even more so when Parry set those words to a stirring melody that also has its roots in folk-song.

Landscape symbolizes the idea of freedom; but who had the freedom to walk through these landscapes? The miners of Nottingham? The dockers of Liverpool? The weavers of Lancashire? Like those descriptions of Venice by Poe and Ann Radcliffe (neither of whom had ever seen their model in reality), the *idea* of such an environment was actually far more significant than being there in person. Political belief, like any other, is driven by emotion—a force that dwells within the unconscious, and which impresses itself upon the world. Landscape therefore represents an *idea*.

Richard Wagner, an artist to whom many respond with a similarly profound sense of recognition as they do to nature itself, was very popular in England, particularly before the outbreak of war with Germany in 1914. Wagner nights at Covent Garden were almost *de rigueur* in Edwardian London. Actor Sir Henry Irving wished to surpass the astonishing stage effects created by Wagner at Bayreuth, and his production of *Faust* at the Lyceum in 1886 was his response to Wagnerian stagecraft. Wagner's influence on British culture was so powerful that it seems appropriate to dwell a little longer on his *Ring* cycle here, as it provides a useful example with which to explore further the power of *conceived*, as opposed to *real* landscape, which is so important in British pagan fantasy. Landscape is the pivot and motivation of the *Ring*: *Das Rheingold* flows *out* of the river Rhine. The landscape is then penetrated (by descending into Nibelheim), and subsequently we rise above it across a rainbow bridge to Valhalla. *Die Walküre* begins with a storm and, after a domestic interlude, ascends once more into the mountains to end in resplendent magic fire. *Siegfried*, as I have already suggested, is a portrait of the fabled Teutonic forest, while *Götterdämmerung* depicts the landscape of civilization only to destroy it in a final deluge, bringing with it a cleansed and resurrected natural world.

Wagner's original approach to the realization of these mythic (because essentially emotional) landscapes on the Bayreuth stage was pictorial realism.

The imitation of nature that characterized the 1876 Festival was designed by Joseph Hoffmann and brought to life by the famed Brückner brothers (the Warner Brothers of their day with regard to their technical sheen). But apparently the performances did not live up to Wagner's ideal. "Next year, we will do it all differently,"[16] he decreed, much to the delight of subsequent conceptual directors who sought to justify their sometimes wayward approaches to Wagnerian *mises en scènes* with those very words. Exactly what Wagner himself wanted to replace his original production designs with remains a mystery, and it is not at all clear whether he was dissatisfied with the naturalistic illusion of reality *per se*, or merely this particular example of it by means of painted flats. Perhaps, judging by a remark recorded in Cosima Wagner's Diaries, he had given up on any satisfactory realization of his imaginative vision: "Oh, I hate the thought of all those costumes and greasepaint! [...] Having created the invisible orchestra, I now feel like inventing the invisible theatre!"[17]

Whatever Wagner had in mind, it wasn't long before independent designers took issue with the conventional spectacle of the steam-shrouded illusions in the Bayreuth *Ring*, and started to suggest that the real landscape of the cycle was actually much more *psychological* than literal: the landscape of emotion, which demanded something much more abstract than the overloaded, conventionally Romantic and, some would say, redundant detail of the original conception. Swiss stage designer Adolphe Appia (1862–1928) entered the arena with his three-dimensional approach involving blocks and steps, which not only complimented the three dimensions of the performers (the two-dimensional flats, he argued, had cancelled them out), but also, by means of subtle lighting effects diffused through walls of gauze, articulated the emotional moods of the musical landscapes far more sympathetically than any amount of Romantic naturalism could achieve. Such naturalism was redundant, according to Appia, because Wagner's thunderstorms and forest murmurs, water and fire were already sufficiently vivid in the music and did not require a literal correlate onstage. What such profoundly emotive tone painting did require was an *emotional* correlation. Appia's abstract landscapes, therefore, articulated his emotional responses to Wagner's musical landscapes.

In this respect, nature imitates art: A landscape only has esthetic value if we can use it to articulate a state of mind. The idea of exploiting landscape to educate, to use it as a means of moral instruction—in other words, as a form of philosophy—has a parallel in the horticultural symbolism of the alchemical rose gardens of the Middle Ages, along with the knot gardens of monasteries, with their evocation of paradise, and the religious symbolism of flowers (the lily, the passion flower and the pansy as symbols of the Holy Trinity). Indeed, the idea of the secret garden was a verdant version of the priest hole for Catholic families in times of trouble. Such landscapes are again projections of human aspiration onto the unknowing and careless framework of nature. The fact that paradise is usually referred to not in cultural but horticultural terms, suggests that since the original concept of the Garden of Eden, we have exploited landscape to express moral and emotional concerns. Landscape has become the screen onto which we *project* our desires; and no better account can be found of the fact that nature truly is indifferent to our activity than in the *Torture Garden* (1899) of Octave Mirbeau. There, amid a paradise of flowers and scents, the most refined of human tortures are enacted, the most refined of cruelties having no impact on nature's most exquisite creations. Mirbeau describes "gentle slopes, sown like lawns, [...] pink crucianella, roses the color known as old rose, and fields of arborescent peonies like sumptuous carpets,"[18] against which he sees carried past "a bundle of bleeding flesh; a sort of human being, whose skin, cut in strips, trailed on the ground like rags."[19] Nature is therefore only ever symbolic and lends her symbols to us with a careless smile. She cannot share in human motivation, still less in our depravities. Her only interest is in what is necessary. Ideals have no relevance to her, still less a meaning, for she cannot comprehend our universe of right and wrong, and smiles alike on saint and sinner, before destroying either if that is her whim.

 I have perhaps labored the point, because all our responses to landscape are fundamentally psychological, and landscape is the primary focus of my approach in this book. Human beings have always lamented the passing of a golden age, but in England this seems to have been intimately tied up with the industrial revolution it initiated. By the turn of the twentieth century, this became pervasive. Kenneth Grahame (1859–1933) entitled his own recollections of childhood *The Golden Age*, prefacing his memories with these words: "A saddening doubt, a dull suspicion, creeps over me. *Et in Arcadia ego*—I certainly did once inhabit Arcady."[20] Folk song collecting, Morris dancing, the country pub, billowing Queen Anne's Lace lining meandering lanes, low horizons and what Philip Hesseltine said of Vaughan William's "Pastoral" Symphony ("A hymn to Pan, with no sound of sorrow"), *The Lark Ascending*, fantasias on "Greensleeves" and themes by Thomas Tallis, teapots and gardens, village greens, cricket matches and warm beer, amateurs and eccentrics, roses around the door and crumpets by the fire, of hedgerows and jam for tea, and the clock at Grantchester still at ten-to-three—all these are part of the myth of England. British patriotic hymns rise through a *crescendo* of emotion just before a musical stiff upper-lip puts a lid on it. "Jerusalem," "I Vow to Thee My Country"—each with their dying fall, their sense of being left high and dry, rather like the manner of British civil servants in India during the Raj. Sentiment, for which the severities of colonial life or the hardships of public school provide no place, always used to simmer secretly in British hearts. Perhaps the British are now past being nostalgic, being merely bewildered, their history now so thoroughly dismembered by modernity that it ceases to have any real cultural significance, living, as so many do, in the perpetual "present" of shopping. There is a difference between cultural continuity and nostalgia. Myth lies somewhere between the two.

One might even be tempted to suggest that the landscape of myth is more significant than the mythic events that unfold before them. The landscape of King Arthur was revived by the Victorians to counteract the landscape of Godless industrialism. Significantly, Gustave Doré's illustrations for Tennyson's *Idylls of the King* (1868) are landscapes rather than conventionally dramatic scenes depicting action and narrative. The events and characters of the poem seem to have been of far less interest to Doré than the settings in which the action takes place, as if he too felt that it was in the latter that the real emotional value of the narratives lie.

Out of the Arthurian revival came the Celtic revival, at the head of which stand writers such as the poet W.B. Yeats (1865–1939) and William Sharp (1855–1905), who also wrote under the pseudonym Fiona Macleod. Macleod's poems and prose pieces are indeed primarily about landscape and its emotional effect. *The Wicker Man* and David Rudkin's pagan and highly political television play, *Penda's Fen*—even Peter Dickinson's series of novels, later televised for children under the title *The Changes* in the 1970s, show just how much landscape has been the principal feature of the pagan revival fantasy: a yearning for pre-industrial society, using landscape to subvert urban authority. "Pagan" originally referred to being "of the village" as opposed to the metropolis, and hence being of the people rather than of the politicians. Landscape can be *subversive*. As Rudkin makes clear in his play, an assault on the landscape (the building of nuclear bunkers beneath it) is an assault on the people's very identity—on their political and imaginative freedoms. It is no accident that a "Christian copper" from the Scottish mainland was chosen as the sacrifice to save Summerisle's apples in *The Wicker Man*, a film that also points out how the worship of nature can lead to dangerously irrational practices, much as Blood and Soil ideology did in Nazi Germany.

"How do I love you?" Stephen, the hero of *Penda's Fen*, asks of England at the very beginning of the play. What kind of patriotism will Stephen follow? The orthodox one, which seems to be a lie, or the pagan one, which seems to be a metaphor for imaginative freedom rather than an appeal to create a community like that presided over by Lord Summerisle? It is through landscape that all this is articulated: the immense emotive power of *place*, of the setting sun, of hedgerows in twilight, of fields of corn, of rain on the river, of the country churchyard, of angels on reed-flanked river banks, and, in other aspects of the Pagan revival, even of Pan himself. In late nineteenth-century Germany, Pan lent his name to an influential art journal featuring the paintings of Arnold Böcklin and Franz von Stuck. In Britain, Pan made his presence felt, appearing in works as diverse as Arthur Machen's *The Great God Pan* (1890), Kenneth Grahame's *The Wind in the Willows* (1908), E.F. Benson's *The Inheritor* (1930) and Dion Fortune's occult romance, *The Goat-Foot God* (1936). There was just as much a cult of Pan as there was of the Grail, and both found nourishment in a simultaneous occult revival, thanks to organizations such as the Order of the Golden Dawn. Its most infamous member, Aleister Crowley, wrote his own hymn to Pan in 1913. Crowley was also fascinated by Frazer's once scandalous *Golden Bough*, and wrote perhaps the first fictional response to that work (predating the more famous Frazer-inspired novels of Mary Renault and Robert Graves), under the title *Golden Twigs* (1916). Crowley's reworking of Frazer also predated T.S. Eliot's use of Golden Bough imagery in his classic modernist poem, "The Wasteland" (1922). Later in the twentieth century, all these strands found their way into the British cinema and television, culminating in *The Wicker Man* and *Penda's Fen* at a time in the 1970s when the very idea of England was under threat from economic depression, modernism, urbanization and technology. When Hammer Films attempted to revive its fortunes in the early years of the twenty-first century, it returned to the tried-and-tested formula of rural horror with *Wakewood*, which looked back to *The Wicker Man* and Hammer's much earlier *The Witches*. *Wakewood* is indeed a brilliant study in the power of landscape in articulating emotion and identity.

Britain might now seem no longer to be defined by its pagan heritage, having suffered from the commercialization and kitschification of its folk traditions. What was once called "folk music," and sung in pubs and harvest festivals, has become the "pop" music that pervades every aspect of British life in shops, restaurants and iPods. The British still gather at ancient sites but worship instead the modern musical gods of the Glastonbury Festival; floral tributes furnish the urban and rural landscape of anonymous roads and motorways, commemorating the dead in a modern form of roadside shrines; while the 1997 death of Princess Diana seemed to echo ancient lamentations over the immolation of a pagan god. Diana's death seemed also to have been a kind of sacrifice on the altar of the popular press. An outbreak of foot-and-mouth disease in 2001 created not only horrific imagery of rural horror with the cleansing by fire of infected cattle, but also a very ancient kind of mass hysteria. Woodland paths were closed and roads were blocked far in excess of the actual threat posed by the problem; and the memory of witch hunts still haunt British life in the shape of DJ and TV presenter, Jimmy Savile, whose breathtaking sexual crimes, immense fame and social prestige many have since suggested were the result of actual magical processes: Savile as a modern-day Aleister Crowley. The corruption of British folk traditions might be typified by the fate of King Arthur. Camelot is now the name of the company that controls the National Lottery, and Arthur, Guinevere, Lancelot and Merlin are the names of Camelot's lottery draw machines.

ONE

The Return of King Arthur

God died in the nineteenth century. Denied by Shelley in 1811, slain by Darwin in 1859 and buried by Nietzsche in 1883, Thomas Hardy read out God's funeral oration in the form of a poem called "God's Funeral" in 1910. God has been reanimated by many a fundamentalist Frankenstein since then; we are now forced to ask ourselves if God really does "belong dead," as Boris Karloff's famous Monster once put it. For many people, of course, God is not dead, and they worry about those who think He is. People in the nineteenth century also worried about the possibility of a Godless universe.

What do you do when someone you love and depend upon, dies? Some people move on. Others go into denial and pretend that nothing has changed. They memorialize. A few mummify the corpse. Others keep the death chamber exactly as it was when the loved one died, which is exactly what Queen Victoria did when she lost her beloved Prince Albert. The revival of interest in King Arthur during Victoria's reign might also be connected to a similar sense of mourning and denial. The crisis of faith created by scientific advances and their implication left an emotional vacuum, which multitudes felt had to be filled if things were not to implode. The religious instinct was still there, but it had increasingly fewer justifications. Hence the rapid construction of so many churches in Victorian England. Evangelism always has something neurotic about it, and Victorian evangelism was particularly neurotic. The fervor with which these neo-Gothic structures were constructed suggests a kind of desperation. When one senses an enemy, one stockpiles arms; when one senses a collapse, one patches the cracks and builds buttresses to contain walls that bulge under the weight of doubt. Victorian church-building was just such a buttress. King Arthur was another, who came to the rescue as legend always said he would.

The Victorians were not the only people to have rallied around the legend of King Arthur to bolster their own confidence and identity. In 1344, Edward III attempted "to recover the memory of King Arthur to restore the honor of the Round Table, that he might inflame the minds of his own lords with military glory."[1] The attempt failed but it led to the creation of the Order of the Garter. Evelyn Eaton's historical novel, *The King Is a Witch* (1965), describes how Edward arranged the pageant:

> Along the riverside and the principal Ways, the houses were hung with silks, and banners of brightly colored cloths and tapestries, representing scenes from the Arthurian legends. Merlin was there, the Knights of the Table Round were there, the Hallows were there, Joseph of Arimathea and Alain the Son of Brons, the Keeper King and Perlesvaus, were there. The Enchantments of Britain were there. Swords, castles, trees, ships, horses, birds, were there. The Grail was there.[2]

In Victorian England, Alfred Lord Tennyson's own feelings of doubt and depression were also drawn by Arthur's magnetic attraction. He could not deny that his beloved friend Arthur Hallam was dead, and Tennyson (1809–1892) was desperate to find a way of dealing with the loss. Life was bad enough without Hallam, but a life without God would surely be unendurable:

> He is not here; but far away
> The noise of life begins again,
> And ghastly thro' the drizzling rain
> On the bald street breaks the blank day.[3]

Tennyson was referring to Hallam's absence here, but his fear that God might also be just as absent was made explicit in a later stanza from *In Memoriam* (1849). This interestingly anticipates Darwin's *Origin of Species* by ten years, inspired as Tennyson had been by Robert Chambers' *Vestiges of the Natural History of Creation*, published in 1844:

> "So careful of the type?" but no.
>   From scarped cliff and quarried stone
>   She cries, "A thousand types are gone:
> I care for nothing, all shall go."

"Nature, red in tooth and claw"—perhaps *In Memoriam*'s most famous line—caused Tennyson much anguish. "Are God and Nature then at strife?" he asked.

> I stretch lame hands of faith, and grope,
>   And gather dust and chaff, and call
>   To what I feel is Lord of all,
> And faintly trust the larger hope.[4]

Tennyson's fears here foreshadowed the existentialists, but they were still only that: fears, not *doubts*. Tennyson preferred to blame Nature, rather than God, who might still not be responsible for Nature's excesses and carelessness. Nietzsche later insisted that as God did not exist, He had nothing to do with Nature's seeming evils; and as there is no God, neither can evil exist in Nature, which is motivated purely by necessities. Tennyson, however, hoped somehow to disentangle God from Nature. Faith eventually triumphed, and it was King Arthur who inspired him to that victory.

Arthur, however, emerged from a murky pagan past, and came to power thanks to the pagan magic of Merlin. Walter Evans-Wentz was firmly of this opinion in his influential 1911 study, *The Fairy Faith in Celtic Countries*:

> The evidence now set forth seems to suggest clearly and even definitively that Arthur in his true nature is a god of the subjective world, a ruler of ghosts, demons and demon rulers, and fairies; that the people of his court are more like the Irish *Sidhe*-folk than like mortals; and that as a great king he is comparable to Dagda the over-king of the Tuatha De Danann. Arthur and Osiris, two ultra heroes and sun-gods, as we suggested at first, are strikingly parallel. Osiris came from the Otherworld to this one, and then returned to the Otherworld, where he is now a king. Arthur's father was a ruler in the Otherworld, and Arthur evidently came from there to be the Supreme Champion of the Brythons, and then returned to that realm whence he took his origin, a realm which poets called Avalon. The passing of Arthur seems mystically to represent the sunset over the Western Ocean: Arthur disappears beneath the horizon into the Lower World which is also the Halls of Osiris, wherein Osiris journeys between sunset and sunrise, between death and re-birth Merlin found the infant Arthur floating on the waves: the sun rising across the waters is this birth of Arthur, the birth of Osiris.[5]

Arthur nonetheless became a Christian champion of all that Tennyson felt was being eroded by industrial modernity. Indeed, Arthur became a personification of Christianity itself, which had similarly grafted its morality, myths and rituals on pagan models, claiming them as its own.

Tennyson was not the first nineteenth-century gentleman to be thus inspired. Chivalry had been made popular by the novels of Sir Walter Scott, and mock medieval tournaments had been staged by eccentrics such as Kenelm Henry Digby (1800–1880) and Archibald Montgomery (1812–1861), the 13th Earl of Eglinton. Digby wrote a best-seller in 1822, *The Broadstone of Honour, or Rules for the Gentlemen of England*, which he professed to be "a guide for manly living"; but Tennyson's attraction to Arthur was perhaps the most personal. He had intended to write an Arthurian epic when he only 24 years old, and like Wagner, who wrote the *Ring* cycle in reverse order, beginning with Siegfried's death, Tennyson started with the "Morte d'Arthur," long before he began work on *Idylls of the King*. The subject of Arthur's death was an ideal way of expressing his grief over Hallam's passing:

> Ah! my Lord Arthur, whither shall I go?
> Where shall I hide my forehead and my eyes?
> For now I see the true old times are dead,
> When every morning brought a noble chance,
> And every chance brought out a noble knight.[6]

Tennyson prefaced the "Morte d'Arthur" with a contemporary metrical conversation between a group of friends one Christmas Eve: a parson, a poet, a host and presumably Tennyson himself. Geology and schisms in the church form one of the topics, which lead inevitably on to the "general decay of faith/Right thro' the world."[7] The lack of an anchor "[t]o hold by" is noted. The fictional poet, by the name of Everard Hall, has already achieved Tennyson's ambition of a 12-volume Arthurian epic but has burned it.

"Why take the style of those heroic times?" he asks,

> For nature brings not back the Mastodon.
> Nor we those times; and why should any man
> Remodel models? These 12 books of mine
> Were faint Homeric echoes, nothing worth,
> Mere chaff and draft, much better burnt.[8]

His friends think otherwise and ask for a rendition of the fragment that one of them rescued from the hearth, and this forms the main body of the poem. The key line in the epilogue that follows the "Morte d'Arthur" is the comparison Tennyson makes between his medieval hero and "a modern gentleman."

"Arthur is come again: he cannot die." And with that pronouncement, "clear church-bells ring in the Christmas morn."[9] The conflation of Arthur, the Victorian gentleman and Christ's birthday form a powerful constellation. Arthur had indeed come again to rescue the Victorians, who were soon to reel and even totter on the brink from the shock of Darwin's implications. But Tennyson's Arthur steadied them and became the model for the Victorian ruling classes. King Arthur was the perfect gentleman, as well as God's ambassador on Earth, allowing Tennyson to give full expression to his bolstered faith. "Yes, it is true," he told his son in 1869, "there are moments when the flesh is nothing to me, when I feel and know the flesh to be the vision, God and the Spiritual the only real and true."

> Depend upon it, the Spiritual *is* the real: it belongs to one more than the hand and the foot. You may tell me that my hand and my foot are only imaginary symbols of my existence, I could believe you; but you never, never can convince me that the *I* is not an eternal Reality, and that the Spiritual is not the true and real part of me.[10]

One. The Return of King Arthur

In *Idylls*, Tennyson's spotlight falls on chivalry—the ideals of hierarchy, obedience, responsibility, generosity, playing the game: all the attributes of *noblesse oblige*, indeed; and these were the qualities of the poem most admired by his contemporaries, who also saw their own work ethic reflected in Tennyson's king. (It was Prince Albert's idea to have Arthurian subjects painted on the walls of the Royal Robing Room Westminster Palace, where the monarch puts on a crown for the opening of parliament.) "England's Michelangelo," as Wilfrid Blunt called the artist G.F. Watts (1817–1904), based one of his most celebrated paintings on Sir Galahad, the "bright boy knight" who, like the hero of Thomas Hughes' *Tom Brown's Schooldays*, never gives up in his struggle against adversity. Sir Galahad was kind of a Boy Scout prototype, and it was perhaps inevitable that prints of Watts' painting were handed out to Eton schoolboys when they left their alma mater, some of them to join the Boer War. (Watts' image was also used to help "sell" the First World War.) And fully in accord with the immense double standard of Victorian ideals regarding the role of women in society (they were either Madonnas or Fallen Women—one slip was enough), Tennyson made Guinevere entirely responsible for Arthur's fall.

Worse, Arthur, like Prince Albert (to whom the poem is dedicated), turns out to be a crashing bore, as anyone would be if they remained completely faithful to these new demanding commandments:

> To ride abroad redressing human wrongs,
> To speak no slander, no, nor listen to it,
> To honor his own word as if his God's,
> To lead sweet lives in purest chastity,
> To love one maiden only, cleave to her,
> And worship her by years of noble deeds.[11]

Tennyson makes Arthur childless to maintain his stainless state. Even Mordred is no longer his illegitimate son. Those who do not live up to his ideals of placing duty before desire are punished. Elaine fails to obey her father and falls in love with Lancelot, ultimately dying from a broken heart. Enid, however, puts up with her suspicious husband Geraint, who falsely accuses her of infidelity and drags her off with him into the wilderness, which she endures submissively and without complaint. Tennyson also made sure that Lancelot, whose dalliance with Guinevere outraged Victorian propriety, suffers suitable pangs of guilt and feelings of self-hatred. She in fact rather resembles Wagner's second wife, Cosima, in her endless self-lacerations:

> The shadow of another cleaves to me,
> And makes me one pollution: he, the King,

> Call'd me polluted: shall I kill myself?
> What help in that? I cannot kill my sin,
> If soul be soul; nor can I kill my shame;
> No, nor by living can I live it down.[12]

Cosima, similarly, was always tormented by the guilt of abandoning her husband Hans von Bülow for the greater genius of Wagner, who was not always kind to her.

Even the end of Arthur resonated with the Victorians, who feared the future that would emerge from their rapidly changing and increasingly Godless world. Alas, their fears were proved correct by history, for after Victoria died, Europe drifted ever closer to the First World War and the destruction of everything hitherto held sacred. However, the bright Christian lamps of virtue and morality did not prove to be as influential on the later Celtic Revival as the wilder shadows in Tennyson's texts—those aspects of landscape and pagan magic, which would ultimately nourish such cinematic visions as John Boorman's *Excalibur* and ultimately the pagan fantasy of *The Wicker Man*. Tennyson's perspective was deeply Christian, but it was the strands of pagan magic and landscape that decorate his Arthurian poems that formed the basis of the Celtic Revival, which increasingly turned away from Christianity. Chaucer had referred to the pagan aspect of Arthurian legend several centuries earlier, in the Wife of Bath's Tale from *The Canterbury Tales,* which Thomas Keightley in his *Fairy Mythology* regarded as "evidently a Fairy tale."

> In oldè dayès of the king Artoúr,
> Of which that Bretons spoken gret honoúr,
> All was this lond fulfilled of faërie;
> The Elf-quene with her joly compagnie,
> Danced ful oft in many a grenè mede.
> This was the old opinion as I rede;
> I speke of many hundred years ago.
> But now can no man see non elvès mo.[13]

Significantly, it was, I think, the pagan element and the succinct but resonantly suggested landscapes in Tennyson's texts that inspired Gustave Doré's famous illustrations for *Idylls of the King* far more than the heroic events, love affairs and Christian morality of the characters. Nearly all of Doré's images feature sublime vistas: seascapes, castles on craggy mountains, dark forests, flowery meadows and romantic waterfalls. Doré (1832–1883) recognized that the power of landscape was far more evocative of the power of myth than its mere events. Some critics felt that Doré's insistence on landscape over action implied that he had not bothered to read the poems.

A horror lived about the tarn, and clave/Like its own mists to all the mountain side. Gustave Doré illustration for Tennyson's *Idylls of the King* (London: Moxon, 1868).

Tennyson was apparently of that opinion too, not being entirely satisfied with the result either.[14] We will never know how far this was the case, but to give Doré the benefit of the doubt, Tennyson's descriptions of landscape, relatively brief though they are, are among the most powerful elements in the poems, and are certainly of immense importance in creating a mythic as opposed to a merely heroic mood.

As I have already mentioned, natural landscapes are of even more importance in Wagner's *Ring* cycle, which was conceived and written at the same time as *Idylls*. Indeed, Tennyson's poetic cycle is really the English equivalent of Wagner's tetralogy, the music of the former residing in Tennyson's remarkably mellifluous diction. There is much to be said for Wagner's use of the alliterative form of Stabreim in his *Ring* texts, but there is no denying that Wagner's texts require the associative magic of his music fully to come to life. This is exactly what Wagner intended, of course, but that is not the case with the notoriously unmusical Tennyson, whose writing is perfectly self-contained. Like the first of the *Ring* dramas, *Das Rheingold*, the story of Tennyson's Arthur begins with water imagery (not that the Idylls themselves follow a chronological order, presenting, as they do, various aspects of the story in non-chronological narrative sequences, often in the form of reminiscence). Thus, the infant Arthur is washed up on the Cornish shore, like a pagan Moses, though Tennyson implies that Arthur is quite literally a gift of the gods, who seem to form the crew or passengers of the ship that brings him:

> It seemed in heaven, a ship, the shape thereof
> A dragon wing'd, and all from stem to stern
> Bright with shining people on the decks,
> And gone as soon as seen.[15]

The ocean, like Wagner's E-flat rumination for the river Rhine, swells and swirls before Merlin, who observes the scene:

> Wave after wave, each mightier than the last,
> Till last, a ninth one, gathering half the deep
> And full of voices, slowly rose and plunged
> Roaring, and all the wave was in flame:
> And down the wave and in the flame was borne
> A naked babe, and rode to Merlin's feet.[16]

Doré captures the scene wonderfully, with towering cliffs and tempestuous waves beneath a brooding sky, with Merlin, the Bard, holding his antique lyre. This image of Merlin is reminiscent of Thomas Gray's earlier description of the Welsh bard Cadwallader in his Pindaric Ode, "The Bard" (1757):

> On a rock, whose haughty brow
> Frowns o'er old Conway's foaming flood,
> Robed in the sable garb of woe,
> With haggard eyes the poet stood;
> (Loose his beard, and hoary hair
> Streamed, like a meteor, to the troubled air)
> And with a master's hand, and prophet's fire,
> Struck the deep sorrows of his lyre.[17]

I swear a vow before them all, that I,/Because I had not seen the Grail, would ride/A twelvemonth and day in quest of it. Doré's illustration for *Idylls of the King* (London: Moxon, 1868).

In John Martin's 1817 painting based on Grey's poem, Cadwallader strides impossibly sublime mountain peaks more reminiscent of the Alps at their most extreme than anything to be found in Wales. Similarly, in Doré's illustration of Tennyson's text, the figures merely decorate the landscape, as will be the case for so many of the rest of the illustrations:

It is landscape that creates the mood and the sense of pagan magic in the air.

A different kind of magic, suggestive of a pagan spring, accompanies the story of Lancelot and Guinevere. May flowers accompany their talk of love as they ride "over sheets of hyacinth/That seemed the heavens up breaking through the earth"[18]—another concise image, which Doré elaborated upon in a magnificent landscape depiction. Tennyson also describes Camelot very much in magical terms, despite its function as a Christian citadel. Built somehow "magically" by Merlin, it is embellished with "many a mystic symbol" along with four zones of statues in the central hall that depict man's evolution: beasts slaying men, men slaying beasts, warriors ("perfect men") and men with "growing wings."[19] Merlin has also created a statue of Arthur. Doré, however, expands the vision, providing us with a truly gigantic castle growing out of rocky crags, worthy of Universal Studios at its most Hollywood Gothic, or King Ludwig II of Bavaria at his most extravagant.

Another powerful setting ("a glen, fray boulder and black tarn") provides the backdrop for Arthur's discovery of a corpse on which he finds the precious jewels he later uses as rewards at tournaments ("A horror lived about the tarn, and clave/Like its own mists to all the mountain side"). Tennyson mentions atmospheric "misty moonshine,"[20] which Doré includes in his accompanying illustration, adding a distinctly Gothic, fog-shrouded castle in the distance. He also depicts the gruesome corpse and even the skeletal rider's equally skeletal horse, giving the lie to suspicions that he had not read the poem.

Tennyson's description of Arthur's royal accouterments is distinctly Celtic, again planting the seed of future developments in the later nineteenth-century Celtic revival movement:

> And from the carven-woe behind him crept
> Two dragons gilded, sloping down to make
> Arms for his chair, while all the rest of them
> Through knots and loops and folds innumerable
> Fled ever through the woodwork, till they found
> The new design wherein they lost themselves,
> Yet with all ease, so tender was the work.[21]

Part of Tennyson's "musical" technique is to repeat certain phrases in the manner of a Wagnerian leitmotif. This applies to natural imagery as much as to the demands of narrative. Thus the line, "And in the meadows tremulous aspen-trees/And poplars made a noise of falling showers,"[22] is reversed a little later as "Of poplars with their noise of falling showers,/And ever-tremulous aspen-trees."[23] In "Merlin and Vivien," the sixth book of *Idylls of the King*, in which Vivien seduces Merlin in a manner that seems to foreshadow Kundry's seduction of Parsifal in Wagner's final music-drama, Tennyson subjects the phrase, "And Vivien answer'd..." to various adjectival metamorphoses, very much in the manner of Wagner's technique. We have "And Vivien answer'd smiling saucily,"[24] "And Vivien answer'd smiling mournfully,"[25] as well as changes in the phrase itself ("And Vivien, like the tenderest-hearted maid,"[26] "And Vivien breaking in upon him,"[27] etc.). Along with this leitmotif approach, much of the natural imagery is also distinctly Wagnerian, with its deep woods and "gloom of stubborn-shafted oaks"[28]—those significantly mythical trees. We have "Gray swamps and pools; waste places of the hern,/And wildernesses, perilous paths,"[29] "green gloom"[30] and "grey dawn," which steals "o'er the dewy world."[31] (Such words seem parallel with Wagner's "Tagesgrauen" [Dawn of Day] interlude in the prelude to *Götterdämmerung*.) Tennyson sometimes exploits his landscape settings metaphorically, here comparing a "terrible war-cry" with falling water:

> For as one,
> That listens near a torrent mountain-brook,
> All thro' the crash of the near cataract hears
> The drumming thunder of the huger fall
> At distance, were the soldiers wont to hear
> His voice in battle, and be kindled by it.[32]

Even Wagner's Valkyries seem to echo Tennyson's lines:

> Borne on a black horse, like a thunder cloud
> Whose skirts are loosened by the breaking storm.[33]

Wagner's thunderstorms in *Das Rheingold* and the Prelude to *Die Walküre* also find their equivalents in Tennyson's "Livid-flickering fork" and "the stammering cracks and claps."[34] This lightning strikes another ancient oak "so hollow, huge and old/It looked a tower of ivied mason work"[35]—another landscape image Doré faithfully illustrates with lustrous lightning in the background, while Merlin rests on the fallen giant, its leaves and branches restless in the wind.

When Percivale sets out on his quest for the Grail, he rides across many landscapes, but Doré chose one particularly resonant scene to illustrate, giving him the opportunity to articulate dappled light and cascading water:

> And on I rode, and when I thought my thirst
> Would slay me, saw deep lawns, and then a brook,
> With one sharp rapid, where the crisping white
> Play'd ever back upon the sloping wave,

> And took both ear and eye; and o'er the brook
> Were apple-trees, and apples by the brook
> Fallen, and on the lawns.[36]

Though Doré omits the apples, and could not resist placing yet more castle turrets in the misty distance of this scene, it is possible to see in Tennyson's imagery and Doré's illustration here, a distant ancestor of the similarly light-dappled apple orchards that blossom in *The Wicker Man*. In all three, the landscape is a crucial aspect of their mythic power.

Mist (or steam), which Wagner employed liberally to cover scene changes at Bayreuth during the 1876 premiere of *The Ring*, also features in Tennyson's catalogue of natural effects, where it is used during the Last Battle to symbolize confusion. Indeed, his description of this battle is a kind of British Ragnarok—Tennyson's own *Götterdämmerung*, indeed, in which "friend slew friend not knowing whom he slew," with "Oaths, insult, filth and monstrous blasphemies."[37] And Tennyson's grand finale matches the sublime heights of Wagner's immolation scene at the end of *Götterdämmerung*. The Lady of the Lake appears to receive Excalibur. Sir Bedivere, beneath "the winter moon,/Brightening the skirts of a long cloud,"[38] hurls it into the waters, where it is received by "an arm/Clothed in white samite, mystic wonderful"[39] (another of Tennyson's marvelous leitmotifs). The Three Queens who take Arthur's body to Avalon on their death barge, raise a cry that "shiver'd to the tingling stars"[40] and float away "like some full-breasted swan" until they are no more than a dot "against the verge of dawn."[41] It is not entirely appropriate that John Boorman accompanied his majestic realization of this scene in *Excalibur* with Wagner's music for Siegfried's funeral, but he could hardly have found any other music of such powerfully mythic resonance.

Tennyson's contemporary Matthew Arnold (1822–1888) was thinking along even more Wagnerian lines in that other pagan revival piece, "Balder Dead," written in 1855 when Wagner was hard at work scoring the text of *Die Walküre*. Arnold's poem also includes references to Valkyries, Odin and Thor, the sun-god Balder being anyway a version of Siegfried. The funeral of Balder represents Arnold at his most Wagnerian:

> Sharp quivering tongues of flame shot out, and leapt,
> Curling and darting, higher, until they lick'd
> The summit of the pile, the dead, the mast,
> And ate the shriveling sails; but still the Ship
> Drove on, ablaze, above her hull, with fire.
> And the Gods stood upon the beach, and gaz'd:
> And, while they gaz'd, the Sun went lurid down
> Into the smoke-wrapt sea, and Night came on.

> [...]
> And as in a decaying winter fire
> A charr'd log, falling, makes a shower of sparks—
> So, with a shower of sparks, the pile fell in,
> Reddening the sea around; and all was dark.[42]

As one would expect, Arnold's poem is a great deal more Norse than Celtic, and also much more pagan than Tennyson's Christianized ideal of Arthur, which "cleansed" the hero-king of his pagan past. Dion Fortune mockingly observed in her novel, *The Goat-Foot God* (1938):

> Don't you know that King Arthur, in the days before he was taken on as a Christian king and an ideal of chivalry, set off with his warriors to harry Hell because the Devil had overstepped the limit? And they chased all through Hell, and upset everything, and Arthur came away with the Devil's big cooking-pot tied on behind as his share of the spoils. [...] Then when Arthur was duly whitewashed when civilization began to be the vogue, he became the very perfect Christian knight and model of chivalry, and the Devil's cook-pot, that Keridwen used to mind, became the Graal.[43]

Fortune's view here had been identified earlier by Evans-Wentz, who traced its origin to the Irish folk epic, *The Book of the Dun Cow*, which describes how Arthur journeyed to "the Welsh Hades world named Annwan, where he, like Cuchulain in Scáth, gained possession of a magic cauldron—a pagan Celtic type of Holy Grail—which furnishes inexhaustible food."[44]

Despite his Christian perspective, Tennyson does include traces of Britain's pagan past and Merlin's Celtic origins in his poem. Along with the suggestions of Celtic decorative art, there are tantalizing glimpses of magical activity, which also helped fertilize later British pagan fantasies. Merlin is described as a wizard who "knew the starry heavens,"[45] and in the tale of an eastern king, which he tells to the seductress Vivien, Merlin speaks of a scrying glass and "elemental secrets, powers/And forces," which gives Tennyson another opportunity for magnificent descriptions of landscape:

> [O]ften o'er the sun's bright eye
> Drew the vast eyelid of an inky cloud,
> And lash'd it at the base with slanting storm;
> Or in the noon of mist and driving rain,
> When the lake whiten'd and the pinewood roar'd,
> And the cairn'd mountain was a shadow, sunn'd
> The world to peace again.[46]

Merlin has acquired a book in which "every square of text an awful charm,/Writ in a language that has long gone by"[47] can be found. Early on in the cycle, Tennyson exposes the Celtic underbelly of his tale with references to fairyland and ancient magic. The Lady of the Lake, who "knows a subtler magic" than Merlin, is somehow both pagan and Christian:

> Clothed in white samite, mystic, wonderful.
> She gave the King his huge cross-hilted sword,
> Whereby to drive the heathen out: a mist
> Of incense curl'd about her, and her face
> Wellnigh was hidden in the minster gloom;
> But there was heard among the holy hymns
> A voice as of the waters, for she dwells
> Down in the deep; calm, whatsoever storms
> May shake the world, and when the surface rolls,
> Hath power to walk the waters like our Lord.[48]

Gareth, who has come to work as a servant at Camelot, wonders if the king be a king at all "or come/From Fairyland" and if the castle "be built/By magic, and by fairy Kings and Queens."[49] An old Seer tells him that "a Fairy King/And Fairy Queens have built the city, son":

> They came from out a sacred mountain-cleft
> Toward the sunrise, each with harp in hand,
> And built it to the music of their harps.
> And, as thou sayest, it is enchanted, son,
> For there is nothing in it as it seems.[50]

Later, in "Guinevere," Tennyson indulges in the sound of "Strange music,"[51] "white mermaiden," "elves" and "spirits of the hills/With all their dewy hair blown back like flame."[52] Such imagery, along with its crucial setting in a mythological landscape, formed the basis for later developments.

The simultaneity of Tennyson's interest in the Arthur myth and Wagner's adaptation of the Nibelungenlied and Norse legends in his *Ring* cycle, along with the grail operas, *Lohengrin* and *Parsifal*, suggest that Jung's theory of the collective unconscious could prove to be true. In their different ways, Wagner and Tennyson created national epics for their respective nations, and both men later inspired the British composer Rutland Boughton (1878–1960) to set the Arthurian legends to music in the form of Wagnerian music dramas, adding that particularly British element of choral music to the proceedings. He was not the only composer attracted to King Arthur. In France, the Wagner-infatuated Ernest Chausson (1855–1899) composed his opera, *Le roi Arthur*, between 1886 and 1895, the love duet in it between Lancelot and Guinevere being strongly influenced by the example of Wagner's *Tristan und Isolde*. Premièred posthumously in 1902, it had magnificent set designs by the Belgian symbolist painter Fernand Khnopff, but was neglected thereafter for many years. Two years after Chausson's opera, the Spaniard, Isaac Albéniz (1860–1909), anticipated Boughton's project with his own Arthurian trilogy, never completed, with an English text by the appropriately named British banker, Francis Burdett Money-Coutts. The latter's *King Arthur* trilogy consists of "Merlin," "Lancelot" and "Guinevere," but Albéniz completed only "Merlin," in April 1902. *Merlin* was only ever staged once, in 1950, though a recording now exists. A key element in it is the use of Gregorian plainchant, anticipating the choral drama of Boughton. But Albéniz also employs a leitmotif system akin to Wagner's approach.

Boughton's Arthurian operas fared little better and have never entered the repertoire since their first performances at the Glastonbury Festivals, which Boughton founded just before the outbreak of the First World War and which continued until the Second. George Bernard Shaw, with whom Boughton corresponded in the hope of raising his profile, was at first dismissive of the project:

> I greatly mistrust your project of a series of Arthurian music dramas. You will simply produce a second-hand Ring. The Ring itself would never have existed had it not been to Wagner an expression of his strongest religious and social convictions; and unless you have equally strong convictions and an equally deep penetration into the social life that surrounds you, you will only waste a great deal of scoring paper which you might employ far better by trying to deal, as Strauss does (not to mention Elgar), with the modern world in a crisp and powerful style, making a clean sweep of the tremolandos and sentimental and grandiose modulations of the nineteenth century.[53]

Later correspondence grew more heated. In November 1908, for example:

> Why do you want to come and play your King Arthur to me? I do not insist on reading my plays to you. Do you suppose that I am an impresario, or that I have influence at the Opera or with music publishers? If so, I assure you you are mistaken. I can do absolutely nothing for you; and your desire to waste my time and your own is not one to be encouraged, especially now that you are married and have a wife to provide for. Get your King Arthur performed if you can; and I will attend the performance if I feel inclined. Until then bend all your energies to achieving the performance; and remember that there are few experiences more trying, even to people whose business it is, than to hear a young composer making a horrible noise at the piano under the impression that he is conveying the beauties of his score to the unfortunate listener. Besides, one knows beforehand by your age and your way of going on that the score will be rubbish, though no doubt the composition of it has helped to educate you, and some scraps of it may come in later on.[54]

Undaunted, Boughton pressed on. There are five operas in the sequence: *The Birth of Arthur*, composed to a libretto by Reginald Buckley in 1908 and 1909, *The Round Table*, on which Broughton collaborated with Buckley on the text, and completed in 1916. For *The Lily Maid* (composed in 1933), *Galahad* (1943–1944) and *Avalon* (1944–1945), Boughton rejected Buckley's libretto and wrote his own. The last two were never performed, though the others did receive premières *The Lily Maid* at Stroud and the first two operas at Glastonbury. He also composed a ballet on an Arthurian theme, *Mystic Dance of the Grail*, in 1913. Broughton had grand plans for his Glastonbury Festival, which he envisaged as an English Bayreuth. Many famous names supported his venture, including Sir Edward Elgar and Bernard Shaw, who by then had been won over to the cause, but these luminaries were not enough to stimulate the funds needed for the Festival Theatre of which he dreamed.

> We are dreamers. That is undeniable. But without dreams nothing can be done. Wagner's dreams necessitated the building of the Bayreuth theatre. Our dramas necessitate the building of a place which Buckley has fitly forenamed the Temple Theatre. That theatre we are intent upon making the centre of a commune. There have been many communes and they have failed—for lack of a religious centre. Our theatre supplies that.[55]

Already in those lines written before the First World War, the way in which the Arthurian cycle was to develop over the years seems to be suggested. As Boughton's biographer Michael Hurd points out, what began as a Wagnerian epic "of kings and queens and unhappy lovers ... ended as a political tracts with strong religious overtones."[56] Boughton confessed to being "bored" by Tennyson, but felt that he had found in Arthur an expression of the British people's "oversoul" and "understood why Wagner had chosen folk subjects which had been produced by that oversoul."[57]

Alas, the Temple Theatre was never constructed. Despite Shaw's advocacy of Boughton at the end of the third edition of his essay, *The Perfect Wagnerite* (1913), funds never came Boughton's way. As Shaw observed, "he attempted to do in Somerset what Wagner did in Thuringia, with the very material difference that Wagner had the King of Bavaria at his back, and Mr. Boughton had nothing material at his back at all."[58] The first performances of *The Birth of Arthur* and *The Round Table* took place in Glastonbury's Assembly Rooms. At just over 50 feet long and 30 feet wide, this is hardly a large hall, and it lacks anything as elaborate as an orchestra pit. (The accompaniment was played on a grand piano.) Astonishingly, the venture was a success. The possibility of creating pagan landscapes on such a small stage was naturally limited, but scene-painting was really unnecessary as Boughton's music was more powerful than any stage illusion. Walking through the empty, rather musty space in the late 1980s, I marveled at what had occurred there, so many years before the mystic associations of Glastonbury drew much larger audiences to immense rock concerts in its surrounding muddy fields.

As Hurd points out, however, the musical style of all five Arthurian operas is not consistent,[59] nor should we expect it to be so, the cycle having been composed over such a long period of time. Despite Boughton's desire to create a specifically British epic, his musical style is indebted to European, particularly German models. However, Boughton insisted that the choral element "is absolutely necessary to the English people."⁶⁰ The musical richness and variety of the cycle as a whole is demonstrated well in *The Round Table,* where Boughton juxtaposes "folk-like simplicity" with Brahmsian harmonies," "Tristanesque chromatics" and "Debussy-inspired whole tones" for the mystical atmosphere required for the Lady of the Lake.⁶¹ These return in the final drama of *Avalon* when Excalibur is thrown back into the Lake from which it came.

King Arthur also inspired many Victorian paintings, which like so much Victorian art (not to mention Wagnerian music drama) went on to inspire twentieth-century cinema. Daniel Maclise (1806–1870) was the first Victorian artist to take up the Arthurian theme for the Moxon edition of Tennyson's poems. His two pictures on the subject proved to be very influential, for they depict the king as imposing, bearded, muscular and entirely worthy of the hero-worship Thomas Carlyle had made fashionable in his celebrated 1841 book on that subject. Joseph Noel Patton (1821–1901) and Walter Crane (1845–1915) depicted Galahad, along with the famous portrait of the errant knight by Watts already mentioned. William Morris (1834–1896) devoted his only oil painting to Guinevere, which complements his poem "The Defence of Guenevere," though his sequel to that poem, "King Arthur's Tomb," is in fact where we should look for landscape imagery, when Launcelot describes his journey:

> Through the fresh wet woods, and the wheat that morn,
> Touching her hair and hand and mouth, and talk
> Of love we held, nigh hid among the corn.⁶²

The mystical elements in Arthurian legend were emphasized by Sidney Harold Meteyard (1868–1947) in his esthetic-occult *I Am Half Sick of Shadows,* based on Tennyson's "The Lady of Shalott," which forms an Arthurian adjunct to his *Idylls.* The Lady, dressed in blue and working at her tapestry in a flower-filled chamber, sits before a gigantic scrying glass in which she sees visions of the world around her, much as an artist secludes him- or herself and, through the almost clairvoyant powers of his or her genius, interprets the world for those who are unable to articulate its mysteries. That Meteyard's Lady is sleeping emphasizes the dream-like, visionary nature of the Romantic artist. Frederick Sandys (1829–1904) also chose the mystical elements in the story for his picture of Morgan le Fey, as did Edward Burne-Jones (1833–1898), who depicted the episode of Merlin and

Vivien. In Burne-Jones' masterpiece, *The Last Sleep of Arthur in Avalon*, a mystical grouping of languid maidens tend to the stricken king who lies beneath an elaborately canopied shrine amid a flowery landscape inspired by the example of Botticelli. Burne-Jones loved this painting and never intended to sell it, spending three days every week at work upon it. Avalon became for him a state of mind, a symbol of the creative act itself, and a landscape of the unconscious indeed:

> I love my pictures as a goldsmith does his jewels. I should like every inch of surface to be so fine that if all but a scrap from one of them were burned or lost, the man who found it might say whatever this may have represented it is a work of art, beautiful in surface and quality of colour.[63]

Burne-Jones was also asked to design Sir Henry Irving's 1890 production of the *King Arthur* play of J. Comyns Carr at London's Lyceum Theater. Bram Stoker recalled the event in his *Reminiscences* of Irving:

> To my own mind it was the first time that what must in reality be a sort of fairyland was represented as an actuality. Some of the scenes were of transcendent beauty, notably that called "The Whitehorn Wood." The scene was all green and white—the side of a hill thick with blossoming thorn through which, down a winding path, came a bevy of maidens in flowing garments of tissue which seemed to sway and undulate with every motion and every breath of air. There was a daintiness and a sense of purity about the whole scene which was very remarkable.[64]

It ran for 105 performances in its first season. In all, there were 191 performances both in England and America before all the scenery and props were consumed by a stage fire in 1898. Irving's approach to production was deeply reliant on setting and effects, anticipating the style of Hollywood in subsequent decades. As his grandson Laurence Irving recalls, these "reached their apotheosis" in the *King Arthur* production:

> Burne-Jones's ethereal and bloodless heroes were clothed in the substantial flesh of the Lyceum Company; he saw his vision of a landscape, half-earthly, half celestial, realized in three dimensions by Hawes Craven and [Joseph] Harker. Comyns Carr's workmanlike libretto ... was set to Sullivan's operatic music, with sonorous and mellifluous recitatives by Irving as Arthur and Forbes-Robertson as Lancelot.[65]

Sir Arthur Sullivan's involvement caused an unintentional moment of comedy, foreshadowing Monty Pythons satire of the story. Appropriate to our theme, it was caused by a lengthy change of scene:

> It was unfortunate that shortly afterwards Sullivan, who, in the orchestra, was enduring with growing impatience an interminable wait during a change of scene behind the lowered curtain, tapped loudly on the music stand with his baton and shouted: "Well—what are we waiting for—Irving, are you ready?"
>
> The green curtain parted. Arthur, in his black Gothic armour, stalked slowly down to the footlights. For a moment or two he peered at the composer over the pince-nez

perched askew on the thin bridge of his nose. "Ready," snapped Irving. "Ready—for *what?*"[66]

Bernard Shaw was even more satirical in his review of this production, which was highly praised by others. While commending Irving on his employment of Burne-Jones and Sullivan, Shaw singled out Comyns Carr:

> [H]ow am I to praise this deed when my own art, the art of literature, is left shabby and ashamed amid the triumph of the arts of the painter and the actor? I sometimes wonder where Mr. Irving will go when he dies—whether he will dare to claim, as a master artist, to walk where he may any day meet Shakespeare whom he has mutilated, Goethe whom he has travestied, and the nameless creator of the hero-king out of whose mouth he has uttered jobbing verses. For in poetry Mr. Comyns Carr is frankly a jobber and nothing else.[67]

In fairness to Comyns Carr, Shaw's comments apply even more to the dialogue of King Arthur's later Hollywood incarnations. While Burne-Jones was transmogrified by Technicolor, many cinematic Arthurian epics favored landscape and the heroic and swashbuckling aspects of the story over sensible dialogue. Most of these films were of either European or American origin, such as *Knights of the Round Table* (dir. Richard Thorpe, 1954), which used authentic Tintagal locations with little imagination. The backdrops of *Prince Valiant*, directed by Henry Hathaway in the same year, are indeed merely that: flat, uninteresting shots of well-known British beauty spots such as Eilean Donan Castle in Scotland and Caernarvon Castle in Wales.

However, some later Arthurian films were made by British directors, who exploited the mythic power of landscape more intuitively. The two most extreme examples of this approach are Jones' and Gilliams' satire, *Monty Python and the Holy Grail* and Boorman's bloody but comparably atmospheric *Excalibur*. Ironically, the mythic landscapes of the Monty Python comedy version are the most powerful. Jones and Gilliam realized that much of the comedic effect relied on the subversion of a richly mythic context. Consequently, they spent a great deal of time not only searching for atmospheric locations in Scotland, which included Glen Coe, Loch Tay, Doune Castle and Castle Stalker at Loch Linnhe, but also filming them in an extraordinarily moody manner. Jones later confessed, when revisiting Loch Linnhe in a documentary for the DVD release of the film, that "the one thing about this place is you just can't go wrong. With skies like this and a setting like this, no matter where you put the camera, it's great." Michael Palin, who accompanied him, agreed: "The landscape up here is free. It's wonderful. You can do these epic things with mountains in the background." But it is how one approaches and adapts the landscapes on offer that makes the difference. During filming, John Cleese told BBC's

Raising the Dragon's Breath. Nicol Williamson as Merlin in *Excalibur* (dir. John Boorman, 1981).

Film Night program, "[T]he jokes tend to be a bit secondary to whether it looks good. So when they say 'more smoke, more smoke,' and this kind of thing—because we've hardly had a shot yet that we haven't had smoke or some arty visual effect—we tend to ask them how many laughs there are in the smoke." But he realized the importance of this, admitting that the two Terrys were "pretty good. They're both visually orientated and very aware of picture composition." And even though spoken in jest, Gilliam no doubt wanted to believe that "Ingmar Bergman is going to be pretty jealous of this one."

Boorman's larger budget failed to make the mythic landscapes of *Excalibur* any more impressive than those in the Python film, impressive though they are; and like Jones and Gilliam, Boorman too relied mostly on mist-shrouded shots of nature. We have mist-filled valleys for the scenes leading up to the rape of Katrine Boorman's Igrayn ("the dragon's breath" as Nicol Williamson's Merlin calls it): Merlin casts his spell from within a stone circle atop a hill, and the subsequent shape-shifting he facilitates (making Uther resemble Igraine's lawful husband) is reminiscent of Siegfried's use of the Tarnhelm in Wagner's *Götterdämmerung* (which makes Siegfried resemble Gunther, facilitating his rape of Brünnhilde).

One. The Return of King Arthur 43

WOODLAND AND WATERFALLS. A scene from *Excalibur* (dir. John Boorman, 1981).

Lush, fern-filled woodland accompanies the discussions between Merlin and Nigel Terry's young Arthur, and sublime waterfalls form a backdrop for the duel between Lancelot (Nicholas Clay) and Arthur. The shining armor and the occult green glow of Excalibur itself are important, but the scenery (some of Ireland's most spectacular regions in counties Wicklow, Kerry and Tipperary) is more eloquent. Some of these scenes verge on the clichés of advertising imagery, such as Lancelot riding through bluebell woods for his encounter with Paul Geoffrey's young Perceval, but clichés are powerful for the very good reason that they are so effective; and what is myth if not an extremely well-worn, though still very effective cliché?

When Lancelot lies under a tree in an idyllic forest setting, we are perhaps meant to think of Siegfried in the "Forest Murmurs" scene of Wagner's *Siegfried* opera—especially as Boorman layers his soundtrack with successive extracts from the Wagnerian canon. (Later, Perceval's lakeside idyll is reminiscent of Siegfried greeting the Rhine-maidens in *Götterdämmerung*'s third act: Lancelot's horse carefully balances the other side of the screen, also reminding the spectator of the artfully arranged compositions of Fritz Lang in his two *Nibelungen* films from the 1920s.) When Arthur breaks Excalibur in a duel with Lancelot, the Lady of the Lady returns it to him in one piece; but she is less mystical than the pool from which she emerges, being presented largely in somewhat unconvincing superimposition. Lancelot later fights with himself over his guilty love for

Guinevere: His naked body grapples with his armored alter ego on moss-clad stones in a gloomy gorge.

Boorman's vision also encompasses dark hills punctuated with flambeaux, starry skies, flowery meadows with raining petals, apple trees in blossom (echoing the pagan imagery of *The Wicker Man*)—even stop-motion flowers in bloom to symbolize Arthur's return to the world after his long sickness. But Camelot is never clearly revealed. We see matte shots of the castle nestling in impressive mountain scenery, but are shown only fairly restricted views of its interiors, perhaps due to budgetary considerations. Boorman seems more interested in the much more powerful natural settings around the castle than in the castle itself.

Landscape plays its greatest role in the final scenes of the return of Excalibur to the lake: Mist rises over the tree-clad slopes of the waters, which ripple as they are parted by the emerging arm of the Lady in white samite, mystic, wonderful. The blood-red disc of the sun hovers overhead and the seascape blends with the lowering skies. Three shots of Arthur's funeral barge complete the film, with light shimmering on the waves. Each shot increases the distance between the viewer and the barge, the final one being disorientating in its effect, as the eye is at first unprepared for the enormity of the change in perspective, the boat being only just perceptible on the vast horizon; and through it all we hear the threnody of Siegfried's funeral music from *Götterdämmerung*.

Excalibur also emphasizes the magical element of the story rather more explicitly than Tennyson or Malory. Helen Mirren's Morgana wants to learn Merlin's magical secrets, and their conversation takes place during the Christian wedding of Arthur and Guinevere, with knights in shining armor and ladies in white robes.

"It's a lonely way, you know, the way of the Necromancer," Merlin explains. "Yes, to know too much. *Lacrimae mundi*: the tears of the world."

"But the power!" Morgana argues. "The joy!"

"Moments, fleeting moments." Merlin insists. "Ah, the days of our time are long buried. The one god comes to drive out the many gods. The spirits of wood and stream grow silent. It's the way of things. Yes. It's a time for men and their ways."

But Merlin's magic has somehow helped to build Camelot, and Merlin has orchestrated the whole story, so the old magic is in fact never far behind the superimposition of Christianity over this pagan past. And later, in the magical duel between Merlin and Morgana, we are shown in no uncertain terms that the old magic is still efficacious. Morgana steals the words of "The Charm of Making" from the old wizard and then promptly traps him in the icy prison of her multi-colored cave, which bears a resemblance to King Ludwig's kitschy Venusberg grotto at Schloss Linderhof.

Technically an American film with a Hollywood Lancelot in the shape of Richard Gere, Jerry Zucker's *First Knight* (1995) features a blue-roofed Camelot, blue-clad serfs and stylized blue-uniformed knights who seem to have strayed from a *Star Wars* adventure; but it understands that British scenery and British weather in particular are vital elements in this very British story. However, Zucker uses all these impressive resources somewhat perfunctorily and with far less narrative conviction than Boorman. We have a funeral at sea and barques set on fire by a flaming arrow, but these fail to summon the pagan majesty of Arnold's *Balder Dead*. We have surging sea around the slate-strewn castle of Malegant, from where Guinevere is by Launcelot, though without any sense of real menace; and both Lancelot and Guinevere are later drenched in a dripping wood, though more for the audience to enjoy the erotic effect this creates than for poetic effect.

By the time we arrive at Antoine Fuqua's *King Arthur* in 2004, the scenery is just as wet but less important than the interminable fighting and shouting, all poetry having been lost in what is really an action movie in fancy dress. In an attempt to portray an historically accurate account of the legend, Arthur is shown here to be a Roman cavalry officer in charge of defending Hadrian's Wall. The story's magical and mystic elements are thus sidelined in favor of a grittier, mud-covered "authenticity" (current fashion seems always to equate the two). But with Ray Winstone's Bors resembling a Cockney gangster and the film's distinctly 21st-century revulsion against the idea of "Romance," which is surely what King Arthur's story is, the film is really neither here nor there. With Guy Ritchie's *King Arthur: Legend of the Sword* (2014), the story becomes no more than a sword-and-sorcery vehicle and collapses under the weight of its own post-modern irony.

Two

Who Is the Grail?

Tennyson reserved his most powerful Arthurian imagery for that section of the *Idylls* devoted to "The Holy Grail." This appeared when Tennyson was 60 years old in 1869, and he regarded it as the most imaginative of his poems:

> I have expressed there my strong feelings as to the reality of the Unseen. The end, when the king speaks of his work and of his visions, is intended to be the summing up of all in the highest note by the highest of human men. These three lines in Arthur's speech are the (spiritually) central lines of the idylls:
>
>> In moments when he feels himself he cannot die,
>> And knows himself no vision to himself,
>> Nor the High God a vision.[1]

Wagner and Tennyson were attracted to the Grail story around the same time. Wagner completed the prose draft of *Parsifal* as early as 1857, two years before the first set of Tennyson's *Idylls* were published, and 12 years before "The Holy Grail" appeared. *Parsifal* proved, in the end, to be Wagner's last music drama (it premièred in 1882) but it had been preceded by *Lohengrin* in 1849. Like Wagner, Tennyson preferred the image of a chalice to the idea of the Grail being a stone, which Wagner's medieval source for *Parsifal*, Wolfram von Eschenbach, had suggested it was. (In Act I, Parsifal asks, "Who is the Grail?" not knowing even that.) Wolfram called it "Lapsit exillis," meaning either a small stone or a conflation of the phrase "lapis lapsus ex caelis"—a "stone fallen from heaven." Wagner conceded that this might have been a reference to a sunstone or a meteoric stone. Or it could be that it was the emerald that fell from the forehead of Lucifer during the war in heaven between God and Satan, which links it with the pearl fixed in the brow of the Indian deity Shiva: a magical third eye that bestows upon one the power of self-knowledge.[2]

The concept of a magical stone is central to the symbolism of the medieval alchemists. The quest to transmute base metal into gold by means of the *lapis philosophorum* was symbolic of a religious quest—more aptly a psychological quest to attain integration with the self. Indeed, the renaissance alchemist Romanus Morienus seemed to understand that the philosopher's stone, like the Grail, was something that can only be found within the psyche. In discussing the nature of the philosopher's stone, he explained:

> [The philosopher's stone] is extracted from *you*: *you* are its mineral, and one can find it in you; or, to put it more clearly, [the alchemists] take it from you. If you recognize this, the love and approbation of the stone will grow within you. Know that this is true without doubt.[3]

That the Grail lies at the heart of our emotional landscape was made startlingly explicit in Hans Jürgen Syberberg's 1982 film version of Wagner's *Parsifal*, the action of which takes place on a gigantic replica of Wagner's death mask. The composer's eye sockets become pools of water, the nostrils inhale the perfume of potted plants that stand in for the flower meadows of Act III, and the whole thing divides in two at the end, when Parsifal gives his command to uncover the grail: an inspired way of demonstrating that landscape is primarily a psychological affair. (This interpretation was reprised by John Boorman in *Excalibur*, when Perceval aids the ailing Arthur: "Drink from the chalice and you will be reborn and the land with you.")

Also unlike Wolfram, Tennyson, basing his poem on Malory's *Morte d'Arthur*, preferred to have the Grail transported to Glastonbury rather than the Spanish castle of Montsalvat, which became the setting for Wagner's *Parsifal*.

> The cup, the cup itself, from which our Lord
> Drank at the last supper with his own.
> This, from the blessed land of Aromat—
> After the day of darkness, when the dead
> Went wandering o'er Moriah—the good saint,
> Arimathaean Joseph, journeying brought
> To Glastonbury, where the winter thorn
> Blossoms at Christmas, mindful of out Lord.[4]

Later in the poem, Lancelot describes how he almost succeeded in the Grail quest:

> O, yet me thought I saw the Holy Grail,
> All pall'd in crimson samite, and around
> Great angels, awful shapes, and wings and eyes.[5]

The Grail was equally important for Tennyson's British contemporaries. Dante Gabriel Rossetti (1828–1882) and Burne-Jones joined with William Morris to paint murals on Arthurian subjects at the Debating

Hall of the Oxford Union. "And what were they going to *do* with the Grail when they found it, Mr. Rossetti?" reads the caption of Max Beerbohm's cartoon, depicting the laconic Benjamin Jowett on viewing the work in progress. Well, the Grail was set to do a great many things. Even Karl Marx used it as a symbol of capitalism in his famous work on the subject:

> Modern society, which, soon after its birth, pulled Plutus by the hair of his head from the bowels of the earth, greets gold as its Holy Grail, as the glittering incarnation of the very principle of its own life.[6]

Marx's ironic inversion of what the Grail should stand for made his point all the more powerful; but if the Grail quest meant anything for Morris, it surely represented its restoration as a symbol of artistic and social values, which socialism would bring to pass. In his poem, "Sir Galahad, a Christmas Mystery," an angel decrees:

> O servant of the high God, Galahad!
> Rise and be arm'd, the Sangreal is gone forth
> Through the great forest, and you must be had
> Unto the sea that lieth to the north:
>
> There shall you find the wondrous ship wherein
> The spindles of King Solomon are laid,
> And the sword that no man draweth without sin,
> But if he be most pure.[7]

Roger Sherman Loomis helps us understand the symbolism in this poem, which is derived from Morris' reading of a ninth-century saga, the *Second Battle of Moytura*:

> Galahad, Bors, Perceval and Perceval's sister discovered a mysterious ship, with not a soul aboard. A Chaldean inscription informs them that the vessel is Faith. Entering, they see a magnificent bed, into the frame of which three spindles of red, white and green wood have been introduced in the form of a cross. At the foot of the bed is a sword of fine workmanship, attached to a belt of coarse hemp. Perceval's sister, who takes the place of the usual hermit as expositor, tells the story and the meaning of the sword, the ship and the spindles. The vessel was built by Solomon, and since Solomon was the builder of the Temple, the vessel symbolizes the Church of the Old Testament. The three spindles were made from the three staves of the Tree of Knowledge, and since the cross of Calvary was made of the same wood, they transform the vessel into the Church of the New Testament. The sword, according to Ephesians, vi, 17, is the Word of God, that is, the Scriptures.[8]

The Grail thus shows us the way, but Morris' poem ends rather pessimistically: "The knights come foil'd from the great quest, in vain;/In vain they struggle for the vision fair."[9] Morris himself was more optimistic, but with the publication of Tennyson's Arthurian poems, he decided to concentrate on other subjects, and his own Grail quest became a mission to create beauty in defiance of the scientific materialism he believed was destroying the power of the individual imagination. Art and politics were inextricable for Morris, forming the ingredients of his social utopia. Explaining in 1894 the reasons why he became a socialist, he expressed his vision of how a sick and unjust society, languishing like Amfortas, the Grail King in Wagner's *Parsifal,* could be healed by the Grail of Art and Legislation:

> What I mean by socialism is a condition of society in which there should be neither rich nor poor, neither master nor master's man, neither idle nor overworked, neither brain-sick brain workers, nor heart-sick hand workers, in a word, in which all men would be living in equality of condition.[10]

The culmination of his friendship with Burne-Jones was when Morris' company, dedicated to the propagation of beauty in the home, received a commission to furnish Stanmore Hall, the residence of Australian mining millionaire, William Knox D'Arcy. Morris asked Jones to design six tapestries based on the Grail legend. "The Failure of Sir Lancelot" brings his career full circle, being very similar to Rossetti's treatment of the same subject in the Oxford mural project. Burne-Jones' wife, Georgiana, described the sequence as follows:

> The first subject is Pentecost morning at the Round Table, when the damsel of the San Graal appears and summons all the knights to the adventure, and suddenly writing comes on the empty chair, the Siege Perilous set by Arthur, where no man may sit but the one who can achieve the adventure. Launcelot is the opposite chair, and points to himself as if asking if he is to sit there. Gawain and Lamorak and Percival and Bors are all there. Then, in the second, the knights go forth, and it is good-bye all round. Guenevere is arming Launcelot. In the third and fourth are the subjects called the "foiling of the knights." Gawain and Ewain are kept from entering, eaten up by the world were they—handsome gentlemen set in this world's glory. Then comes Launcelot's turn in the fourth—eaten up not by coveting of glory but eaten up he was, and his heart set on another matter. So he is foiled—dreams he comes to the chapel and has found it, but not a glorious one as he thought it would be, but a ruined and broken one—and still he cannot enter, for one comes and bars the way. And then comes the ship—which is as much to say that the scene has shifted, and we have passed from out of Britain and are in the land of Sarras, the land of the soul, that is. And of all the hundred and fifty that went on the Quest, three only are chosen and may set foot on that shore, Bors, Percival and Galahad. Of these, Bors and Percival may see the Graal far off—three big angels bar their way, and one holds the spear that bleeds; that is the spear that entered Christ's side, and it bleeds always. You know by its appearing that the Graal is near. And then comes Galahad who alone may see it—and to see it is death, for it is seeing the face of God.[11]

It is fitting that Wagner's wife, Cosima, sat for Burne-Jones, who apparently drew—or began to draw—her portrait, in 1877. George Eliot, who had known Cosima's father, Franz Liszt, when in Weimar, arranged the meeting, and commended Cosima to Burne-Jones as "a rare person worthy to see the best things, having her father's quickness and breadth of comprehension."[12] Wagner had been engaged to conduct at the Royal Albert Hall, and Cosima had accompanied him. She had three sittings with the artist (her English was excellent) and recorded the experience in her diary, seemingly unaware of how much Burne-Jones had in common with her husband (Burne-Jones had painted a version of the Tannhaüser legend in his 1869 *Laus Veneres*): "To the studio of the Pre-Raphaelite painter Burne-Jones. Pretty, delicate pictures, he himself very pleasant."[13] On his part, Burne-Jones had not always been an admirer of Wagner's music, but when he heard extracts from *Parsifal* performed at the Albert Hall in 1884, he enthused, "I nearly forgave him—he knew how to win me. He made sounds that are really and truly (I assure you and I ought to know) the very sounds that were to be heard in the Sangraal Chapel, I recognized them in a moment and knew he had done it accurately."[14]

Wagner explained his earlier sound portrait of the Grail in the Prelude to *Lohengrin* in a program note, describing his idea of this magical object in terms comparable to the socialistic ideals of Morris, though with a far greater emphasis on the human need for Love rather than economic equality:

> From a world of hatred and discord it seemed as though love had vanished: no longer was there a single human community in which it still showed itself clearly, dispensing beneficent laws. Yet amidst the bleak concern for profit and possessions, a concern which regulates all our worldly dealings to the exclusion of all else, the human heart's unquenchable longing for love was finally rekindled by the urge to assuage a need, longed for and sought after under the name of the "holy Grail."
> Perfumes of ravishing sweetness well forth from its womb: entrancing fragrance wafts from within it like clouds of gold, usurping the onlooker's startled senses and filling the innermost depths of his quivering heart with wondrously hallowed emotion. The Grail sends forth the sunbeams of the sublimest love like the steady flame of a heavenly fire, so that every heart begins to beat in the fiery glow of eternal ardour.[15]

Tennyson's Grail poem is filled with astonishingly vivid flashes of landscape, astonishing because he again creates these impressions with very few words. Admittedly, he is attempting to create the near-delirious experience of Percivale's quest, but the imagery is all the more powerful and evocative for that. We move, kaleidoscopically, from "deep lawns, and then a brook"[16] filled with the apple trees (again we might think of *The Wicker Man*), past the "plowshare in the field,"[17] which gleams in the light of the Grail, "a mighty hill, and on the top, a city wall'd: the spires/Prick'd with incredible pinnacles into heaven," and "a lowly vale./Low as the hill was high,"[18] but having glimpsed the Holy Grail, Percivale loses it, and is plunged back into the night:

> Blood-red, and sliding down the blacken'd marsh
> Blood-red, and in the sleeping mere below
> Blood-red. And in the strength of this I rose,
> Shattering all evil customs everywhere,
> And past thro' Pagan realms, and made them mine.[19]

Tennyson's montage of the varied locations of Percivale's quest is almost cinematic in its effect, and is far more disorientating than Boorman's misty, muddy equivalent in *Excalibur*, impressive though Boorman's vision is. Like Tennyson before him, he suggests the confusion of the Grail quest itself with symbolic imagery of stunted forests, thick with tangled undergrowth:

> The lightning here and there to left and right
> Struck, till the dry old trunks about us, dead,
> Yea, rotten with a hundred years of death
> Sprang into fire.[20]

Boorman also includes forbidding crows beneath a watery sun, marshes, flaming moorland and a snowy mountaintop on which Perceval discovers the frozen corpse of a knight who has preceded him, its hands still raised together in prayer. Unfortunately, despite the always thrilling accompaniment of Wagner's *Parsifal* Prelude, the use of the actor David de Keyser as the voice of the Grail does remind British viewers of a certain age of the long-running television advertising campaign De Keyser voiced for the pain-killer Anadin. "What is the Grail? Whom does it serve?" he asks, in the same tone as "Headache? Tense nervous headache?" But Boorman effectively uses artificial means, drawn from surrealism, to suggest the mystical environment of the Grail Chapel at which Perceval finds himself: an immense birch tree illuminated by floodlights against the severe blackness of the night, reminiscent of these lines in Tennyson:

> And in the blast there smote along the hall
> A beam of light seven times more clear than day:
> And down the long beam stole the Holy Grail
> All over covered with a luminous cloud.[21]

A British Grail fantasy from 1933 more firmly connects the Christian idea of the Grail with its pagan origins. John Cowper Powys' immensely long novel, *A Glastonbury Romance*, is primarily a naturalistic story, though one flashed through with mystical visions, and in it he refers to the ancient Arthurian myths, relating the Grail to the Cauldron of Anwyn. That particular legend had inspired the eccentric British composer Joseph Holbrook (1878–1958) to compose an operatic trilogy on the subject between 1909 and 1928. As we have seen, the occult novelist Dion Fortune was also keen to reveal the pagan origin of the Grail in *The Goat-Food God*, a novel to which we will be returning when we invoke Pan in Chapter Six. Fortune describes the Grail as a horn of plenty, with "an inexhaustible source of supply for all and sundry. However much they ate out of it, and whatever sort of parties Arthur gave, the cauldron always filled up again, and everyone found it contained his favourite recipe."[22]

The Grail plays a much more central role in Powys' *Glastonbury Romance*, which is once more a work rooted in and largely justified by its evocation of landscape. As Powys explains in his preface, the book is a study of "the effect of a particular legend, a special myth, a unique tradition, from the remotest past of human history, upon a particular spot on the surface of this planet together with its crowd of inhabitants of every age and of every type of character."[23] Some of those characters react against the Grail legends so associated with the town. Philip Crow, an industrialist, loathes the mystical aura of the town, which he regards as obstructive to his progressive and highly materialistic plans for the place. He is opposed by a mystical preacher called Geard, who plans to make Glastonbury a mystery center and place of pilgrimage, constructing an imposing arch over the Chalice well, and organizing an Arthurian pageant complete with "booths and tents and bands."[24] This not only looks forward to the Glastonbury rock festivals of our own day but also has something of the kitsch medievalism that Hitler would organize for the Munich Days of Art four years after Powys' novel was first published. Unnervingly, Crow would like to wipe the place clean "both of its under-nourished rebellious populace and of its morbid relics, and then set to work, as inevitably as a beaver returns to its job after the flood, to build up an industrial centre out of the richest tin ore and out of the most scientific dye works anywhere on earth."[25] Not only does this in general terms anticipate the Nazi atrocities that were already happening when *A Glastonbury Romance* was published, but the reference to Crow's "dye works" chimes alarmingly with IG Farben, the pharmaceutical and dye-making corporation so intimately involved in the manufacture of the Zyklon B gas that was destined for the death chambers of Auschwitz. Crow's lack of sympathy with the landscape is therefore equated with his lack of connection with humanity and the cosmic order, as with the tragic symbolism of Goethe's Oak. Such disconnection with the mythic power of the landscape will return as one of the central issues in Rudkin's *Penda's Fen*.

In stark contrast, Mr. Evans, who is persuaded to perform the role of Christ on the Cross at Geard's Pageant, suffers a seizure because of it. Indeed, he feels himself to embody the landscape around him:

His body projected itself under the pain in great waves of filmy chemical substance. It flung forth this filmy substance in streams, in torrents, in a mighty, rushing rain! And then there arrived a moment when Mr. Evans knew that his body was the whole hill, the whole field, nay! the whole wide-stretching landscape.[26]

He may have been performing the role of Christ, but the result is, for him, a deeply pagan experience. He becomes simultaneously Zeus, Prometheus and the vulture that pecks out Prometheus' liver. In a virtuoso chapter describing the various dreams of Glastonbury's inhabitants, Geard's daughter, Persephone, dreams she has actually become a tree, like a latter-day Daphne:

Persephone dreamed that green leaves were growing out of her feet and out of her shoulders and that she was standing stark naked in the centre of a group of silver-barked birch trees who were all, like herself, slim, naked girls with green leaves growing out of their heads and green leaves growing out of their feet.[27]

A host of other characters have their own responses to the legend. Sam Dekker has a vision of the Grail, like a latter-day Percivale: "He saw a globular chalice that had two circular handles. The substance it was made of was clearer than crystal; and within the water was a shining fish."[28].

The fish is a symbol of Christ, but again, Powys is keen to conflate the Christian and pagan aspects of the Grail, having Mr. Evans insist, "It obviously *does* refer to that ancient heathen Grail, far older than Christianity, which redeemed ... and always will redeem ... everyone who understands it...."[29]

The Grail is also described as "that fragment of Beyond-Time fallen through a crack in the world ceiling upon the Time-Floor" and as "a piece of the Absolute."[30] But the emphasis on landscape in this novel is of most concern to our theme. Powys was firmly of the belief that landscape *is* myth. The "very low-lying character of the country" around Glastonbury makes it "a fatal receptacle for the superstitions of two thousand years! Into this blue-purple vapour, into the bosom of these fields lower than the sea, floated, drifted upon the wind, all those dangerous enervating myths."[31] Powys describes the mystery of Glastonbury as "etheric."[32] This "Insula Avallonia" embodies the myth as well as generating it; and Cordelia, Geard's other daughter, is well aware of this:

She was certainly wrestling with a soil and with the growths of a soil that were more soaked in legends than any other hillside in Wessex. Legends seemed to thicken around her as she struggled blindly on between these budding apple trees. The fresh spring grass at the feet of these trees seemed in that darkness to be growing out of an earth that yielded to each step she took.[33]

Cordelia's father is convinced that Glastonbury is no less than a "reservoir of world magic,"[34] which had been unused. He intends to revive it and somehow cause a "crack in Cause and Effect"[35]—as succinct a definition of magic as one is ever likely to find. He also intends to perform miracles himself, attempting to cure an elderly woman of cancer by plunging her in the waters of the Grail Fountain: "[T]his chalybeate fountain on this particular hillside had been the scene of such a continuous series of mystic rites, going back to the neolithic men of the Lake Village, if not to the still more mysterious race that preceded them, that there had come to hang about it a thick aura of magical vibrations."[36]

But Powys is critical of Geard and Evans, whom he describes as "atheists towards the life-giving Sun-God," their ideas representing "the victory of vapour over light and of dampness over heat!" He accordingly relates their characters to the landscape around Glastonbury Tor where their conversation takes place: "A landscape of green and grey, a landscape with all hard outlines obliterated, was what just suited these three fantastical human beings. A common relaxation, a common inertia, a common langour descended upon them as they sat there, gazing down on that pastoral scene."[37]

Neither of them are true pagans in their theological abstractions, and they represent "everything that separates our race from nature." For Geard, God is an "ambiguous Emperor of the Cosmos," whose power he aims to channel by plunging "the Bleeding Lance of his mind into the half-dead cancer,"[38] and this attempt to redeem corrupt matter extends to Mr. Evans' belief that Nature itself is in need of redemption: "Something has come into it from outside." From his Christian viewpoint, it is "the Incarnation that transforms Nature." Evans actually loathes Nature, insisting that "God is outside Nature ... altogether outside ... creator of it ... but often loathing it as much as I do! I feel sometimes that Matter is entirely evil.... Something has taken up Matter into Itself.... Matter is no longer spare from Spirit. It has become the living flesh of Spirit."[39]

Charles Williams (1886–1945), an associate of C.S. Lewis and Tolkien, included very little landscape in his somewhat turgid Grail adventure, *War in Heaven* (1930). In this occult detective story, black magician Gregory Persimmons attempts to use the Holy Grail as a channel of power with which to destroy his enemies—and ultimately the world itself. Williams' approach rather anticipates the way in which the Indiana Jones movies exploit holy artifacts such as the Ark of the Covenant and the Grail in the name of action-adventure entertainment. Just as the Ark of the Covenant comes to life at the end of *Raiders of the Lost Ark* (dir. Steven Spielberg, 1981), the Grail in Williams' novel pulsates with magical power as Persimmons summons the spirit of the boy he intends to sacrifice: "A fantastic bubble of tinged cloud seemed to appear, moving upward from the Graal, and the bubble thickened and became mist and shaped itself into a form and face. The Graal was duly visible in a faint green light, through which and over which the recalled spirit took on a mortal covering." Soon after this, the divine nature of the chalice asserts itself:

> The faint glow round the Vessel faded and vanished; and all the moving darkness of the room seemed to direct itself towards and to emerge from the thickest core of night which beat in the Cup, as if its very heart were beating there. One moment only they heard and felt that throbbing heart, and then suddenly from it there broke a terrific and golden light; blast upon blast of trumpets shook the air; the Graal blazed with fiery tumult before them; and its essence, as at last that essence was touched, awoke in its own triumphant and blinding power.[40]

Williams, who had belonged to A.E. Waite's Fellowship of the Rosy Cross, firmly believed in what he was fictionalizing. He also possessed a perhaps disturbing knowledge of esoteric wisdom; but it is quite possible to interpret the Grail in *War in Heaven* as just one aspect of that psychological landscape of chaos and integration that lies within the individual psyche. We are all Grails, capable of creativity or self-destruction depending on how we are used and how we use ourselves, and consequently the Grail is closely related to the great Hermetic quest of alchemy.

As we have seen, Wolfram von Eschenbach thought of the Grail as a stone along the lines of the *lapis philosophorum* sought by the alchemists. Indeed, if the emerald from the brow of Lucifer was in fact another manifestation of the Grail, it is also related to the celebrated Emerald Tablet of Hermes Trimegistus, the great alchemical theoretician, whose most resonant phrase is "Quod superius est sicut quod inferius et quod inferius est sicut quod superius" ("That which is above is as that which is below and that which is below is as that which is above"). Long ridiculed, the Hermetic quest was rescued for the history of ideas in the twentieth century by Jung, who identified the psychological importance of what had previously been considered merely a chemical process. Jung identified alchemy's ultimate aim to unify of the female and male aspects of the psyche (the so-called animus and anima) by means of sun and moon symbolism. The symbolism of alchemy really concerns the integration of the unconscious, by means of the alchemical process itself. Alchemy emphasizes the importance of balancing the microcosm and macrocosm—in other words, our unity with, dependence upon and symbolization of the natural world as an objectification of psychological process.

However, Jung's explanation had already been formulated by an obscure Victorian, Margaret Atwood, whose sole book, *A Suggestive Enquiry into the Hermetic Mystery* (1850), was subsequently withdrawn from the public for fear that she had revealed too much.

Atwood, like Jung after her, quoted the alchemist Romanus Morenius as a key to revealing the hidden meaning of the quest: "Hæc enim res ex te extrahitur—This matter, O king, is extracted from thee."[41] This did not mean "some gold found sticking between a dead man's teeth" as Atwood suggests it might have been misleadingly intended to imply, but was rather an indication that the quest was largely concerned with psychological integration. Just as the symbols of Wagner's *Parsifal*—the Grail itself and the spear—are partly sexual, so the stone of the philosophers and the gold it is supposed to be able to transmute out of lead are symbols of the golden wisdom of self-knowledge. In his re-telling of Eschenbach's epic in *Parzival and the Stone from Heaven* (2001), Lindsay Clarke describes the Grail as a symbol and vehicle of healing. When, after his long pilgrimage in search of wisdom and insight, Parzival returns to the Grail castle, he is able to cure Anfortas, the sick leader of the Grail community; but it is really Parzival's compassion rather than the Grail that cures him: "Parzival stood transfixed as he watched this miracle of healing taking place before his eyes. In the same instant the whole chamber glowed luminous with the radiance of the Grail." Clarke has Parzival understand that the Grail is "the soft, protective chamber of a womb in which unborn twins, one male, one female, were floating in peace."[42]

Balance is also required between man and his environment, as Clarke points out in his afterword to the *Parzival* novel:

> Meanwhile much of the population of the earth erodes the natural environment in a struggle for profit or subsistence, and in the prosperous north-west, like a deep basenote trembling under everything, there is a sense of impending disaster. We know we've got things wrong. We don't know what to do about it.[43]

This is where the significance of landscape connects the quest to our theme. Atwood's life and her solitary alchemical volume had inspired Clarke's 1984 novel, *The Chymical Wedding*, in which he creates a narrative continuum between the researches of a fictionalized Atwood and a present-day attempt to recapture the psychological meaning of alchemy as a means of saving humanity from self-destruction. Significantly, Clarke is keen to set up a strong sense of place in his opening chapters, with highly charged descriptions of the Norfolk landscape in which both stories unfold. Against these evocations of the natural world, so powerful in their associative resonance of both ecological and psychological harmony, he contrasts on several occasions the sudden and earth-shaking intrusions of fighter jets from a local Air Force base. The threat of nuclear annihilation is offered as a magnification of that psychological fragmentation experienced by the main character—a writer out of tune with himself and those he loves. The writer encounters an elderly poet who is attempting to discover the lost secret of the character based on Atwood. The poet clearly explains that the contemporary world is as out of balance as the psychology of the writer he befriends, if that is quite the right word for the fractious and uncomfortable relationship they develop. Materialism, he argues, has diverted us from what is psychically necessary to us:

> [T]he physicists smash their way into the mirror of matter, and what do they find? That it breaks. That matter is fissile, right? Remarkable! Except that alchemy has always known this. It also understands that the more we are entranced by the dance of matter the more we fall victim to its fissile nature. It's not only the atom that splits. *We are in the mirror. Consciousness splits too. It shatters like china.*[44]

The threat of nuclear annihilation is symptomatic of the psychological imbalance thrown up by contemporary materialism—and the rejection, as nonsense, of the profound psychological truths embedded in the Hermetic quest. In this respect, Clarke is reiterating what Rudkin and his director, Alan Clarke, discuss so eloquently within the pagan-pantheistic context of *Penda's Fen*: the necessity to acknowledge and restore the balance between the physical and psychological, past and present, nature and man. Rudkin emphasizes the political aspect of this rather more than Clarke does in his novel, but the parallel remains. As we shall see, Rudkin has a radical poet expose the government's lies and the secret nuclear bunkers hidden under the elegiac rolling Gloucestershire countryside, which is so powerfully associated with Elgar's truly patriotic music. (It is patriotic in the sense of it being rooted in landscape rather than in the State, which merely appropriated it.) The implication is the same as Clarke's: We must claim back our landscape from those who strip us of our heritage, just as we must claim our psychic needs from the life-draining forces of materialism around us.

The structure of Clarke's Romance (his own designation) fluctuates between the Victorian past and the 1980s, the narratives of each aspect echoing each other to create that sense of historical continuity, which is also part of Clarke's theme: the realization that without a sense of the past, we have no identity in the present, and that without a connection with the rhythms and realities of the natural world we can sustain a society neither ecologically nor emotionally. An awareness of our pagan past nourishes the secular present, even if it bypasses the Christian intermediary, which was largely becoming redundant in Atwood's time and which Clarke demonstrates as being moribund in our own. The church in the present-day sections of the novel no longer has a congregation large enough to sustain a local priest. The priest who does officiate is peripatetic, dividing his pastoral care between other communities, and he no longer occupies the derelict and uninhabitable village rectory.

The church itself contains the pagan statue of a crudely carved fallen woman, pointing to her own sexual organ. This carving had deeply troubled the Victorian priest we meet in the time-shift sections of the novel. Known as Gypsy May, it summons memories of a mental breakdown suffered by the priest during his time in India. "Someone should have advised him that this church was distinguished from all other by a grotesquely unchristian feature," Clarke's narrator insists. "But why should they have troubled to do so? He alone knew the true nature of the mental turmoil he had suffered in India. He alone could have anticipated that what might seem to others no more than an antique curiosity would be to him a memorandum of despair."[45] The priest's dilemma somewhat resembles that of Miss Mayfield (played by Joan Fonteyn) in Hammer's *The Witches*. She too has suffered a breakdown caused by heathen iconography, this time in Africa. When she returns to England, she is befriended by a defrocked priest (Alec McCowen) who surrounds himself with Christian iconography, thus setting up a similar tension between paganism and Christianity. But the Victorian priest in *The Chymical Wedding* learns that both the physical and spiritual must be balanced with each other—and this is largely the meaning of alchemy itself.

At one stage in Clarke's story, the present-day, peripatetic rector of Munding, Neville Sallis, explains that holy sites are often built on ancient mounds: "A lot of churches round here are built on them. Under the patronage of St. Michael now—victory over the pagan serpent and all that."[46] This reference to the pagan serpent brings me to the intriguing, if somewhat breathless Gnostic theories of Philip Gardiner, which developed out of the equally controversial theories of Henry Lincoln, Michael Baigent and Richard Leigh in their best-seller, *The Holy Blood and the Holy Grail* (1982). Gardiner's proposal is that the Holy Grail is not "merely" a metaphor of the bloodline of the House of David (i.e., the womb of Mary Magdalene), as Lincoln *et al.* had suggested, but in fact the symbolic vessel of a *real* elixir formed somehow from serpent venom—thus explaining the widespread serpent cult underlying all modern religions and the pervasive symbolism of the caduceus not only in medical terms but also magical iconography. Whatever truth this theory has, it is certainly in the tradition of British pagan fantasy. One of its most powerful fictional precedents is Bram Stoker's 1911 novel, *The Lair of the White Worm*: Its vivid, if also somewhat lurid narrative echoes what Clarke's fictional Neville Sallis has to say about "the pagan serpent."

Stoker's novel also uses landscape to create a sense of mythic resonance. His idea of the shape-shifting snake woman Lady Arabella March, fascinating though it is, is nowhere near as powerful as his descriptions of the environment around the country estate of Castra Regis in a part of what was once known in Roman times as Mercia. This he describes as "the heart of England." Stoker's Sir Nathaniel de Salis (an interesting coincidence given the name of Clarke's cleric) explains:

> I want you to bear in mind the trend of the ground, for some time sooner or later, we shall do well to have it in our mind's eye when we are considering the ancient traditions and superstitions, and are trying to find the *rationale* of them. Each legend, each superstition which we receive, will help in the understanding and possible elucidation of the others.... The very heights and shapes and materials of these hills—nay, even of the wide plain that lies between us and the sea—have in themselves the materials of enlightening books.

Sir Nathaniel indeed goes on to mention King Penda (at least twice) as "the reactionary to Paganism," and goes into some detail about the history of the topography we are about to visit:

> That to the east, where the trees are, lower down—that was once the location of a Roman temple, possibly founded on a pre-existing Druidical one. Its name suggests the former, and the grove of ancient oaks suggests the latter [...] The old name translated means "Diana's Grove." Then the next one higher than it, but just beyond it, is called "*Mercy*"—in all probability a corruption or familiarization of the word *Mercia*, with a Roman pun included.[47]

It is in Diana's Grove—built over the old pagan temple with its foul-smelling well—that Lady Arabella dwells, having the opportunity to slither in her snake-form through subterranean tunnels. Stoker explains the geology too:

> Now the clay is easily penetrable, and the original hole probably pierced a bed of china clay. When once the way was made it would become a sort of highway for the Worm. But as much movement was necessary to ascend such a great height, some of the clay would become attached to its rough skin by attrition. The downway would have been easy work, but the ascent was different, and when the monster came to view in the upper world, it would be fresh from contact with the white clay. Hence the name, which has no cryptic significance, but only fact.[48]

But the White Worm does indeed have a great deal of cryptic significance, suggesting a phallic horror, which, when linked to a foul-smelling hole, suggests Stoker had certain sexual qualms. Indeed, the novel ends with the dynamiting of the well at Diana's Grove, implying a kind of sexual purification:

> The rent, torn and dislocated stonework looked worse than before; the upheaved foundations, the piled-up fragments of masonry, the fissures in the torn earth—all were at

the worst. But the horrid mass of slime and the sickening remnants of violent death were gone.[49]

As in *Dracula*, the sexual anxiety revealed by the tale has been overcome and neatly removed. It is, in effect, the mirror image of the kind of integration advocated by Clarke. One might say that Stoker's novel is a Grail romance in reverse, in which the holy vessel (the well) is destroyed, and the lance (or worm) is chopped up.

The 1988 Ken Russell film, *The Lair of the White Worm*, makes even more symbolic use of landscape. We begin with a long shot of the gaping entrance to an immense cave (in fact, "Thor's Cave" in Staffordshire), which immediately suggests the sexual meaning of the story. This is emphasized when Russell takes us inside the caverns, with their distinctly vaginal resonance, though these spaces could also represent the gut of the all-consuming worm itself: "A lovely place for a picnic," as Catherine Orenburg's Eve Trent points out. The opening shot of the action again roots the film in the landscape that generates the story: We see Peter Capaldi's appropriately named archaeologist, Angus Flint, dig up an immense prehistoric snake skull—Russell's take on the similar opening of *Blood on Satan's Claw*. Later, he references the scene in Disney's *The Jungle Book* (1968), in which Ka the snake hypnotizes Mowgli: Amanda Donohoe's snake woman, Lady Sylvia Marsh, is found draped over the branch of a tree in a distinctly antediluvian forest with moss covered trees. She slithers down and takes Eve back to her place for a bite.

Alan Garner's *The Owl Service*, which was also filmed for children's television, is conceivably another kind of Grail romance in that it, like the Hermetic Quest, is about the resolution of psychological imbalance and the reconciliation of sexual discord. Like *The Chymical Wedding*, it juxtaposes two love triangles from different periods, the past informing the present. Alison, who is on holiday in Wales with her half-brother, Roger, and the housekeeper's son, Gwyn, discovers a dinner service in the attic of their holiday home. Garner's inspiration for this device was a design by Christopher Dresser, which can be interpreted either as a series of stylized owls or as flowers depending on the direction from which it is viewed. Alison traces the images, interpreting them as owls. She then makes paper models of them, after which the designs miraculously disappear from the plates themselves. Thus is the psychological disturbance from a distant past unleashed. The plates had been made by others in an attempt to contain that disturbance; and when another attempt at containment is discovered in the form of a mural, revealed by falling plaster in the house, there is no stopping the chain of events.

The mural depicts a woman made of flowers who is in fact a representation of Blodeuwedd, the magical maiden fashioned out of flowers in the Welsh epic, *Mabinogion*: "So they took the blossoms of the oak, and the blossoms of the broom, and the blossoms of the meadow-sweet, and produced from them a maiden, the fairest and most graceful that man ever saw."[50] When Blodeuwedd betrayed her husband, Lleu Llaw Gyffes, with her lover, Gronw Pebr, she was condemned by her creator, who intended her for Lleu, to be transformed into an owl.

> "...I will turn thee into a bird; and because of the shame thou hast done unto Lleu Llaw Gyffes, thou shalt never show thy face in the light of day henceforth; and that through fear of all the other birds. For it shall be their nature to attack thee, and to chase thee from wheresoever they may find thee. And thou shalt not lose thy name, but shalt be always called Blodeuwedd." Now Blodeuwedd is an owl in the language of this present time, and of this reason is the owl hateful unto all birds. And even now the owl is called Blodeuwedd.[51]

Lleu killed Gronw with a spear, which legend has it pierced a standing stone behind which Gronw was defending himself. The standing stone remains and provides another gateway through which the past invades the present. This occurs literally when Roger takes a photograph of the stone. When the photograph is developed, an image of Lleu raising the spear is revealed.

The sexual tensions between Lleu, Gronw and Blodeuwedd are re-enacted by Roger, Gwyn and Alison. Roger's mother has brought shame on the family after an affair. Roger's father, Clive, has since remarried and has taken his new wife's daughter into the family, hence Alison's status as stepsister to Roger. Gwyn's mother, the housekeeper, once hoped to marry Clive's cousin, Bertram, who previously owned the holiday home in which they are staying, but Bertram died in a motorcycle accident, and Gwyn's mother is cheated of her inheritance. There are consequently three "re-enactments" of the ancient tragedy, and Garner implies that such re-enactments have been taking place throughout the ages because the ghost of Blodeuwedd has been unable to rest. Neither has the violence of the men she loved.

Roger takes a condescending attitude to the working-class aspirations of Gwyn, and is appalled by Gwyn's romantic intentions towards Alison. Alison also remains aloof, though somewhat teasing in her attitude toward Gwyn's advances. The tensions reach a climax in a storm. Alison becomes increasingly possessed by the owl form of Blodeuwedd's ghost. As feathers swirl around the room, Roger suddenly realizes that the only way to break the cycle is to forswear hatred and prejudice and to insist that the owls are not owls at all but rather flowers. He shouts his insight at Alison and instead of feathers, the room is filled with petals. The spell has been broken by forswearing conflict and looking at the designs as flowers, not owls. "What made you think those plates could be anything else? Why didn't you cut the pattern into flowers right at the start, you silly girl?" Roger asks, as Alison recovers from the ordeal.

We see here, though in disguised form, the key elements of the Grail quest: a magical vessel containing power that can be misused. Here it is a dinner plate rather than a goblet, and it is absorbed by Alison, after having traced the pattern. The plate therefore becomes an aspect of her, and as much a symbol of the anima—even of the womb—as the goblet Grail. There is also the spear of Lleu, which echoes the lance that wounds Amfortas in Wagner's *Parsifal* and the Fisher King in the Arthurian Grail romances, along with the theme of reconciliation and renunciation, which leads to redemption in the end.

Once again, the landscape described so eloquently in mythical terms by Garner, conveys much of the meaning of his tale. Though his approach is largely based on dialogue, Garner, like Tennyson before him, is able to convey profound evocations of location with relatively short passages. Even though much of the TV adaptation takes place inside the holiday home, the landscape is more in evidence as a setting (the main title sequence significantly begins with a photograph of the tree-crowned hill from which Lleu killed Gronw). The story is *embodied* in the landscape. At the beginning of the second chapter, Roger is lying beside the stone of Gronw. Three short sentences are all Garner needs to convey the mythic quality of a landscape unchanged since ancient times: "The mountains were gentle in the heat. The ridge above the house, drowned with a grove of fir trees, looked black against the summer light. He breathed the cool sweet air of the flowers."[52] Here, Garner summons the sense of an enclosed valley from which the tragedy cannot escape, the sense of oppressive summer heat, symbolizing the oppression of the legend, and, last but not least, the key to the riddle: the scent of flowers. Immediately after this description, Roger senses the ancient lance thrust through the hole in the stone. The past has indeed come back to life.

In Chapter Five, this sense of the landscape embodying and ushering forth the ancient tragedy is eloquently suggested in another evocation:

> There were no clouds, and the sky was drained white towards the sun. The air throbbed, flashed like blue lightning, sometimes dark, sometimes pale, and the pulse of the throbbing grew, and now ... he felt that the trees and the rocks had never held such depth, and the line of the mountain made his heart shake.[53]

Huw is found amid this landscape invoking the ghost of Blodeuwedd: "Come, apple-sweet murmurer, harp of my gladness, come summer, come [...] She's coming, [...] she won't be long now."[54] The TV adaptation accompanies these words with a memorable shot looking up at the trees, which are flooded with green light. Like Garner's prose descriptions, the shot doesn't last long, but is quite sufficient, in its mythic juxtaposition with the predominantly domestic settings, to create the necessary sense that the myth is embodied in the landscape itself. And green light brings us to the Green Knight...

Three

The Green Man Cometh...

On New Year's Day, in the anonymous 14th-century Middle English poem, *Gawayne and the Grene Knyghte,* a Green Knight rides into the banqueting hall of King Arthur's court. His clothes, his horse, his skin—even his beard are green, and he asks the knights if any of them is brave enough to decapitate him and agree to allow him the opportunity to return the compliment the following year. The knights are understandably wary and silent; Arthur is about to accept the challenge to save the honor of the court when at the last moment Gawain steps forward. The Green Knight bares his neck, Gawain raises his sword and the head is cut clean off. It is soon picked up, however, and replaced on the Knight's shoulders by the Knight himself, who then climbs back onto his horse and reminds Gawain of their bargain.

The poem later explains that the Green Knight is actually one Bertilak de Hautdesert, transformed by the magic of Morgan le Fey, Arthur's malevolent sister, who set up the whole charade to test the mettle of the knights and to frighten Queen Guinevere to death.

It is tempting to go beyond the story's "logical" explanation and interpret the Green Knight as a manifestation of the pagan Green Man—that powerful archetype of the forces of Nature, or the passing of the seasons and of the season's eventual renewal of life. In this light, the challenge of the Green Knight becomes a metaphor of the challenge each year offers us: Have we the courage to seek our own destiny through the passing years, to slay the old year in winter at risk of being slain ourselves, and to welcome the renewal of life with the spring?

There is still a great deal of uncertainty about whether this was the original meaning of the work—and even the word "green" may have been a mistranslation of the Irish word "glas" which can mean both green or gray; but one of the Irish stories on which the poem partly draws concerns the hero Cuchulain. As in King Arthur's Court, Cuchulain's warriors argue amongst themselves as to who is the bravest, whereupon a wild man with a huge beard enters the hall and offers the same challenge as that of the Green Knight: Only Cuchulain is brave enough to risk his own neck. The story formed the basis of Yeats' "Heroic Farce," *The Green Helmet* (1910). Yeats' representative of the "Green Man" is rather confusingly described as a Red Man, but his role is similarly redemptive, as he explains at the end of the play:

> *Red Man:*
> I have not come for your hurt, I'm the Rector of this land,
> And with my spitting cat-heads, my frenzied moon-bred band,
> Age after age I sift it, and choose for its championship
> The man who hits my fancy.
> *[He places the Helmet on Cuchulain's head]*
> And I chose the laughing lip
> That shall not turn from laughing whatever rise or fall,
> The heart that grows no bitterer although betrayed by all;
> The hand that loves to scatter; the life like a gambler's throw;
> And these things I make prosper, till a day come that I know,
> When heart and mind shall darken that the weak may end the strong,
> And the long remembering harpers have matter for their song.[1]

There are two feature films based on the Green Knight story. Both were directed by Stephen Weeks, who is perhaps better known for his work on the Jekyll and Hyde adaptation, *I, Monster* (1971). The first version appeared in 1973, with Nigel Green as the Green Man and Murray Head as Gawain. In 1984, it was somewhat unnecessarily remade as *Sword of the Valiant*, with a larger budget and starring Sean Connery as the Green Knight. Peter Cushing puts in a brief appearance and Ronald Lacey repeats the role he took in the first film. The 1973 version has a low-budget charm, though its Romantic score by Ron Goodwin and the somewhat theatrical costumes, along with the even more theatrical settings of Castel Coch and Cardiff Castle cause the proceedings to totter on the brink of Monty Python's Arthurian satire, but without the somber, Bergman-like imagery of that film. Crucially, it departs from the 14th-century text by ignoring the magical deception of Bertilak, making a clear distinction between the character based on him and the Green Knight. Weeks' Green Knight grows old at the end and withers away like Dickens' Ghost of Christmas Present—yet another manifestation of the Green Man. (Dickens' Ghost similarly appears at the end of the year and wears a holly wreath on his head with a "genial face," "sparkling eyes," "open hand" and "cheery voice."[2] The Ghost is also a kind of human horn of plenty, or Grail, bringing holly, mistletoe, red berries, turkeys, geese, poultry, etc.) That Weeks' Green Knight fades away like this, further enhances the interpretation Weeks wishes us to take of the Knight as representing the seasons and the turning of the year. Indeed, he organizes the film into four clearly marked sections, each introduced by medieval-style illuminated manuscripts depicting Spring, Summer, Autumn and Winter. Morgan le Fey is replaced by a beautiful and entirely benign maiden called Linet (Ciaran Madden), and the film ends with a narration that concisely explains the moral:

> Now Gawain understood the aim of his quest: He had prayed for knighthood and the nature gods had taken heed. Green Knight was sent to ripen his untutored youth and reveal to him, through trial and ordeal, the mystery of life. To each his seasons, to each his moments of defeat and glory, of loving and losing, of death and joyful rebirth, that his time on this earth might be fulfilled with courage and the purity of heart that befits a man. Thus ends the tale of Gawain and the Green Knight.

Sir Harrison Birtwhistle's 1991 opera, *Gawain*, is altogether a grimmer affair and much more faithful to the original poem. The musical style is rather more challenging than Ron Goodwin's mainstream film score for Weeks' first film version of the story, being in Birtwhistle's characteristically atonal idiom (many aspects of which would nonetheless fit quite comfortably into a film score, if topped and tailed with more traditionally Romantic gestures). The interpretation of Gawain is different too: He is presented as much more of a flawed hero, more selfish, more fearful of death and guilty of deception. Morgan le Fey is returned to the story, sowing discord at Camelot, and altogether there is a much more contemporary cynicism at work, undermining the Victorian ideals that inform Weeks' cinematic versions.

The Green Knight story is also echoed towards the end of Lindsay Clarke's *The Chymical Wedding*, in which, as we have seen, a cantankerous elderly poet, Edward Nesbit, has been investigating the Hermetic researches of a long-dead Victorian spinster. He learns that this researcher had been romantically involved with an unhappily married Christian cleric, who committed suicide as a consequence of their affair. Similarly disillusioned over his own life and the seeming failure of the Hermetic quest's promise of sexual and psychological harmony, Nesbit takes on the guise of the Green Knight, thrusting two branches of holly into his hair, before dragging Alex Darken, the man who has cuckolded him, to the now deserted parsonage of the long-dead Victorian vicar. This he calls the Green Chapel, and it is where the vicar committed suicide. In a travesty of the Victorian tragedy, Nesbit intends to kill himself with the cut-throat razor employed by the unhappy rector. Fortunately, this is avoided, but the pagan reference to the

Green Knight adds a weight and frisson to the incident, enriching its meaning.

Whatever his real significance, the Green Man has much in common with the life-rejuvenating qualities discussed by Frazer in *The Golden Bough*. With regard to the Slavic tradition of Green George, "a young fellow clad from head to foot in green birch branches," Frazer writes:

> At the close of these ceremonies the Green George, that is an effigy of him, is thrown into the water. It is the aim of the lad who acts Green George to step out of his leafy envelope and substitute the effigy so adroitly that no one shall perceive the change. In many places, however, the lad himself who plays the part of Green George is ducked in a river or pond, with the express intention of thus ensuring rain to make the fields and meadows green in summer.[3]

The Green Man appears in many Christian churches, imparting his message of wholeness and continuity. One might add that each time we watch Errol Flynn, or any other actor portraying Robin Hood in films, peering through the leafy boughs of Sherwood Forest, we are also catching a glimpse the Green Man of old. Robin Hood's connections with the Green Man and Robin Goodfellow (the Puck of Shakespeare's *A Midsummer Night's Dream*) are admittedly contentious— along with his supposed blood sacrifice for the good of the land, which we will be exploring in Chapter Eight; but in his desire to balance rich and poor, to create justice, and live in harmony with nature, there does seem to be a connection with the great pagan archetype. With our own ecologically challenged world, the Green Man has

NATURAL FORCES. The Bamberg Green Man (photograph by Johannes Otto Först/Wikimedia Commons).

also lent his name to the political Green movement, calling out to us for the need to rebalance our relationship with nature. His spirit has therefore been present all the way along our journey so far, even though he might not have revealed himself in person. He informs the sublime nature music of Wagner, in *Parsifal* and the *Ring*, both of which warn us of the danger of living outside the requirements and rhythms of the natural world. In Clarke's *Chymical Wedding*, Alex Darken openly speaks of his need to encounter him. At the beginning of the story, separated from his wife and suffering from writer's block, Darken has taken refuge in a remote Norfolk village. He wanders around the copses "where starlings thronged, where willow and alder brooded over a flooded marl-pit or hankered for the river's edge," and reaches for the promise of renewal, which he calls the Green Man. Whenever he seems to be on the brink of finding him, the Green Man retreats into the woods. "But this," he continues, "if ever, was the season of the Green Man, and this almost medieval wood was Green Man country."[4]

Quintessential image of pagan unity with nature that this pagan figure is, it is hardly surprising that the inn where locals gather in *The Wicker Man* is also called The Green Man. So is the pub in Kingsley Amis' satirical ghost story, *The Green Man* (1969), which is haunted by the ghost of seventeenth-century occultist, Thomas Underhill (his surname alone suggests a diabolic nature). Amis' model here would seem to be M.R. James' ghost story, "Number 13," which is set in a contrastingly *Danish* hotel room, though one that is similarly haunted by a comparable dabbler in the black arts, Nicolas Francken. (When the story was adapted by Pier Wilkie for the BBC in 2006, the action was relocated to England.) In Amis' novel, Underhill conjures a distinctly malevolent Green Man to seduce the hero's daughter, a development that undermines the pagan idea behind the archetype: Many Green Men are indeed unnerving, representing the forces of nature over which we have no control, but they are not demonic. In the Granada TV adaptation of Amis' novel, the Green Man superficially resembles Tolkien's Treebeard in *The Lord of the Rings*—the tree-like "Ent." However, the Ents serve Nature not the Devil.

Tolkien's description of Treebeard does indeed suggest the traditional iconography of the Green Man:

> ... a large Man-like face, almost Troll-like..., very sturdy with a tall head, and hardly any neck. Whether it was clad in stuff like green and grey bark, or whether that was its hide, was difficult to say.... The lower part of the long face was covered with a sweeping grey beard, bushy, almost twiggy at the roots, thin and mossy at the ends. But at the moment the hobbits noted little but the eyes. These deep eyes were now surveying them, slow and solemn, but very penetrating. They were brown, shot with a green light.[5]

The Green Man's presence in trees also informs Algernon Blackwood's "The Man Whom the Trees Loved" (1912) and "The Willows" (1907) Both tales explore our ambivalent relationship with nature, which is far more powerful than we are. "The Man Whom the Trees Loved" is perhaps less complex than "The Willows," but it is equally as unnerving. It describes the absorption of its main character, Mr. Bittacy, by the forest that surrounds him. To the horror of his conventionally Christian wife, he becomes part of what he loves and which loves him in return; but Blackwood makes a distinction between the "friendly" cedar tree in Bittacy's garden (a protective sentinel) and the trees in the forest surrounding the garden, which are more threatening, and sentinels of a different kind. Garden trees are "despised and pitied" by forest trees, because they are constrained by civilization.

Various theories are put forward, such as the idea that trees had once been capable of locomotion, being somehow creatures of a different sort, but which had lost the power of movement through indolence. It might also be that trees have a consciousness of their own, and that they really only come into their own at night; during the day, like vampires, they sleep. There are other Gothic elements: Woodcutters are "a race of haunted men"—executioners, indeed.

Gradually, the forest advances upon Bittacy. His wife dreams that a tree "whispered with ten thousand soft lips of green"[6]—an image of a Green Man if ever there was. Later, in "some unkind, resentful, hostile way," the trees gaze at her "with their myriad, vast sight,"[7]—lines which suggest the kind of Green Man that can be seen on the pedestal of the famous equestrian statue at Bamberg Cathedral in Germany. This is one of the most unnerving Green Men ever carved, whose fierce gaze emerges from curling acanthus leaves. William Anderson is quite right when he suggests that "[t]he most you could hope for in any dealings with him is that he should be on your side.... The Green Man here warns against the crushing of natural instincts in an unbalanced attempt to maintain control."[8] And this, of course, is what Blackwood's tale is partly about. Terrified, Mrs. Bittacy wishes to deny the forces of nature, whereas her husband is utterly unable to resist his pagan instincts. Balance is therefore needed in our negotiation with them.

The way in which the trees from the forest seem to be advancing on Bittacy's house also has something of the deeply unnerving effect of the stone monoliths that surround the dream house in Catherine Storr's 1958 novel, *Marianne Dreams*, to which I will return. Blackwood describes the forest trees as "sentinels set visibly about the limits of a camp that itself remained invisible."[9] They are far more threatening than Tolkien's Ents;

Blackwood suggests that the forest trees can move of their own accord: "The trees stood up—the whole beleaguering host of them stood up—and with the uproar of their million branches drummed the thundering message out across the night. It seemed as if they had all broken loose."[10]

More complex, perhaps, is Blackwood's most famous tale of all, "The Willows." Here, the trees are described as "symbols of the forces that are against us."[11] They are sinister in themselves, but gradually the two protagonists realize that the real threat is an entity from the fourth dimension which resents their presence on a remote island in the middle of the Danube, where the men have taken refuge for the night during a canoeing trip. Blackwood begins by describing the swaying, "continually shifting" willows, which somehow "give the impression that the entire plain is moving and *alive*."[12] Of course these trees are alive, but Blackwood suggests by the italics that they are also *conscious* in some way.

Later, the narrator perceives shadowy figures amid the willows, but "wholly independent of the swaying of the branches" and he "seemed to be gazing at the personified elemental forces of this haunted and primeval region."[13] These forces are not so much a personification of nature, like a Green Man, but something from beyond nature—something altogether alien. "I suddenly found myself overtaken by a vast sense of terror. From the shadows a large figure went swiftly by."[14] Whatever these figures are, they appear to resent the travelers to the extent of damaging their canoe and, in the end, killing another man, who acts as a kind of lightning conductor for the hostile force.

Here, Blackwood responds to the pagan power of landscape by interpreting it as an emanation from some kind of alternative reality; but, like the idea of the Green Man, this approach is really only a way of expressing the mystery of natural forces that are rooted *in* landscape. The instinct from which images of the Green Man are borne is the same, merely its interpretation differs. Almost as if writing a critical commentary on his own imaginative approach, Blackwood has his narrator explain: "When common objects in this way become charged with the suggestion of horror, they stimulate the imagination far more than things of unusual appearance."[15]

I have walked through a corn field in the middle of the night and been similarly unnerved by the rustling, gently swaying movement of the willow-like stalks, reminiscent not only of Blackwood's willows but also of the scene in a celebrated Val Lewton horror film, which suffers from the unpromising title of *I Walked with a Zombie* (dir. Jacques Tourneur, 1943). The movie is set on the Caribbean island of Saint Sebastian and the scene in question depicts the moonlit journey of Frances Dee's Betsy Connell, who takes the sick, somnambulant wife of a plantation owner to a voodoo ceremony, in the hope that the voodoo priest may cure her. They walk through a plantation as through some ancient vegetative temple, encountering a truly frightening figure of Darby Jones' Carre-Four, a mute Negro with bulging eyes who points the way to the houmfort, where the ceremony takes place. Inspired as the film was by Charlotte Brontë's *Jane Eyre*, it too may stake a claim in the soil of British pagan fantasy.

And there are other tendrils trailing behind the Green Man in British music and film. Arnold Bax's tone poem, *The Tale the Pine-Trees Knew* (1931), like Sibelius' rather more terrifying musical portrait of the Finnish forests in *Tapiola* (1926), is a kind of hymn in praise of the disturbing power of the Green Man. The Green Man also appears as a living statue in Peter Greenaway's film, *The Draughtsman's Contract* (1982). As a symbol of the forces of nature that has no respect for the formality and artificiality of the 17th-century aristocratic garden landscapes depicted in the film, this anarchic character is a kind of vandal—even a revolutionary. He replaces an obelisk, standing on its pedestal himself, and then urinates. Towards the end of the film, he dismounts from a bronze horse, making the statue redundant, as it no longer commemorates anyone. He then bites into and spits out a pineapple as a gesture of contempt for the elite society, which that once rare and expensive fruit represents. But it is almost as though Greenaway is telling us to spit out the film as well—cautioning us not to take it too seriously.

The Green Man is even present in the ironic commentary on 1960s culture that is Michelangelo Antonioni's *Blow Up* (1966). In this, a fashion photographer (David Hemmings) haunts the surreal solitude of a London park to observe some unexplained but presumably nefarious goings-on between a woman (Vanessa Redgrave) and a man who is perhaps her lover. No music is required here—and neither is there any dialogue. The sinister and pregnant mood of the scene is very largely conveyed by the sound of wind in the trees. The unnerving quality of this sound is something we have all experienced for ourselves. Even when watering flowers in my garden in the evening light, the rustling of ash trees towering over me has a melancholy, even frightening quality. It is the voice of the Green Man whispering.

The warning glance of the Green Man beneath the Bamberg Rider has also inspired what one might term eco-science fiction. John Wyndham's *The Day of the Triffids (1951)* is a Green Man tale gone wrong, in which nature takes revenge on humanity. The majority of the population in this story is made sightless by a shower of significantly *green* meteors. The carnivorous plants of the title, themselves the result of bio-engineering, can also blind their victims with their own poison, as well as being able to move and communicate amongst themselves. Thus does Wyndham create a metaphor for our ecological blindness. The landscape in the novel is predominantly an urban one, which the Triffids, like nature itself, are intent on colonizing by force. Consequently, Wyndham, following Blackward's example, is careful to create a familiar picture of London, made unfamiliar by events.

> Even Hyde Park Corner, when I reached it, was almost deserted. A few derelict cars and lorries stood about on the roads. Very little, it seemed, had gone out of control when it was in motion. One bus had run across the path and come to rest in the Green Park; a runaway horse with shafts still attached to it lay beside the artillery memorial against which it had cracked its skull. The only moving things were a few men and a lesser number of women feeling their way carefully with hands and feet where there were railings, and shuffling forward with protectively outreached arms where there were not. Also, and rather unexpectedly, there were one or two cats, apparently intact visually, and treating the whole situation with that self-possession common to cats. They had poor luck prowling through the eerie quietness—the sparrows were few, and the pigeons had vanished.[16]

The novel ends bathetically, with only the hope that it will be possible to drive the Triffids back from the land they have usurped; but the irony is that it is surely humanity that has usurped the land from nature. Worse, it has corrupted nature by breeding the Triffids, which turn upon their creators. A not particularly faithful screen adaptation appeared in 1963, directed by Steve Sekely, but the story was better served by a BBC TV treatment in 1981, directed by Ken Hannam. It similarly exploited shots of familiar London landmarks devoid of traffic and pedestrians.

We might extend the influence of the Green Man to other literary examples of characters seeking union with the forces of nature. D.H. Lawrence's *Women in Love* (1921) contains a striking scene, made even more explicit by Ken Russell in his 1969 film adaptation. In the movie, Birkin (Alan Bates) runs naked through open country, wandering among "thickets of hazel, many flowers, tufts of heather, and little clumps of young fir-trees, budding with soft paws." It is wet and he wants to touch everything, "to saturate himself with the touch of them all." He walks among the primroses, "his legs, his knees, his arms right up to the arm-pits, lying down and letting them touch his belly, his breasts.... He went through the long grass to a clump of young fir-trees, that were no higher than a man. The soft sharp boughs beat upon him, as he moved in keen pangs against them, threw little cold showers of drops on his belly, and beat his loins with their clusters of soft-sharp needles."¹⁷

Lawrence's vision was given an even stronger homosexual connotation in E.F. Benson's *Raven's Brood,* in which Dennis feels compelled to go out running in the dark. Dennis is a lusty young farmer, deeply attached to another lad called Willie. (Willie is referred to as "Dennis's Willie" in a euphemism Benson was surely conscious of when he was writing). Though Dennis also has eyes for a girl and hopes to marry her, his love for Willie remains the stronger attraction. Dennis, like Birkin, gets wet and muddy in his desire to be united with the landscape, and by implication the Green Man himself:

MASTER BATES. Alan Bates goes native in Ken Russell's *Women in Love* (1969).

> The rain had begun to fall thick again, and still the uncomprehended rapture grew, and he must shout as he ran. His skin dripped with the sweat of his swift going, and he paused to strip off the encumbering jersey which close clung to him, and he gasped to feel the cool wet pricking on his back and chest and shoulders.... He threw himself face-downward, bare-chested, on a bed of sprouting bracken, and lay there panting, while the arteries throbbed in his throat and temples. He flung wide his arms and legs, as if to wrestle with the earth his mother, or hold her in strong embrace, and with his spread fingers he dug into the soft soil, and with his teeth he bit the sappy fern stems.¹⁸

If the Green Man had been watching, he would have been well pleased.

Four

Tristan and Isolde

The Celtic legend of Tristan and Iseult reached its most compelling modern expression in Wagner's epoch-making music-drama of 1865. So powerful was Wagner's profoundly psychological approach to this ancient myth that anyone who wished to make a new version of the story thereafter could hardly avoid being compared with Wagner's treatment. The immense impact of the music was a cultural thunderclap, and it still rumbles in our own time in a film such as Lars von Trier's apocalyptic *Melancholia* (2011), where the *Tristan* prelude invests the proceedings with a depth and meaning the film might lack without it. Even Wagner was astonished by his own creation, writing from Venice to his muse and lover Mathilde Wesendonck:

> Child! This Tristan is turning into something *terrible*!
> This final act!!!--------------
> I fear this opera will be banned—unless the whole thing is parodied in a bad performance—: only mediocre performances can save me! Perfectly *good* ones will be bound to drive people mad,—I cannot imagine it otherwise. This is how far I have gone!!![1]

So overwhelming was the effect of this work that in 1965, Elliot Zuckerman entitled his centenary study of its cultural reception *The First Hundred Years of Wagner's* Tristan, implying, quite rightly, that there would be plenty more Tristanizing in the second hundred. Even the 2006 *Tristan and Isolde* film directed by Kevin Reynolds negotiates Wagner by studiously ignoring it, both musically and in its gritty, anti–Romantic approach, which is nonetheless romantic with a small "r," in a way deemed appropriate for apparently more hardened, though in fact far more sentimental millennial audiences.

British versions of the story at the end of the nineteenth and the beginning of the twentieth centuries could hardly dissociate themselves

THE LANDSCAPE OF MYTH. Sophie Myles as Isolde in Kevin Reynolds' *Tristan and Isolde* (2006).

entirely from the mythic power of Wagner's music. Intriguingly, however, the spirit of the age had stimulated Wagner and Matthew Arnold to address the Tristan story within two years of each other. (Arnold's poem, "Tristram and Iseult," appeared in 1852, while Wagner first conceived his own *Tristan und Isolde* in 1854.) The two responses are very different, not least in Wagner's decision to feature only one Iseult. (In the original tale there are two: Iseult of Ireland and Iseult of Brittany.) Wagner also has Tristan and Isolde already in love before the love potion merely removes their restraint. In stark contrast, Arnold includes both Iseult of Brittany and Iseult of Ireland, and the love potion is wholly responsible for what happens:

> Iseult of Brittany?—but where
> Is that other Iseult fair,
> That proud, first Iseult, Cornwall's queen?
> She, whom Tristram's ship of yore
> From Ireland to Cornwall bore,
> To Tyntagel, to the side
> Of King Marc, to be his bride?
> She who, as they voyaged, quaff'd
> With Tristram that spic'd magic draught,
> Which since then for ever rolls
> Through their blood, and binds their souls.[2]

In 1882, Algernon Charles Swinburne published his long blank verse poem, *Tristram of Lyonesse*, which he had begun many years earlier. Written for cash when he was "'pressed to death' for money and he complained frequently of his lack of 'tin,'"[3] it failed to ignite the controversy and adulation of his earlier work. According to his biographer Edmund Gosse, "The amatory completion of *Tristram* was not objected to by anybody. What was objected to in the poem, alas, was its lack of vital interest."[4] But it contains some striking seascape imagery in tune with our theme:

> The soft hoar bloom
> Of springtime olive-woods, the warm green gloom
> Of clouded seas that swell and sound with dawn of doom,
> The keen thwart lightning and the wan grey light
> Of stormy sunrise crossed and vexed with might,
> Flash, loom, and laugh with divers hues in one
> From all the curved cliff's face, till day be done.
> Against the sea's face and the gazing sun
> And whensoever a strong wave, high in hope,
> Sweeps up some smooth slant breadth of stone aslope,
> That glowed with duskier fire of hues less bright,
> Swift as it sweeps back springs to sudden sight
> The slender of the moist rock's fervent light,
> Fresh as from dew of birth when time was born

Four. Tristan and Isolde

> Out of the world-conceiving womb of morn.
> All its quenched flames and darkling hues divine
> Leap into lustrous life and laugh and shine
> And dark into swift and dim decline
> For one brief breath's space till the next wave run
> Right up, ripple down again, undone,
> And leave it to be kissed and kindled by the sun.[5]

Other British versions of the tale appeared in subsequent years. We have seen how Sir Henry Irving had produced a King Arthur play by the art critic and playwright J. Comyns Carr (1849–1916) at the Lyceum Theater in London. Irving's co-star in the production, Ellen Terry, later made a great impression in Irving's production of *Macbeth*, wearing a costume that had been designed by Carr's German wife. An enthusiastic Wagnerian, Carr went on to arrange the first British performance of *Parsifal* at Covent Garden in 1914. Meanwhile, his four-act play, *Tristram and Iseult*, appeared in 1906, very much in the manner of Shakespeare without Shakespeare's wit. First performed at the Adelphi Theater in 1906, it starred the Canadian actor, Matheson Lang, and the English Lily Brayton in the title roles. Carr's detailed stage directions reveal his training as an art critic and his desire to create esthetic drama, in which the stage picture is just as important, if not more important, than the words. Act I opens in "A narrow bay surrounded by rocky shores."

> At the back to R. a shelving ledge of rock forms a natural quay, by the side of which is moored the ship in which TRISTRAM is to set sail for Ireland. The vessel is set diagonally, with its raised stern turned to the audience, the remainder being hidden by a rising wall of rock, behind which it finally glides out of view at the fall of the curtain. Down these rocks to R. descends a steep path leading from the castle, the ramparts of which are seen in perspective. The centre of the stage forms the fringe of the little bay stretching away to the cliffs that overlook the open sea.[6]

Carr also requires lavish interiors, though one scene is set on deck at sea, and the love scene (Carr's equivalent of Wagner's "Liebesnacht" in *Tristan*) is set in a forest:

> ISEULT'S bower in the forest. The entrance that leads to the dwelling is down stage R., and the dwelling itself is either wholly hidden by trees or merely suggested by a portion of the turret seen above the trees. Beyond this entrance rises a rocky eminence down which is a practical path that leads to the stage. It is overgrown with trees, through which the rays of the moon fall on the scene. This rocky mound forms the nearer bank to a little stream that falls behind it and flows across the scene from R. to L.; and another bank rises beyond and projects further on to the stage. In the centre a shelving bank borders the stream which lies here in a quiet pool, and then flows on till it falls into the bay that is seen between the trees on L. There are no entrances on L., which can be treated as though the rocks rose again with the stream running beyond them downwards to the bay. The general effect of the scene is of an enclosed dark woodland bower intersected by a rivulet.[7]

Scenery also plays a powerfully dramatic role in the tableau at the end of the play when the ill-fated lovers die in one another arms:

> While the Chorus is heard, the stage completely darkens and the scene changes to the final tableau. During this change, which is conducted to the accompaniment of the spirit voices, from the hollow pool behind the two figures of TRISTRAM and ISEULT rises the form of ISEULT OF THE WHITE HANDS, whose figure is lit by a single shaft of light. When the change is complete, the bank upon which they are reclining forms a jutting head of land that is backed by a wide expanse of moonlit sea, and the ghostly ISEULT is seen bending over the prostrate forms of the two LOVERS, her white arms and hands outstretched in the moonlight.[8]

This version of the famous story was followed in 1917 by the play of another art critic, Arthur Symons (1865–1945), whose *Tristan and Iseult* was dedicated to actress Eleonora Duse, the celebrated lover of Gabrielle D'Annunzio, with an accompanying quotation (in Italian translation) from Act III of Symons' play: "Non sentite il sangue delle rose stillare/Tra le mie dita nella vostre due mani?" ("You do not feel the blood of the roses burn/Between my fingers into both your hands?"). This imagery is of a much more overtly decadent kind that one encounters in Wagner's text, and reflects Symons' advocacy of *fin de siècle* esthetics. He too restores the two Iseults: Iseult of Brittany who loves Tristan like a wife and Iseult of Ireland who loves him like a mistress. Influenced by Wagner's example, Symons suggests that Iseult of Ireland's love for Tristan prefigures the love potion. At first she professes to hate him for having murdered her uncle, Morold, but she later asks the queen of Ireland:

> Why could I not kill Tristan? I had the will [....]
> Mother I hate him! he has spilt our blood.
> Why is it that my eyes follow his eyes,
> As a hound follows his master?[9]

When the potion unleashes their passion for each other, Symons effectively uses a landscape of blinding light as a metaphor for their emotions:

> Look, Tristan, there is nothing here but light:
> Light in the sky, light in the hollow sea,
> The encircling and caressing light of the air!
> Light eats into my flesh and drinks me up:
> I am a cup for the immense thirst of light;
> I cannot see you, Tristan, for the light.[10]

Iseult's imagery here forms an intriguing counterpoint to the kind of Wagnerian staging techniques that were being developed by Appia around the same time, with all that concealed lighting diffused through immense panels of gauze surrounding the performance space. Iseult certainly describes a landscape here, but it is very much a psychological one. Wagnerian imagery also informs Iseult of Brittany's desolate sea imagery, as she attends to the wounded Tristan at the end of the play: "I see the grey sea and the grey sky."[11] This is surely an echo of the Shepherd's line "Öd und leer das Meer!" ("Bleak and bare the sea!") in Wagner's *Tristan* poem, which was subsequently quoted by T.S. Eliot in *The Wasteland*. A more concise and effective evocation of landscape it would be hard to find, and this is presumably why Eliot was so drawn to it as shorthand for his own landscape of disillusionment and collapse.

Thomas Hardy (1840–1928) began his *The Famous Tragedy of the Queen of Cornwall* around the same time as Symons began work on his Tristan play, but did not finish it until 1923. He even supplied his own sketch of "An Imaginary View of Tintagel Castle at the Time of the Tragedy" as a frontispiece, giving a clear idea of the maritime landscape he had in mind. It required "no theatre of scenery," but another sketch depicts an "Imaginary Aspect of the Great Hall at the Time of the Tragedy" in the event of a theater performance. He does, however, specify an "arch in the back-centre (a doorway or other opening may counterfeit this) through which the Atlantic is visible across an outer ward,"[12] again emphasizing the importance of the landscape of the sea as a resonant accompaniment to the drama, which had been so important to Wagner before him. Indeed, imitating the form of "A Play for Mummers," he prefaced the proceedings on the title page with a brief quotation from the medieval *Tristan* poem of Gottfried von Strassburg, Wagner's original source material:

> Isot ma drue, Isot m'amie.
> En vos ma mort, en vos ma vie!

Merlin is present in the cast, along with "Chanters" who form a kind of chorus, described as "Shades of Dead Old Cornish Men and Women," and Iseult the Fair competes with Iseult the Whitehanded for the affections of Tristan. Hardy elaborated the text for Rutland Boughton, who wrote music for an operatic version of the play at Glastonbury in 1924, which Michael Hurd believes to be perhaps Boughton's finest work.[13] Boughton and Hardy hit it off personally: "I think I like that man as much as anyone I have ever met," Hardy told his wife,[14] complimenting Boughton's musical version as "a glorification of the play."[15] The critics tended to agree: According to the *Manchester Guardian*, "Mr. Boughton's music almost glitters with psychological insight, but at first hearing one requires a quick mind to perceive even one half of the subtlety that binds the characters in past and present events, binds them and hurries them to their violent end."[16]

Four years after Hardy published his *Queen of Cornwall*, the poet laureate John Masefield (1878–1967) published his own *Tristan and Isolt* drama. He begins with the death of Kolbein, who has enslaved Marc as a puppet king, having murdered Marc's brother, sired Tristan with that brother's wife and then had her killed. Later, Kolbein is killed by Tristan. The latter role was played in the original 1927 performance by John Laurie, later to be associated with the role of Private Frazer in the popular BBC comedy series, *Dad's Army*. Although Tristan is a serious role, Masefield also includes some farcical elements in direct contrast to the Wagnerian monolith he had still had to negotiate to make the play his own. Accordingly, he introduces a Swineherd called Hog, his wife Sowkin and their son Pigling, which gives Masefield the opportunity for some splendid low humor:

> Our Easter duty of March black-puddings, lord.
> There, sire, a love of a pudding, as black as medicine,
> And thick and soft as a lady's thigh: do feel I.
> There's something to lean on in a day of trouble.[17]

Later, there is a comic scene involving the attempted theft of a pig by some courtiers, the object of which is to humiliate Tristan, but this backfires.

Again, Tristan acknowledges that he loves Isolde long before drinking the potion: "I cannot look on her face without loving her."[18] And in this version, Brangwen, Isolt's servant, is ordered to take her mistress' place in the marriage bed with Marc, as Isolt cannot endure the thought of intercourse with anyone but Tristan. This is very different from Wagner's account, but Tristan's lines, "Would God/To-morrow might never dawn" and Isolt's "It may never dawn./The world may end,"[19] are deeply resonant of Wagner's day/night imagery in the music-drama with which this story in still most associated.

In Isolt's final lament, Masefield, like his predecessors, brilliantly employs landscape imagery to create a suitably mythical resonance:

> The brook will run down
> Over the shingle to sea; and the corncrake call;
> And the honeysuckle, up in the glen, drowse sweetness:
> And the moon come over the hill: mother will have them,
> Not I: I shall not have them. What shall I have?
> Some sky for the two wild swans to be wing in wing,
> Some holly thicket for the stag and his deer,
> Some space in heaven, where I, the comet, will seek
> My mate, past withering orbs and moons gone blind,
> For centuries to come.[20]

This tradition of using landscape to generate mythic resonance returned in Kevin Reynolds' 2006 film version of *Tristan and Isolde*. It opens with shots of brooding skies over bald mountains, with wind whistling on the soundtrack and a shivering rabbit sheltering amid dry grasses, no doubt symbolizing the vulnerability of all the characters in this film's depiction of an unpredictable, treacherous and violent society. Two figures (young Tristan and his father, played by Thomas Sangster and Richard Dillaine) are then shown walking through a vast landscape of valley and towering mountains as a backdrop to the main title of the film itself. In this somewhat hipster version of the ancient tale (featuring a great many beards, leather jerkins and the mumbling of such contemporary-sounding phrases as "by all means," "thanks," "I'll be back" and "It's fine"), it is barely five minutes before we have a brutal fight sequence in which Tristan's parents are killed. The funeral of Tristan's mother is again framed by tall cliffs. Wide skies climb over Isolde when she expresses her desire to see England, followed by a spectacular chase and ambush scene set in another part of the forest. The ensuing dead bodies are then placed on barges and set off over the sea. The flaming arrows shot at them to set them alight, echo both Jerry Zucker's *First Knight* and Matthew Arnold's rather more spectacular "Balder Dead":

> Then the wind fell, with night, and there was calm;
> But through the dark they watched the burning ship
> Still carried o'er the distant waters on,
> Farther and farther, like an eye of fire.
> And long, in the far dark, blazed Balder's pile;
> But fainter, as the stars rose high, it flared;
> The bodies were consumed, ash choked the pile.[21]

Tristan, believed killed, is in fact one of the drifting corpses, but he has only been poisoned, and the flames do not appear to have burned him. He drifts towards Ireland where Isolde finds him on a magnificently billowing shore. Waves roll in with Wagnerian momentum, and the first kiss of the lovers, some scenes later, also takes place on the elegiac beach. They eventually part on the sea, with Reynolds' camera riding the waves; and, later, when Tristan takes Isolde back to Cornwall as King Marke's bride, another sea journey is inevitable. On her wedding day, Isolde floats on a barge towards her husband, dressed in white, her arms outstretched like the Lady of the Lake.

All this sea and water imagery not only also features in Wagner's poem for *Tristan und Isolde*, but was also used by Wagner as a metaphor of music itself in his important essay, "Das Kunstwerk der Zukunft" ("The Artwork of the Future," 1850):

> Music encircles her sister [dancing and poetry] in affectionate entwinement; they are the *shores* by means of which she, the *sea*, unites two continents.
> ... Not yet may we give up our figure of the idea as music's being. If *rhythm* and *melody* are the shores at which the tonal art meets with and makes fruitful the two continents of the arts primevally related to it, then tone itself is the primeval fluid element, and the immeasurable expanse of this fluid is the sea of *harmony*. Our eye is aware only of its surface; its depth only our heart's depth comprehends. Up from its bottom, dark as night, it spreads out to its mirroring surface, bright as the sun; from the one shore radiate on it the rings of rhythm, drawn wider and wider—from the shadowy valleys of the other shore rises the longing breeze which agitates the placid surface in waves of melody, gracefully rising and falling.[22]

Sea imagery is really the strongest connection Reynolds' film has with its Wagnerian counterpart; but what it lacks musically, it makes up for in the poetic use it makes of landscape, which punctuates the violent action of the first half of the film. One particularly arresting shot shows a tall obelisk atop dark cliffs against the sea—an image that has nothing to do with the story, but which nonetheless exudes usefully mythical resonance. A later close-up of the full moon achieves the same effect.

Five

Celtic Twilight

King Arthur having led the way, late-Victorian Britain found itself in the midst of Scotch mists, Welsh wizards and Irish legends. Ironically, this was partly due to the fact that Arthur's Christian mission had failed. Despite appearances to the contrary, Christianity itself was failing. No matter how many pre-Raphaelite churches the Victorians built, God was increasingly absent. How to fill the void? The old gods, awoken, would eventually haunt the twentieth-century consulting rooms of Jungian psychotherapists, encourage the growth of homeopathy and meditation, and stimulate a reaction against the satanic mills of Christian industrialism by encouraging a return to nature. For the Victorians, occultism was another solution, one that Irish poet W.B. Yeats enthusiastically embraced. He enrolled in the recently formed Order of the Golden Dawn and later the Theosophical Society of Madame Blavatsky, whom he knew in person. There was also the nationalist question. Ireland had long desired Home Rule. A nationalist revival, hand in hand with the vacuum left by a God in retreat, led to a revival of the old gods from a time long before the Act of Union.

Along with a Nationalist revival came a Celtic revival, which inspired Scottish and Welsh writers as well. But like all copies and pastiches, this revival was rather different from the genuine article. The genuine article merely provided a model, reinterpreted in the light of modern needs. In this respect, the Celtic Twilight writers, artists and musicians who gathered around Yeats' example find their equivalent in the fantasy castles of King Ludwig and the "mythic" operas of Wagner, which inspired Ludwig in the first place. This is not to say that revivalist art is not powerful and affecting, but it is as well to realize what it is not. As Frank Delancy puts it, Yeats "and others who names crop up in any discussion of the Irish 'Celtic Twilight' movement wrote—with very rare exceptions—in English, and had no native working knowledge of Gaelic."[1] The point of reviving Celtic memories was both an escape from reality and a contradictory desire to create a revitalized society. It did not spring from the people but from modern intellectuals and artists. An earlier, eighteenth-century example of this occurred when James MacPherson (1736–1796) managed to hoax the whole of Europe with his literary forgeries, claiming they were translations of genuinely ancient writings by the Celtic bard, Ossian, the most famous of which is "Fingal." Ironically, Ossian had far more of an impact on continental Europe than in Britain. Napoleon devoured Ossian's poems; Goethe translated them into German and quoted from them in his 1804 novel, *The Sorrows of Werther*; Ingres covered an immense canvas devoted to Ossian, and the man who had voted against Berlioz winning the Prix de Rome, Jean-François Le Suer, completed a phenomenally successful opera, *Ossian—ou Les bardes*, in 1804.

In Britain, Ossian's impact was less intense. Theater audiences had been able to enjoy "a grand historic, dramatic pantomime in two acts" called *Oscar and Malvina*, with music by William Shield (completed by William Reeve), first performed in 1791. (Oscar was Ossian's son; Malvina, the son's bride.) The music became popular enough to feature as the Overture to J.R. Planché's adaptation of John Polidori's tale, "The Vampyre," in 1820. It was an appropriate borrowing, as this play was also set in Scotland, the vampire himself uniquely wearing a kilt. The production's playbill made much of the "authentic" Scottish scenery "including correct Views of the BALSITICK COLUMNS of The Island of Staffa, with The GROTTO and CAVE of FINGAL,"[2] later to be made even more famous in Mendelssohn's *Hebrides* Overture in 1830. Inevitably, the influence of Sir Walter Scott's Romantic "Waverley" novels, with their celebration of Scottish landscape and history, lay behind all of this as well, but Ossian had prepared the ground for Scott's later success. Ossian's influence also made itself felt in the first two names of Oscar Fingal O'Flahertie Wills Wilde.

MacPherson's Ossian was important not so much from a literary as from a political point of view. After the defeat of Scottish nationalist hopes at Culloden, Ossian gave back a cultural identity to a defeated people. "In effect," writes Delaney, "a Bard had been re-born (born had they but known) and whatever the miserable political realities Celtic song rang out again, the glorious past had come to life."[3] One of the key aspects in all of this was McPherson's conflation of heroism with landscape as we see in these four examples:

> Like autumn's dark storms pouring from two echoing hills, towards each other approached the heroes. Like two deep streams from high rocks meeting, mixing roaring on the plain; loud, rough, and dark in battle meet Lochlin and Inis-fail. Chief mixes his

strokes with chief, and man with man: steel, clanging, sounds on steel. Helmets are cleft on high. Blood bursts and smokes around. Strings murmur on the polished yews. Darts rush along the sky. Spears fall like the circles of light, which gild the face of night: as the noise of the troubled ocean, when roll the waves on high.[4]

The little hills are rolled in its course, the rocks are half-sunk by its side. But Cuthullin stood before him, like a hill, that catches the clouds of heaven. The winds contend on its head of pines, the hail rattles on its rocks. But, firm in its strength, it stands, and shades the silent vale of Cona. So Cuthullin shaded the sons of Erin, and stood in the midst of thousands.[5]

As a hundred winds on Morven; as the streams of a hundred hills; as clouds fly successive over heaven; as the dark ocean assails the shore of the desert: so roaring, so vast, so terrible, the armies mixed on Lena's echoing heath.[6]

Beside a stream of roaring foam his cave is in a rock. One tree bends above it. The rushing winds echo against its sides. Here rests the chief of Erin, the son of generous Semo. His thoughts are on the battles he lost. The tear is on his cheek.[7]

But Celtic identity crosses national borders; it applies to many nations and peoples, and Celtic legend has cross-fertilized European culture. All through the years in which the earlier British Tristan plays were being written, Yeats was hard at work redefining the ancient Celtic legends of Ireland. In his 1931 poem, "Coole and Ballylea," he identified himself as one of the "last Romantics" and had used Irish legend to channel his hatred of English materialism, explaining, "[T]he Celt, never having been meant for utilitarianism, has made a poor business of it...."

We hated at first the ideals and ambitions of England, the materialisms of England, because they were hers, but we have come to hate them with a nobler hatred.... We hate them now because they are evil.[8]

In his early epic poem from 1889, "The Wanderings of Oisin," nationalism, magic and myth combine in a way that foreshadows many of Yeats' later Celtic works. He symbolized these nationalistic tensions in the story of a demon who enchains a beautiful lady. Oisin, or Ossian, has spent a century among the Sidhe. He defeats the demon and then travels to an island of forgetfulness where he is awakened after another century and determines to return to Ireland; but as soon as he sets foot on the soil of his homeland which is now a Christian country, his 300 years catch up with him. Throughout the poem, landscape again plays an important mythologizing role:

And I rode by the plains of the sea's edge, where all is barren and grey,
Grey sand on the green of the grasses and over the dripping trees,
Dripping and doubling landward, as though they would hasten away,
Like an army of old men longing for rest from the moan of the seas.[9]

Oisin was the son of Fionn mac Cumhaill, from whose own legend derives the brief cameo appearance of the Salmon of Knowledge in *The*

Wicker Man. In Fionn's story, a salmon eats nine hazelnuts and gains the whole of the world's knowledge, and whoever eats the salmon will also gain that knowledge, which Fionn does. Yeats does not discuss this legend in *The Wanderings of Oisin*, but he does include a resonant line that echoes it: "Have a speed like the speed of the salmon herds." In *The Wicker Man*, the salmon takes the form of a costume to be worn by one of the inhabitants of Summerisle during the May Day celebrations, which lead to the sacrifice of Edward Woodward's unfortunate Sergeant Howie.

The title of Yeats' 1893 collection of faery and folklore stories, *The Celtic Twilight*, economically encapsulates it all, for "twilight" can mean both the glimmerings of dawn as well as the onset of darkness. It is a condition between light and dark, and thus a metaphor for the parallel state of consciousness he hoped would lead to national renewal. Consequently, in his play, *Countess Cathleen* (1899), Cathleen sells her soul to the devil to save the Irish peasants from starvation. *The Land of Heart's Desire* (1894) also combines the occult world of fairies with a nationalist agenda.

Yeats dreamed of founding an Occult Nationalist Order, and even considered purchasing an abandoned castle on the island in the middle of Lough Key at Roscommon to serve as its headquarters. Despite it being in fact a nineteenth-century folly, the place nonetheless had an undeniably mythical and Romantic resonance for him:

> The situation at the centre of the lake, that has little wood-grown islands, and is surrounded by wood-grown hills, is romantic, and at one end, and perhaps at the other end too, there is a stone platform where meditative persons might pace to and fro. I planned a mystical Order which should buy or hire the castle, and keep it as a place where its members could retire for a while for contemplation and where we might establish mysteries like those of Eleusis and Samothrace; and for ten years to come my most impassioned thought was a vain attempt to find philosophy and to create ritual for that Order.[10]

The opening poem of Yeats' collection, *The Rose* (1893), expresses his desire to sing of things Irish and Mystical. He invokes the mythical figures of Cuchulain, Fergus, Druids and "old Eire." Accordingly, poems about Fergus and the Druid and Cuchulain immediately follow. Cuchulain, born of a virgin, was bound to a pillar and shot through with arrows, his blood fertilizing the earth; but in "Cuchulain's Fight with the Sea," Yeats tells of how Cuchulain mistakenly kills his own son before wrestling with his own psyche, symbolized by the sea.

Reversing the story of Oedipus, this story also has much in common with the Finnish story of Kullervo, who impregnates his sister and consequently falls on his sword. Sibelius felt that story to be the most suitable with which to express the National Romantic agenda of his first major work, the *Kullervo Symphony*, in 1892. Yeats' line "Cuchulain I, mighty Cuchulain's son" is similar to a much reiterated line in *The Kalevala*, "Kullervo Kalervon poika" ("Kullervo, son of Kallervo"). What Kullervo did for Sibelius, the Cuchullain legend did for that musical equivalent of Yeats, Arnold Bax (1883–1953). Bax's positive infatuation with Irish legend belies the fact that he was actually born in the London suburb of Streatham; but after his studies at the Royal Academy of Music he moved to Ireland and even wrote poetry for a while under the pseudonym of Dermot O'Byrne. His last orchestral foray into this Irish subject matter, *The Garden of Fand*, a musical sea-scape strongly influenced by the example of Debussy's *La Mer*, dates from 1914. Fand, the daughter of the sea lord Manannan, seduces Cuchullain who, somewhat in the manner of the Russian legend of Sadko, forgets his earthly wife Emer and lives in the sea "Garden" with Fand. Bax's purpose here was again to suggest a mythical landscape rather than tell the story in musical terms. It is consequently a symphonic impression of the sea, given a mythological mood by association. So many of Bax's other works reflect the contemporaneous mood of Yeats' Celtic Twilight: *In the Faëry Hills* (1909), *Spring Fire* (1913), *November Woods* (1917) and *Tintagel* (1917–19) are all Celtic landscapes in musical form.

Yeats continued *The Rose* with a "Faery Song" and the famous "The Lake Isle of Innisfree," which encapsulates Yeats' desire for a mystical retreat. Of all of Yeats' poems, it is one of the most evocative invocations of mystical landscape, replete with the purple glow of noon, the glimmer of midnight, the bee-loud glade, evenings filled with linnet wings, and the lapping waters of the lake. "Countess Cathleen in Paradise" is followed by "The Man Who Dreamed of Faeryland," which is exactly what Yeats did all his life. The titles of these poems are often what invest the texts with their mythic resonance: The titles are essential contextualizers.

In his next collection, *The Wind Among the Reeds*, there is a "Song of Wandering Aengus," the Celtic Eros, who plays his harp and is accompanied by singing birds. Again, the title adds mythic resonance to a poem that is not specifically about Aengus at all, being rather a magical eclogue and reminiscence of lost or perhaps longed-for love. Landscape is again used to evoke the pagan, with references to a hazel wood, apple blossom in the hair of the girl invoked by the poet, and the hollowed and hilly lands through which he wanders. Succinct and carefully chosen imagery, often no more than two words (such as "dappled grass" through which the poet desires to walk with the girl he imagines), create entire vistas of landscape, which encapsulate a state of mind; and it would seem that the state of mind cannot exist without the landscape. The landscape must come first to inspire the mood. It then becomes a metaphor *of* the mood.

In another poem from this collection, "The Hosting of Sidhe," Yeats' vision of the Sidhe is in marked contrast to the popular view of fairies up to that time. The nineteenth century had been the great era of spiritualism, a movement imported from America where it had been born in 1848 with the hoax perpetrated by the Fox sisters, which even their later confession did nothing to harm. The Victorians, troubled by religious doubt, harried by science and desperate for meaning beyond mere materialism, had consequently been fascinated by fairy imagery, as Jeremy Maas has explained:

> Fairy painting was close to the centre of the Victorian subconscious. No other type of painting concentrates so many of the opposing elements in the Victorian psyche: the desire to escape the drear hardships of daily existence; the stirrings of new attitudes towards sex, stifled by religious dogma; a passion for the unknown; psychological retreat from scientific discovery; the latent revulsion against the exactitude of the new invention of photography.[11]

Fairy painting, often an articulation of landscape for magical effect, attracted the attention of many artists of the time, inspired as they often were by the fashion for spectacular fairy ballets and Shakespearean productions, which went to town on fairy "effects." This was, after all, the age of Mendelssohn's music for *A Midsummer Night's Dream*. Even Wagner, whom I have so often mentioned in parallel with developments in Britain, wrote his own fairy opera, *Die Feen*, in 1834. (It was not actually performed until 1888, five years after his death.)

Richard Dadd (1817–1886), who later suffered from mental illness, leads the distinguished list of British artists who worked in the fairy field. Joseph Paton (1821–1901), Daniel Maclise (1806–1870) and the opium-inspired John Anster Fitzgerald (1819–1906, known as "Fairy Fitzgerald") helped to create the predominate Victorian image of gossamer-winged fairyland. Richard Doyle (1804–1883) was also fascinated by elves, pixies, goblins and butterflies. His brother Charles, whose alcoholism landed him in a lunatic asylum, was the father of Sir Arthur Conan Doyle (1859–1930), who later championed the celebrated Cottingley fairies affair.

The Cottingley fairies have themselves inspired several films. The British-made *Photographing Fairies* (dir. Nick Willing, 1997) takes a more ambivalent approach to the possibility of fairies actually existing in its parallel narrative, in which a disillusioned and grief-stricken photographer eventually comes to believe that the fairies of a similar so-called hoax, originally regarded to have been an hallucination, might well be genuine.

If classical ballet gave the impression of defying gravity, gossamer wings attached to the tutus of its ballerinas, pantomime went even further with hidden wires and machinery; but this idea of fairies having wings is a relatively modern invention, first suggested by Alexander Pope in the second canto of his long poem, *The Rape of the Lock* (1714):

> Some to the sun their insect-wings unfold,
> Waft on the breeze, or sink in clouds of gold;
> Transparent forms, too fine for moral sight,
> Their fluid bodies half dissolved in light,
> Loose to the wind their airy garments flew,
> Their fluid bodies half dissolved in light,
> Thin glittering textures of the filmy dew,
> Dipt in the richest tincture of the skies,
> Where light disports in ever-mingling dyes,
> While ev'ry beam new transient colours flings,
> Colours that change whene'er they wave their wings.[12]

It is from Pope, therefore, that Barrie's Tinkerbell, all of Walt Disney's fairies and even the psychedelic ones in *Photographing Fairies* ultimately derive. Yeats, however, tapped into a different and older fairy tradition. These creatures did not sport wings and were less benign, as Shakespeare hints in *A Midsummer Night's Dream*. Though Queen Mab, the fairies' midwife, is described in *Romeo and Juliet* in charmingly diminutive and harmless terms as "no bigger than an agate-stone/On the fore-finger of an alderman," the *Midsummer Night's Dream* fairies are potentially more disturbing. Puck is a version of the hobgoblin Robin Goodfellow, known for his mischievous jests as well as the help he might lend to farmers and busy housewives. Titania is "proud Titania," and Oberon is "jealous"—in Puck's words, "passing fell and wrath." When roused, as Oberon is at the beginning of the play, "elves, for fear,/Creep into acorn-cups and hide them there."[13] Such characteristics link Shakespeare's fairies with the Sidhe—that proud and terrible faery race, which rides out on the Eve of St. John from their home on the banks of the river Boyne, their aim being to enlighten poor mortals by converting them to their own religion. Evans-Wentz quotes Eugene O'Curry's observation that "the term (*sidh*, pron. *shee*) as far as we know it, is always applied in old writings to the palaces, courts, halls or residences of those beings which in ancient Gaelic mythology held the place which ghosts, phantoms, and fairies hold in the superstitions of the present day."

In modern Irish tradition, "'the People of the *Sidhe*,' or simply the *Sidhe*, refers to the beings themselves rather than to their places of habitation. Perhaps partly on account of this popular opinion that the *Sidhe* are a subterranean race, they are sometimes described as gods of the earth or *dei terrinei*, as in the *Book of Armagh*; and since it was believed that they, like the modern fairies, control the ripening of crops and the milk-giving of cows, the ancient Irish rendered to them regular worship and sacrifice, as the Irish of to-day do by setting out food at night for the fairy-folk to eat."[14]

Yeats was not alone in his Celtic quest. Maud Gonne, the woman with whom he was infatuated and whose later marriage to another man devastated him, was equally enthusiastic about mystical Irish nationalism. (She wrote, "If only we could make contact with the hidden forces of the land it would give us strength for the freeing of Ireland."[15]) So too were George Russell (1867–1935, known as "A.E.") and William Sharp who, like Arnold Bax after him, felt the need of a pseudonym—in Sharp's case "Fiona Macleod"—fully to express his Celtic side. In 1897, these individuals formed a London-based group under Yeats' leadership dedicated to "visionary exploration." Yeats believed Russell had "extraordinary clairvoyant powers,"[16] and "A.E."'s poetry is almost entirely of a mystical and visionary nature. Sometimes, it is specifically allied to the Irish Celtic cause, as in "Children of Lir," "A Call of the Sidhe," "On Behalf of Some Irishmen Not Followers of Tradition" and "In Connemara." Less specifically entitled poems also refer to characters from Celtic mythology, which the notes at the end of his Collected Poems gloss. Among others, these include Aengus, Balor, Dana, Lu, Fomor and … Etain.

The name of Etain has a particular resonance for us as she appears in Fiona Macleod's play, *The Immortal Hour*, which was later transformed into Rutland Boughton's phenomenally successful opera of the same name. In it, the role of Etain was originally played by Gwen Ffrangcon-Davies (later to appear in Hammer's *The Witches* and *The Devil Rides Out* [dir. Terence Fisher, 1968]). Etain, a faery princess, wanders into the world of men, marries their king, Eochaidh, and is later lured back to her faery world by means of the celebrated Faery Song: "How beautiful they are, the lordly ones." This became popular in its own right. Like many people of her own generation, my mother knew the song but had no idea about Boughton, still less of Fiona Macleod before I introduced the opera to her. The charm of the melody, however, should not blind us to the warning in the words themselves that these fairies are "proud and are terrible." Evans-Wentz traces the origins of the Etain story to *The Book of the Dun Cow*, in which Etain and Midir make their final departure through the somewhat less romantic conduit of a chimney. Eochaidh rushes out to see two white swans flying over Tara, bound together by a golden chain.[17]

Sharp almost grew to believe that Fiona Macleod was an individual entity, and he kept the secret of her real identity a closely guarded secret.

His wife, Elizabeth, explained that the Fiona Macleod phase "belongs to the last 12 years of William Sharp's life, the formative influences which prepared the way for it went back to childhood."

> Though "the pains and penalties of impecuniosity" during his early struggles in London tended temporarily to silence the intuitive subjective side of his nature in the necessary development of the more objective intellectual "William Sharp"—critic, biographer, essay and novel writer as well as poet—he never lost sight of his desire to give expression to his other self.... But the secret was totally guarded by the small circle of friends in whom he confided. "'Fiona' dies" he was wont to say, "should the secret be found out."[18]

Even Yeats believed in Macleod's existence, and for "her" sake he even agreed to call his Mystical Order "Celtic" rather than "Irish,"[19] for the persona of Macleod was derived from Sharp's Scottish ancestry and "her" tales, prose poems and dramas were predominantly Scottish or mythically Scottish in setting. Sharp and "Macleod" also shared Yeats' occult agenda, and Yeats wrote to Macleod regarding the kind of dramas he envisioned for what eventually became the Abbey Theater:

> My own theory of poetical or legendary drama is that it should have no realistic, or elaborate but only a symbolic and decorative setting. A forest, for instance, should be represented by a forest pattern and not by a forest painting. One should design a scene, which would be an accompaniment not a reflection of the text. This method would have the further advantage of being fairly cheap and altogether novel. The acting should have an equivalent distance to that of the play from common realities.[20]

After her death, *The Writings of "Fiona Macleod"* was issued by Heinemann in eight volumes. The titles of these books express much of their mystical Celtic agenda: *The Dominion of Dreams, The Divine Adventure, Where the Forest Murmurs*; but fascinating though these mood pictures are, it is fair to say that Macleod's fame today rests on the play, *The Immortal Hour*, which does indeed conform to Yeats' distinctly symbolist ideals about drama, and also has a good deal in common with Maeterlinck's approach, particularly in *Pélleas et Mèlisande*. Like Mèlisande, Etain is discovered in an amnesiac state in a wood. She is found by Eochaidh, just as Mèlisande is discovered by Golaud. Eochaidh marries Etain, only to lose her again, as happens with Golaud and Mèlisande. Macleod explained that the story "symbolised, I think, the winning of life back to the world after an enforced thralldom: the renewal of Spring: in other words, Etain is a Gaelic Eurydice, Midir a Gaelic Orpheus who penetrated the dismal realm of Eochaidh, and Eochaidh but a humanized Gaelic Dis."[21]

Another important character is Dalua, the Dark Faery Fool, "whose falling shadow even causes bewilderment and forgetfulness."[22] As members of the Sidhe, Macleod's faery-folk are not only "proud and terrible" but also have "fierce blue eyes." (Macleod's vision went on to inspire the Elves of Tolkien's *The Lord of the Rings* [1954], who are described as being "very tall," "grave and beautiful" and "clad wholly in white."[23]) The famous Faery Song lures Etain back to the world from which she came, leaving Eochaidh lamenting the destruction of his dreams: "My dreams! my dreams! Give me my dreams!" Dalua touches him, and he falls into the "Dream of Death."

When Boughton adapted Macleod's drama, he incorporated various of her other poems to expand upon the possibility of exploiting the choral writing with which he hoped to create his distinctly English version of Wagnerian music drama. The work also contains some of Boughton's most magical and atmospheric writing: Wagnerian orchestral sonorities combined with impressionistic pentatonic harmonies. Particularly effective is his music for a magical fountain of beauty and dreams, sparkling with glockenspiel and fluttering flute. Harps ripple, alongside repeated figures in the strings, the atmosphere of which is comparable to Tennyson's scenes describing the Lady of the Lake:

> I see a Fountain and within its shadow
> A great fish swims, and on the moveless wave
> The scarlet berries float: dim mid the depths
> The face of One I see, most calm and great,
> August, with mournful eyes.[24]

A voice from the fountain urges Eochaidh not to entangle his fate in the world of faery-lore, and to return to his own world before it is too late; but Eochaidh is not to be deterred. The scene is one of the great set pieces of Boughton's opera. So too is the pomp of the marriage ceremony, which is introduced by an extended *a cappella* choir of Bards, Druids and Warriors. Boughton here incorporated several of Macleod's poems such as "The Bells of Youth" and "Green Fire" to create a pageant of choral splendor, which is very much a response to the marriage scene at the end of the second act of Wagner's *Götterdämmerung*.

Midir's "I am a song" is very much a set-piece aria, referencing the mystical Salmon of Knowledge within the context landscape:

> I am a song
> In the Land of the Young
> A sweet song:
> I am Love.
>
> I am a bird
> With white wings
> And a breast of flame
> Singing, singing.

> The wind sways me
> On the quicken-bough:
> Hark! Hark!
> I hear laughter.
>
> Among the nuts
> On the hazel-tree
> I sing to the Salmon
> In the faery pool.
>
> What is the dream
> The Salmon dreams,
> In the Pool of Connla
> Under the hazels?
>
> It is: There is no death
> Midir, with thee,
> In the honeysweet land
> If Heart's Desire.[25]

It could well be Aengus himself singing here, and a visual parallel to this moment can be found in the painting by the Celtic Revival Scottish artist, John Duncan (1866–1945), whose *Angus Og* of 1908 similarly sings of love "putting a spell on the calm of the sea." Naked but for a ribbon around his ribs, with outstretched wings, the red-haired god raises his arms and sings out over the rocky crags of the coastline. Duncan in fact illustrated a four-part publication called *The Evergreen*, which was organized by Sharp and his publishing partner, Patrick Geddes. This was intended to be the beginning of a Celtic library series, but the project foundered after negative criticism, even though Duncan's work was praised.[26] Duncan even heard Yeats read his own poetry,[27] and his Celtic Revival paintings often provide a visual parallel to the moods summoned by Yeats, Sharp and Russell. Duncan's Celtic subjects include *Merlin and the Fairy Queen*, *Tristan and Isolde* (1912), *The Children of Lir* (1914), a pencil drawing of *Cuchulainn* (inscribed "CUCHULAINN I care not though I last but a day if my name and my fame are a power for ever!"), a depiction in chalk of a *Fairy Enthroned*, a crayon drawing of the *Head of a Celtic God* and, perhaps most famous of all, his large painting of *St. Bride* (1913), who is carried over the sea by two angels so that she may witness the birth of Jesus in the Holy Land.

Duncan's painting, *The Riders of the Sidhe* (1912), attractively complements Yeats' earlier poem, "The Hosting of the Sidhe" (1899), in which the fairies come between men and the hopes of their hearts and the deeds of their hands. They are, indeed, a Celtic version of the Moirai, or Fates of ancient Greece. Accordingly, as Duncan's biographer, John Kemplay, explains, the fairies in *The Riders of the Sidhe* each carry a symbol of fate:

> The first rider in the procession carries the symbol of wisdom (the tree of life); the second rider, the symbol of love (the Grail cup of the heart of abundance and healing); the third rider, the symbol of the will in action (the sword of power); and the fourth rider, the symbol of the will in its passive form (the crystal that reveals the past and the future).[28]

In his earlier career, Duncan had explored Arthurian terrain in *The Taking of Excalibur* (1897), in which Merlin rows Arthur out onto the magical lake, where a fierce Lady of the Lake holds the sword aloft, accompanied by an even fiercer sea serpent. Duncan also depicted *Deirdre of the Sorrows* in a compact, tightly constructed chalk drawing. This legend similarly appealed to Boughton, who originally conceived a ballet on the subject but later revised to form his second symphony in 1927. The three movements tell a story comparable to that of Tristan and Isolde: Dierdre, betrothed to King Conochar, is enamored of Naisi. The lovers elope (in the symphony's second movement) and finally are united in a kind of Liebestod.

Ultimately, the Celtic Revival was a retreat from reality in search of a cult of beauty. "O where are thy white hands, Heart o' Beauty?"[29] Macleod asks in a poem whose title, "Heart O' Beauty," says it all. "Dim face of Beauty haunting all the world," writes Macleod in another:

> Fair face of Beauty all too fair to see,
> Where the lost stars down the heavens are hurled,
>   There, there alone for thee
>   May white peace be.
>
> For here, where all the dreams of men are whirled
> Like sere torn leaves of autumn to and fro,
> There is no place for thee in all the world,
>   Who drifts as a star,
>   Beyond, afar.[30]

"Who dreamed that beauty passes like a dream?"[31] Yeats asks in "The Rose of the World." "Ah, faeries, dancing under the moon,/A Druid land, a Druid tune!"[32]—those were his hopes for an Ireland he longed for in "To Ireland in the Coming Times." But "A.E.," who shared this vision perhaps even more intensely, understood that Beauty, "the breath of Beauty," is a delicate thing in a world that has other concerns:

> I saw how all the trembling ages past
> Moulded to her by deep and deeper breath,

> Neared to the hour when Beauty breathes her last
> And knows herself in death.³³

All these visionaries longed for the Land of Heart's Desire, which finds its most eloquent musical expression in Boughton's setting of Midir's words in *The Immortal Hour*:

> Go, look for it:
> Lost name, beautiful:
> Strayed from the honeysweet
> Land of Youth.
>
> I am Midir, Love:
> But where is my secret
> Name in the land of
> Heart's desire?³⁴

There is a great deal of repetition in Celtic Twilight texts: reiterated expressions of longing for natural and metaphysical beauty, for roses, for Hidden Fire, for twilit seas, for rainbows. Whether in spring or winter, sunshine or rain, it is through landscape that the Celtic Twilight finds and describes the Land of Heart's Desire. The landscape stands as a metaphor for a state of mind, as is made quite clear in "Flame on the Wind," one of Macleod's most extraordinary poems:

> O wind without that moans and cries, O dark wind in my soul!
> I would I were the wet wild wind that's blowing to the Pole!
> I'd seek the plunging bergs of ice to cool my flaming heart...
>
> O Flaming Heart,
> I'd drown you deep where the great icebergs roll!
> I'd follow on thy beating wings the wings of the wild geese,
> I'd seek among the plunging hill the phantom-flight of peace...
> O is there peace for hearts of fire in gloom and cold and flight—
> Torches of night
> 'Mid swaying bergs that grind the trampling seas?³⁵

Macleod is above all a landscape artist, and in other collections she resorts to prose-poems, rather than the more sustained narratives, such as *Pharais* and *The Mountain Lovers* with which Sharp began Macleod's career. But even in *The Mountain Lovers* there is a preoccupation with the power of landscape, as in this superb description of a storm over the sea:

> It was a night for the peat-glow. Outside, the darkness was intense. The thunderstorm had rolled heavily away, though the far hills still held an echo. But a great wind had arisen, and blew across the heights with a sound like the trumpets of a mighty host. From the forest came a vast tumultuous sigh, as of the moaning sea.³⁶

In *Tragic Landscapes*, the human element is largely rejected in favor of the narrative of landscape itself—a tempest, mist and "summer-sleep," as is the case in the "Nature Essays" from *Where the Forest Murmurs*, which describe forests, grasses, tides, summer clouds, dusk and so forth, but very little human action. Macleod's self-sufficient descriptions here are settings for stories that never happen:

> Isolated, in one of the wildest and loneliest mountain-regions of the Highlands of Ross, I know a hill-tarn so rarely visited that one might almost say the shadow of man does not fall across its brown water from year's end to year's end. It lies on the summit of a vast barren hill, its cradle being the summit of a vast barren hill, its cradle being the hollow of a crater. Seven mountains encircle Maoldhu from north, south, east and west.
>
> When the wind blows, one hears its lamentation falling across the hill-solitudes and down through the mountain-glens with a sound as of a myriad confused sobs and cries, a sound that is now a forlorn ecstasy and now the voice of the abyss and of immeasurable desolation.[37]

It was Edgar Allan Poe who originated this sort of esthetic landscape writing, in tales such as "The Domain of Arnheim" (1846) and most particularly "Landor's Cottage" (1849), which he concludes with the statement, "It is not the purpose of this work to do more than give, in detail, a picture of Mr. Landor's residence—as I found it."[38] But Macleod invests her Scottish landscapes with a mythic grandeur lacking in Poe's primarily esthetic approach.

Landscape is also central to the genre of the ghost story, the ghostly element usually emerging from a detailed description of locale. M.R. James' "A Warning to the Curious" (1925), for example, concerns the discovery of a buried crown said to guard the English coast against invaders. The amateur archaeologist who finds it is haunted by the ghostly keeper of the crown who pursues him until it is replaced; but it is James' description of the unnerving Suffolk landscape in which the story unfolds, that is the essential element in the tale. (It was brilliantly realized on film in Laurence Gordon Clarke's 1972 BBC television adaptation.) James fully understood the power of landscape as the generating principle of the narrative, and though he drew back from Macleod's self-sufficient descriptions, he nonetheless created portrait landscapes that were even more powerful because less self-consciously poetic than Macleod's:

> On your left (you are now going northward) is heath, on your right (the side towards the sea) is a belt of old firs, wind-beaten, thick at the top, with the slope that old seaside trees have; seen on the skyline from the train they would tell you in an instant, if you did not know it, that you were approaching a windy coast. Well, at the top of my little hill, a line of those firs strikes out and runs towards the sea, for there is a ridge that goes that way; and the ridge ends in a rather well-defined mound commanding the level fields of rough grass, and a little knot of fir trees crowns it.[39]

This landscape, already rather arresting, becomes menacing at night:

> There was nothing to be seen: a line of dark firs behind us made one skyline, more trees and the church tower half a mile off on the right, cottages and a windmill on the horizon on the left, calm sea dead in front, faint barking of a dog at a cottage on a gleaming dyke between us and it: full moon making that path we know across the sea: the eternal whisper of the Scotch firs just above us, and of the sea in front. Yet in all this quiet, an acute, an acrid consciousness of a restrained hostility very near us, like a dog on a leash that might be let go at any moment.[40]

James' story is a reworking of the Celtic legend of Bran, a supplementary element of which inspired Joseph Holbrooke's symphonic poem, *The Birds of Rhiannon* (1926), and which the Victorian Celtic scholar, Alexander Macbain, described in his study of Celtic mythology:

> Manannan, the son of Lir, is in the Welsh Myths one of the seven—that mystical number, so common in the old Welsh poems—who escapes from Ireland on the death of his brother, Bran, the blessed, king of Britain. Returning with the head of Bran, the seven heroes found the throne usurped by Cassibelaunus and retired to Harlech, where the birds of Rhiannon kept them enchanted by their music for seven years; and after this they feasted for 80 years more at Gwales in Penvro, from which place they set out to London and buried Bran's head with its face to France. As long as Bran's head was left there facing France no invasion of Britain could be successful. Unfortunately Arthur exhumed the head, declaring that he would maintain the country against any foe without the need of supernatural safeguard.[41]

Lir, whom Macbain reminds us was the father of Bran, was originally a sea God akin to Poseidon, and was later humanized as Lear, the king made famous by Shakespeare. Another of the names for Lir was Lud, and Lud has inspired a more contemporary response from Iain Sinclair in his poetic rumination on the urban landscape of London's churches, *Lud Heat* (1975):

> Lud was the mythological king of Britain who is supposedly buried beneath London's Ludgate, and whose name is one of the etymological contenders for the place name of the capital. Heat is a term used throughout Sinclair's intratext ... to denote energy, malign or benign, often associated with certain places, and persisting through time.[42]

Sinclair's belief (rather than mere theory, it would seem) is that buildings such as Nicholas Hawksmoor's series of baroque churches in London are "generators" of energy or, as Allen Fisher suggests, it is "because of these lines of energy, that certain situations occur."[43] These "situations" include the crimes of Jack the Ripper, the Ratcliffe Highway murders of 1811 (commemorated by Thomas de Quincy in his essay, "On Murder Considered as One of the Fine Arts" in 1827) and, in more recent times, the ritualistic battering to death of Abraham Cohen in the summer of 1974, on Cannon Street Road, which was marked with three ritualistic coins "laid at his feet, as they were in 1888 at the feet of Mary Ann Nicholls, the first Ripper victim."[44] These occult interpretations of place and coincidence, now part of what is termed "psycho-geography," are another way in which landscape has been used to articulate myth—in this case, *urban* landscape. Poe, Baudelaire and Arthur Machen were all progenitors of this now influential trend in both literary and popular culture, ranging from Peter Ackroyd and W.S. Sebald to the magus of counter-culture, Alan Moore, whose graphic novel, *From Hell*, inspired Allen and Albert Hughes' 2001 film starring Johnny Depp. In Machen's *The London Adventure—or The Art of Wandering* (1924), one of psycho-geography's seminal texts, Machen explained, "I try to reverence the signs, omens, messages that are delivered in queer ways and queer places, not in the least according to the plans laid down either by the theologians or the men of science."[45]

From our point of view, it is appropriate that Sinclair, who followed in Machen's footsteps, chose Celtic myth for the foundations of his own vision. His vision of London is therefore built on a specifically mythic landscape, which generates his (often quite incoherent) psycho-geographic fantasies. Incoherence is, indeed, part of its *raison d'être*, for Sinclair's approach is largely subjective in its attempt to form order out of chaos by means of coincidence. This is largely the program of all mythologies, to say nothing of conspiracy theories, all of which require some meaningful grounding in a so-called "hidden" (or occult) truth. Such a conflation of emotional response with the need for connection and myth has always been a dangerous game to play.

Anthony Shaffer was keen to point out these dangers in his screenplay for that cinematic re-working of Celtic myth and psycho-geography that is Robin Hardy's *The Wicker Man*. It appeared in 1973, two years before Sinclair's *Lud Heat*, but Sinclair makes no mention of this film in his text, despite references to Hammer horror films in general and Hammer's *Frankenstein and the Monster from Hell* (dir. Terence Fisher, 1974) in particular.

Often interpreted as a film in praise of paganism over the stultifying nature of a particularly puritanical version of Christianity, *The Wicker Man* is anti-religion altogether, as its human sacrifice at the end makes abundantly clear. Accordingly, Shaffer sets up a complex interplay and comparison between Christian and pagan motifs: the Eucharist is paralleled in the scene when young Myrtle Morrison (Jennifer Martin) is forced by her mother May (Irene Sunters) to endure the placement of a frog in her mouth to take away her cough. The maypole, which schoolmistress, Miss Rose (Diane Cilento), explains is an overt symbol of the penis, is an inversion of the Christian ideal of marriage, which attempts to contain such erotic drives within the confines of a "sacrament." The generative power symbolized by the cavorting of a hobbyhorse is a pagan equivalent of the Virgin Mary, whom, as Summerisle points out to a shocked Sergeant Howie when observing the ritual of parthenogenesis, was "herself impregnated by a ghost." The Hand of Glory, used to lull Howie into a trance-like sleep, also has its Christian parallel in the use of incense and altar candles. The libation to the god of the sea—a barrel of wine rolled out into the ocean waves— is balanced by shots of Howie drinking Christ's blood in the Eucharist scene at the beginning of the film. Even the crucifixion is paganized in the final scenes when Howie is sacrificed in the Wicker Man itself.

A great deal of the ritual and belief systems of the film also derive from Frazer's *Golden Bough*, and I will be addressing these later, but here I would like to explore the importance of landscape as a method by which *The Wicker Man* generates its mythic power. Much of the film is actually framed within domestic settings—streets, courtyards, harbor, village greens, schoolhouse and Lord Summerisle's castle. This not only creates the required sense of claustrophobia, but also a feeling of normality, which makes the gradually apparent abnormality and ultimate horror of the situation all

CHRISTIAN COPPER COMES A CROPPER. Christopher Lee as Lord Summerisle in the climax of *The Wicker Man* (dir. Robin Hardy, 1973).

the more powerful. However, the film is topped and tailed with impressive landscape sequences, which both contextualize the action and enhance the pagan mood of its shattering conclusion. We begin with Howie's seaplane taking off, accompanied by the stern vocals of "I am come to the low country." Howie flies over islands, cliff faces, moorland, small islands covered in moorland, mountains with strange finger-like peaks; and then, with the change in music to the much warmer sound of "Corn Rigs," we see cultivated terraces, apple blossom, palm trees and finally the village buildings in which so much of the subsequent action is to take place. The opening journey is a metaphor of the difference in religious belief from the stern Christian mainland of Howie and the seductive dangers of the pagan system at work on Summerisle, and it all achieved entirely through landscape and music.

The film's final scenes are also almost entirely based on landscape as well—the imposing shots of the Wicker Man itself being contextualized by the roaring sea around its clifftop position, and the fiery setting sun during its destruction. This is a film about the land itself—its fertility, its produce, and the livelihood of those who work upon it. The idea of the Wicker Man derives from the slender evidence of Caesar who left an account of Druidical practices, which forms the only substantial information we have about the practices of the so-called Druids. Later speculation has fleshed out Caesar's account, and much of what we think of as being Druidical, such as the Welsh tradition of the Gorsedd and Eisteddfod, are nineteenth-century improvisations. The landscape is really the only thing we can be certain about.

Perhaps because of the power of landscape in *The Wicker Man*, the film has also inspired the desire among many of its fans to track down the locations where it was shot. There are *Wicker Man* tours in Kirkcudbrightshire, just as there are Jack the Ripper tours in the East End of London and *Dracula* tours in Whitby, where Bram Stoker set part of his novel. Whitby is now a meeting place for Goths, and there is an ever-growing trend among horror film fans for tracking down movie locations. A friend of mine once sent me an email recounting just such adventures in London, which contained this particularly poignant paragraph:

> I found the other bridge much further away at the very end of the track, deep in the bushes, with an even more elaborate stone balustrade, also now removed. The close by stone gazebo had also been demolished long ago. If you have a copy of *The Oblong Box*, you can watch Vincent Price and Hilary Dwyer walk and kiss on that bridge. It was so strange to be alone there in the bushes on an overgrown and neglected bridge and know that Vincent Price was once there in 1969. If I hadn't done my meticulous research beforehand, I would never have recognized the place and I would never have realized the connection.[46]

Five. Celtic Twilight 101

This new kind of sightseeing is another aspect of psycho-geography. Guide books have been produced, and weekend location quests regularly take place: Psycho-geography takes many forms. Allan Brown borrows a phrase from George Steiner to help explain this phenomenon, "morbid ingenuities," and argues that the phrase "seems to capture a range of mind-sets and reflexes, habits and actions. So much that confronts us now is morbid in nature, and so many of the ways this morbidity is furthered displays unmistakable ingenuity."[47] To explain what he means by this, Brown discusses a fragment of the original Wicker Man structure in his possession:

> It looks innocent enough, if a trifle silly: a blameless souvenir, a token of remembrance. But this mouldering bit of wood also has the power to spark a host of associations. Is it fanciful to be reminded of holy relics like the fragments of the True Cross which were virtually a currency in early Christian Europe; or the fingers, toes and other off-cuts of saints which lie in museums to this day?
>
> I don't think it is. Both are reliquaries; both are invested with a certain magic by those who covet them. The magic derives from the proximity of the object (whether holy or as secular as a certified chunk of *The Wicker Man*) once had to the thing that is worshipped; in the case of the True Cross, the Saviour himself. To own or touch the object is to feel the presence of the Loved One as it breaks from its own realm and enters ours.[48]

Location hunting—discovering the specific landscape enshrined in the peculiarly magical terrain of British horror films—provides a similar sense of connection with the mythic aura they project.

Landscape continues to inform the pagan horror film. When Hammer Films rose from the dead in the twenty-first century, the company celebrated its return with *Wakewood*, a mirror image of *The Wicker Man*, in which Timothy Spall's village elder is a kind of yeoman Lord Summerisle, presiding over a pagan ritual that brings a dead girl back to life. Juxtaposed with her father's bloody veterinary work in the suitably Celtic depths of a remote Irish village, the magical re-birthing of the child is rooted in the gore of reality; but the ceremony also binds her parents—and the child—to the locale of the village, defined by the sinister wind turbines surrounding it, in a highly imaginative mythologizing of the prosaic. Our first view of these turbines shows them crowning a hill, rather like the "Druid" stone circles that Alexander Macbain famously discusses towards the end of his book. (After sifting the various theories as to their origin, Macbain discounts all theories as to their having anything to do with Druids; but it is the association, erroneous or not, with perceived Celtic practices that informs the imagery in *Wakewood*.) There is another, genuine stone circle later in the film, which seems to be a kind of graveyard, but the turbines are more powerful and more sinister, especially with their accompanying, amplified "swish."

Wakewood is a horror film, and therefore a negotiation with death. But it also addresses the horror of birth, comparing the bloody birthing of a calf with the equally visceral re-birthing of a dead girl. The use of landscape, bringing with it all the sonorous echoes of paganism, is crucial. Hence, we are subjected to the four elements: a great deal of rain and snow, the often bloody earth, wind in the turbines and fire at the re-birthing ceremony. The idea of being bound to a particular location is another articulation of the concept of psycho-geography: These things happen in *Wakewood* and only there. The re-born child can only live for the three days granted to her, providing she remains there. Her destiny is bound to the landscape, just as, so the Iain Sinclairs amongst us would argue, the Ripper murders were intimately connected with, indeed dependent upon the locale in which they took place.

In Laurie Brewster's 2013 horror film, *Lord of Tears,* landscape plays a central role in what is fundamentally another ghost story. It is also a conflation of Poe's "Ligeia" (a woman returns from the dead), Hitchcock's *Psycho* and *The Birds* (dripping taps, murder in the bath, flocks of birds perched and fluttering), Garner's *The Owl Service* (the legend of the Owl Man himself) and *The Wicker Man* (sacrificial killing). It tells of a schoolteacher haunted by the ghost of his former nanny. The nanny was sacrificed to Moloch by the teacher's father. By doing so, the father entered a pact with

ENFANT TERRIBLE. Ella Connolly as the unnatural Alice standing amid stones in *Wakewood* **(dir. David Keating, 2011).**

dark forces to keep his terminally ill wife alive; but all this is really no more than a premise on which to hang some extremely evocative and mist-soaked shots of Scottish landscape. These are far more eloquent, poetic and gripping than the interior shots, the performances and even the impressive nightmare sequences. The Owl Man who also haunts the protagonist (Euan Douglas) is nowhere near as unnerving as the wind in the trees, the rising mists on the horizon, the stern waters of the loch, the startled flocks of birds and the wild and troubling woods. Brewster films all these with a loving attention, which is curiously lacking when he moves indoors. Indeed, the esthetic underlying the whole project does seem to be along the lines of Macleod's prose poems. One gets the impression that Brewster's response to landscape was what inspired the film, for which a narrative had then to be found to justify it.

Brewster has explained that he wanted to make a specifically Scottish horror film, and he certainly achieved this. "In some Japanese horror films," he explains, "they use a lot of their own mythology so I was thinking that, in Scotland, we have our own rich culture and history, so why should we not use it in a modern horror film?"[49] A family that sacrifices a young woman to Moloch, whether or not he manifests himself as an Owl Man, is hardly an inherently Celtic theme, however, despite the Celtic glosses that are superimposed upon it; but there is nothing more Gaelic than the locations caught so atmospherically by Brewster's cinematographer, Gavin Robertson, which truly follow in the tradition of Fiona Macleod's prose poems. The same thing might be said for Neil Marshall's 2002 werewolf romp, *Dog Soldiers*. Most of the film was shot in Luxembourg, but the helicopter shots of the soldiers arriving in the remote Scottish Highlands were exactly what they purported to be, and the lonely spirit of the place is far more frightening than any animatronic werewolf could ever be.

Six

The Garden of Pan

Pan became very fashionable in Britain at the end of the nineteenth century and continued to be so even after the First World War. Novelist W. Somerset Maugham was well aware of Pan's power over this transitional culture:

> In a hundred novels his cloven hoof left its imprint on the sward; poets saw him lurking in the twilight on London commons, and literary ladies in Surrey nymphs of an industrial age, mysteriously surrendered their virginity to his rough embrace. Spiritually they were never the same again.[1]

If popularity is the ultimate accolade, Pan's triumph over British sensibilities was surely crowned in Lionel Monckton's 1909 musical, *The Arcadians*, which ran for just over 800 performances at London's Shaftesbury Theater, making it, at the time, the third longest run for any musical on Earth. It was even filmed in 1927. The plot features a band of idealistic Arcadians descending on corrupt modern London with the aim of transforming it into a place of sweetness and light like their homeland. Their mission ultimately fails, London remaining as prosaic as ever. This being a British musical, it also features horses, jockeys and (cashing in on the craze for aviation) a plane crash for good measure; but its most famous song, "The Merry, Merry Pipes of Pan," became a well-established paean the Goat-Foot God.

Continental composers with somewhat higher esthetic aspirations, such as Debussy and Ravel, were even more enchanted with Pan's piping. Franz von Stuck and Arnold Böcklin were keen to paint him. Writers Thomas Mann and Friedrich Nietzsche responded to the call of this pagan figure, who represented so many things to so many people: sexual freedom, homosexuality, nature worship, political freedom, hedonism, escapism, terror—even black magic. Pan's popularity in Britain also rode the wave of the Celtic Revival. Indeed, in the pages of a story by Fiona Macleod, Pan appears as the Dark Fool, Dalua. The weather is dank and dreary here, unlike that of Pan's native Greece, but Pan/Dalua still plays his pipes:

> One night when Dan Macara was going over the hillside of Ben Breacan, he saw a tall man playing the pipes, and before him a great flock of sheep.
> It was a night of the falling mist that makes a thin soundless rain. But behind the blur was a rainpool of light, a pool that oozed into a wan flood; and so Macara knew that the moon was up and was riding against the drift, and would pull the rain away from the hill.
> ... The man did not look round as Dan Macara drew near. The pipes were shadowy black, and had long black streamers from them. The man wore a Highland bonnet, with a black plume hanging from it.
> The wet slurred moonshine came out as the rain ceased. Dan looked over the shoulder of the man at the long, straggling crowd of sheep.
> He saw then that they were only a flock of shadows.
> ... Dan Macara ran forward, and strove to grasp the man by the shoulder; but with a crash he came against a great slab of granite, with its lichened sides wet and slippery with the hill mist. As he fell, he struck his head and screamed. Before silence and darkness closed in upon him like two waves, he heard Dalua's mocking laughter far up among the hills, and saw a great flock of curlews rise from where that shadows had been.[2]

This Celtic version of Pan similarly causes panic—a word that is derived from the name of the horned and hairy one. But it would seem that it is landscape that really generates the panic and ecstasy, which the god merely personifies. It is the panic induced by stillness on a summer afternoon, alone in the woods, when everything is so calm it seems inevitable that something violent or unexpected will occur: the calm before the storm. Panic can equally as well be inspired by the kind of lonely moorland Macleod describes. Even if only a personification of natural forces, Pan is always present.

The followers of Pan in Britain very much believed that the Goat-Foot God should return to live in the urban present. Oscar Wilde (1854–1900) was one of the first of these modern British writers to lament the contrast between Pan's ancient world of pagan pleasure and the restraints of prosaic modern London:

> O goat-foot God of Arcady!
> This modern world is grey and old,
> And what remains to us of thee?

Wilde compares the "dull and dead" Thames to Pan's native olive woods and "vine-clad wold"—states of mind, once more finding their topographical equivalents. In the second of his two villanelles on the subject, Wilde implores Pan to "leave the hills of Arcady," for the modern world "has need of thee."[3] Earlier, in his Newdigate prize-winning poem, "Ravenna," Pan, in his natural woodland setting, is again placed in opposition to the poet's contemporary world, where only a "fond Hellenic dream" seems possible amid the evening chimes of the convent's vesper bell:

> The pine-tops rocked before the evening breeze
> With the hoarse murmur of the wintry seas,
> And the tall stems were streaked with amber bright;—
> I wandered through the wood in wild delight.
> So startled bird, with fluttering wings and fleet,
> Made snow of all the blossoms; at my feet,
> Like silver birds, the pale narcissi lay,
> And small birds sang on every twining spray.
> O waving trees, O forest liberty!
> Within your haunts at least a man is free,
> And half forgets the weary world of strife:
> The blood flows hotter, and a sense of life
> Wakes i' the quickening veins, while once again
> The woods are filled with gods we fancied slain.
> Long time I watched, and surely hoped to see
> Some goat-foot Pan make merry minstrelsy
> And the reeds! some startled Dryad-maid
> In girlish flight! or lurking in the glade,
> The soft brown limbs, the wanton treacherous face
> Of woodland god![4]

Illustrator, Aubrey Beardsley, so much associated with Wilde, also evoked Pan as a symbol of sexual freedom in his story, *Venus and Tannhäuser*, in which he includes an altar to Pan as part of an elaborately artificial stage spectacle:

> The curtain rose upon a scene of rare beauty, a remote Arcadian valley, and watered with a dear river as fresh and pastoral as a perfect fifth of this scrap of Tempe. It was early morning, and the re-arisen sun, like the prince in the "sleeping Beauty," woke all the earth with his lips.
> ... Suddenly, to the music of pipe and horn, a troop of satyrs stepped out from the recesses of the woods, bearing in their hands nuts and green boughs and flowers and roots and whatsoever the forest yielded, to heap upon the altar of the mysterious Pan that stood in the middle of the stage.[5]

Even D. H. Lawrence, at quite the opposite esthetic pole, invokes Pan for comparable sexual reasons at the end of *Lady Chatterley's Lover* (1928), arguing that the masses should "acknowledge the great god Pan. He's the only god for the masses, forever. The few can go in for higher cults if they like. But let the mass be forever pagan."[6]

Perhaps the most popular and immediately recognizable British manifestation of Pan takes us to what might seem the least likely place one would expect to find him, for it was in London's Kensington Gardens that

Six. The Garden of Pan

PAN EUROPEAN. Cover design by Franz von Stuck for *Pan* magazine, 1895.

Peter Pan made his debut in J.M. Barrie's novel, *The Little White Bird* (1902). In this book, Peter was rather different from his later incarnations in Barrie's play, *Peter Pan, or the Boy Who Wouldn't Grow Up*, and the novelization of that play (titled *Peter Pan and Wendy*). The six *Little White Bird* chapters concerning the original Peter Pan were later extracted and issued as a gift book (with illustrations by Arthur Rackham) as *Peter Pan in Kensington Gardens*. Here, he is described as a seven-day-old baby, but a baby that steals other babies; and this worrying aspect of his nature relates Peter to another aspect of Celtic culture, for it was very probably Yeats' poem, "The Stolen Child" (1889), that gave Barrie the idea:

> Come away, O human child!
> To the waters and the wild
> With a faery, hand in hand,
> For the world's more full of weeping than you can understand.[7]

The third chapter of *Peter Pan and Wendy* is indeed subtitled "Come Away! Come Away!"[8] and in *Peter Pan in Kensington Gardens*, Peter also rides a goat, as well as playing the pipes:

> Peter's heart was so glad that he felt he must sing all day long, just as the birds sing for joy, but, being partly human, he needed an instrument, so he made a pipe of reeds, and he used to sit by the shore of the island of an evening, practicing the sough of the wind and the ripple of the water and catching handfuls of the shine of the moon, and he put them all in his pipe and played them so beautiful that even the birds were deceived.[9]

Peter also plays his pipes to his abandoned mother. His name brings together Christian and pagan associations: the founding father of the Christian Church and the satyr the Church later demonized as the devil himself. He therefore embodies many tensions, not so far removed from the pagan–Christian duality at the heart of Tennyson's *Idylls of the King*. Neither is Peter entirely benign. He is intimately associated with death and sets out on his goat (a singularly demonic animal) to collect babies who fall from their perambulators. Peter is seven days old but also immortal:

> His age is one week, and though he was born so long ago he had never had a birthday, nor is there the slightest chance of his ever having one. The reason is that he escaped from being a human when he was seven days old; he escaped by the window and flew back to Kensington Gardens.[10]

Peter is presumably dead but also alive—a kind of undead baby, and what Solomon Caw, the wise old bird he encounters in Kensington Gardens, calls "a Betwixt-and-Between."[11] These aspects of Peter's character are of course developed in his later incarnations, but it is landscape that concerns us here, and the landscape of Peter Pan is an urban one.

Kensington Gardens, in the heart of London, is tamed nature. At 4.00 p.m. on a dark November day, the leaves are still reddening on the trees. As the daylight fades, the lamps begin to glimmer along the winding paths, which now disappear into darkness, creating the uniquely urban effect of artificial light on natural foliage. There is nothing in nature like this. The light from converted gas lamps illuminates the trees like burning bushes. Though parks are artificial, they can be even more mysterious than dark forests, for far more occurs in them and there are just as many places in which to hide. The Goat-Foot God might therefore feel equally well at home in a park as a wood.

Matthew Arnold had also evoked Pan in his poem, "Lines Written in Kensington Gardens":

> In this lone open glade I lie,
> Screen'd by deep bough on either hand;
> And at its head, to stay the eye,
> Those black-crown'd, red-boled pine-trees stand.
>
> Birds here make song, each bird has his,
> Across the girdling city's hum.
> How green under the boughs it is!
> How thick the tremulous sheep-cries come!
>
> Sometimes a child will cross the glade
> To take his nurse his broken toy;
> Sometimes a thrush flit overhead
> Deep in her unknown day's employ.
>
> Here at my feet what wonders pass,
> What endless, active life is here!
> What blowing daisies, fragrant grass!
> An air-stirr'd forest, fresh and clear.
>
> Scarce fresher is the mountain-sod
> Where the tired angler lies, stretch'd out,
> And, eased of basket and of rod,
> Counts his day's spoil, the spotted trout.
>
> In the huge world, which roars hard by,
> Be others happy if they can!
> But in my helpless cradle I
> Was breathed on by the rural Pan.[12]

Kensington Gardens are represented here as a haven from the strain of the urban, whereas for Barrie the park represents an imaginative haven from reality. It is a place inhabited by fairies, where the trees walk about and converse after Lock-Out Time when the public has gone away.

A charming musical portrait of Kensington Gardens after lock-out was composed in 1918 by Harry Farjeon (1878–1948), a long-serving professor at the Royal Academy of Music. His immediately appealing *Peter Pan Sketches* for piano are yet another testament to the popularity of Barrie's creation. "Mamie in Kensington Gardens After Lock Out" forms the second piece in the suite, in which fairy effects are created by playful *acciaccatura* marked "Light and fairy-like," while the awakening trees are suggested by a unison passage in lower register ("*p* and without much tone, but rather pompously and with well-marked phrasing"). The first piece describes "The Wendy Bird." The third is a portrait of the crow, "Solomon Caw" ("Soberly: rather pompous"), with repeated staccato thirds to suggest a pecking motion, later developing into an ostinato marked "chattering." This is followed by "Peter at His Mother's Window" (an Andante to be played "rather sadly"). It is dedicated to Barbara Rackham, the daughter of *Peter Pan*'s famous illustrator, Arthur Rackham; a passionate outburst in the middle of this tender lament suggests deeper layers of emotion before dissolving through a tearful tremolo and returning to the sad material of the opening. The final piece, "Peter and His Shadow," passes through many emotions over its four short pages, reflecting Peter's mercurial character. We start *poco lento*, with tremolos and a terse descending four-note motif marked "duskily and gloomily," then embark on an *Allegro con spirit* section marked "mysteriously," moving on to being played "boldly and with spirit," "gradually with less courage," "plaintively," "riotously" and "frisky and lively," before ending *fortissimo*, "playfully and with mischief."

That Barrie should have chosen Kensington Gardens rather than any other London park is partly due to the connection the place had with his own life and the family of Arthur Llewelyn Davies, whose boys—in particular Peter Llewelyn—inspired the tale; but Kensington Gardens also has an arcane interest of their own. It was in Kensington Palace that King George I brought a wild boy he had discovered in woods near Hamelin (the German town associated with its own infamous child-snatcher). Given the name "Peter," he was regarded as a noble savage, and became something of a celebrity, even inspiring a satire by Jonathan Swift. That George II's consort, Queen Caroline, later took an interest in the boy and also laid out Kensington Gardens in the form of Masonic patterns such as the square, compass and pentagram, suggests the possibility of psycho-geographical connections in the manner of Iain Sinclair: Kensington Gardens as a place of magical transformation presided over by a Pan-like baby. The fairy folklore of Kensington Gardens is certainly curiously considerable, and was well-known to the poet Thomas Tickell (1685–1740), who referred to it in his 1722 poem, "Kensington Gardens":

> The landskip now so sweet we well may praise:
> But far far sweeter in its ancient days,
> Far sweeter was it, when its peopled ground

Six. The Garden of Pan

> With Fairy domes and dazling tow'rs was crown'd.
> Where in the midst those verdant Pillars spring,
> Rose the proud Palace of the Elfin King;
> For ev'ry edge of vegetable green,
> In happier years a crowded street was seen;
> Nor all those leaves, that now the prospect grace,
> Could match the numbers of its Pygmy race.[13]

The northern boundary of Kensington Gardens adjoins Bayswater Road, the name of which probably derived from an early medieval tenant of the land called Bainiardus. The area's many medicinal springs were therefore associated with Bainiardus, and the abbreviation of the name, when combined with the waters, resulted in the designation, Bayswater. These springs gave rise to various holy wells, two of which were dedicated to St. Agnes and to St. Govor. They are still to be found in Kensington Gardens and were known to Barrie.

Unlike Barrie's *Peter Pan* play, which has been adapted in several American-made films, *Peter Pan in Kensington Gardens* has not attracted much cinematic attention, but it is possible to connect it with other examples of film and television if we claim Barrie's placement of Pan in Edwardian London as an aspect of psycho-geography. Barrie's conflation of pagan past with metropolitan present was re-imagined by Nigel Kneale in *Quatermass and the Pit* (originally a BBC TV series first broadcast over Christmas and the New Year in 1958–1959, and filmed nine years later by Roy Ward Baker for Hammer Films). Kneale's conceit for this Quatermass story is that a certain area of London appears to be haunted, subject to poltergeist activity and consequently abandoned. The area surrounds Hobbs Lane Underground station, which is closed for renovation. A pentagram is discovered in a spacecraft that is unearthed there, along with the remains of what turn out to be Martians—horned, locust-like creatures not unlike the popular iconography of devils (or of Pan). Human skeletons with skulls suggesting a far greater brain capacity than normal are also found, prompting Quatermass to theorize that the Martians, finding their own planet unable to sustain them, visited Earth and attempted to transfer their own psychic abilities into the ape-like ancestors of humanity, expanding the brain capacity of these early humans in the process. Unfortunately, along with the psychic abilities some people still possess, humanity has also inherited the Martians' more violent and irrational instincts.

The idea that part of London might be haunted, like the fictional Hobbs Lane and the real Kensington Gardens, was also taken up by P.J. Hammond in "The Meddlers" (dir. John Russell, 1972), an episode of the children's TV series, *Ace of Wands*: A property developer is intent on intimidating the

AWFULLY WEIRDLY. Aubrey Beardsley illustration for the "Keynotes" edition of Arthur Machen's *The Great God Pan* (London: John Lane, 1894).

Six. The Garden of Pan   113

inhabitants of a local market so that he can demolish the old buildings. The tension of the story derives from the way this fairly mundane plot is articulated through a series of grotesque characters: a preacher with his own mobile pulpit, a trio of sinister street musicians, and the corpulent property developer himself. There are also odd noises and the suggestion that the market is "jinxed" with arson, fruit going rotten overnight, and other apparently supernatural occurrences all given credence by the psychic hero, Tarot, played by Michael Mackenzie. "So many people look scared," he observes. The property developer is made to resemble Aleister Crowley, with a shaven head and sinister manner. Like an Ann Radcliffe Gothic novel, these supernatural suggestions are given a rational explanation in the end, but the point of the story is to convey the idea of an urban landscape blighted by its past history: Psycho-geography in the form of children's tea-time entertainment.

This approach was pioneered by Arthur Machen in his story, *The Great God Pan*, which is really the first important modern tale on the subject. It has nothing whimsical about it and pretends to be a scientific account of the spirit of Pan taking over the soul of a young woman with horrifying consequences, even though Pan himself does not appear to the reader. It is largely set in an urban landscape, which does rather resemble the "cursed" environments of Hobbs Lane and the market in "The Meddlers." It is also Machen's response to the Whitechapel murders of Jack the Ripper. But it begins with pastoral descriptions of "the odour of the woods, of cool shaded places, deep in the green depths, drawn forth by the sun's heat; and the scene of the good earth, lying as it were with arms stretched forth, and smiling lips."[14] Machen then describes a mystical union of the individual with the landscape:

> all things mingled, the form of all things but devoid of all form. And in that moment, the sacrament of body and soul was dissolved and a voice cried "Let us go hence."[15]

Landscape imagery is also used to describe the changing expression of Mary, the girl subjected to the Pan experiment. Her expression during it resembles "the changes of the hills when the summer clouds float across the sun."[16] Whatever it is that she sees (Machen is sensibly non-specific here), it is terrifying enough to turn her into a "hopeless idiot."

There are other pastoral recollections, such as the one set in "the long dim vista of the green causeway in the forest,"[17] but the remainder of the tale, relating how the corrupt child of the unfortunate Mary, like a female Jack the Ripper, is catastrophically involved in the lives and violent deaths of several other characters, is almost entirely set amid the grimy boarding houses of London. Machen is adept at comparing city landscapes to those in nature. Ashley Street, for example, "looked as dark and gloomy as a forest in winter."[18] He also ably demonstrates that it is quite possible to play out "an old mystery … in our day, and in dim London streets instead of amidst the vineyards and the olive gardens"[19] The tale ends with a return to the landscape in which it began, but it is described in terms of exquisite corruption, with reference to "the heavy perfume of the elder, whose mingled odour is like the odour of the room of the dead, a vapour of incense and corruption."

> I stood at the edges of the wood, gazing at all the pomp and procession of the foxgloves towering amidst the bracken and shining red in the broad sunshine, and beyond them into deep thickets of close undergrowth where springs boil up from the rock and nourish the water-weeds, dank and evil.[20]

Pan is evidently not a benign figure here, being a personification of what the narrator describes as lying "beyond the veil of horror one dare not express" and "energies I do not understand."[21]

Pan became so pervasive in British culture that he turned up metaphorically in novels that have little or no connection with the god or his cult. I have already mentioned *Lady Chatterley's Lover*. Similarly, E.M. Forster's *The Longest Journey* (1907) concerns Rickie, an unsuccessful author who brings out a collection of tales called *Pan Pipes*, inspired by his vaguely pagan response to landscape:

> I had a great idea of getting into touch with Nature, just as the Greeks were in touch; and seeing England so beautiful, I used to pretend that her trees and coppices and summer fields of parsley were alive. It's funny enough now, but it wasn't funny then, for I got in such a state that I believed, actually believed, that Fauns lived in a certain double hedgerow near the Gog Magogs, and one evening I walked round a mile sooner than go through it alone.[22]

Pan also appears in Somerset Maugham's early novel, *The Magician* (1908). Inspired by an encounter with Aleister Crowley in Paris, Maugham's villain is occultist, Oliver Haddo, who seduces the unfortunate heroine, Margaret Dauncey. During an hypnotically induced hallucination ("Her brain reeled. It seemed to her that Haddo bade her cover her face. She gasped for breath, and it was as if the earth spun under her feet"[23]), Margaret finds herself in a strange landscape:

> No moon shone in the sky, but small stars appeared to dance on the heather, vague night-fires like spirits of the damned. They stood in a vast and troubled waste, with huge stony boulders and leafless trees, rugged and gnarled like tortured souls in pain. It was as if there had been a devastating storm, and the country reposed after the flood of rain and the tempestuous wind and the lightning. All things about them appeared dumbly to suffer, like a man racked by torments who has not the strength even to realise that his agony has ceased.[24]

Out of this nightmare terrain, a pageant of the dead appears before her, followed by the arrival of "a monstrous, goat-legged thing, more vast than the creatures of nightmare. She saw the horns and the long beard, the great hairy legs with their hoofs, and the man's rapacious hands. The face was horrible with lust and cruelty, and yet was divine. It was Pan, playing on his pipes, and the lecherous eyes caressed her with a hideous tenderness."[25] The novel was filmed by Rex Ingram in 1926. Made in France for MGM and starring the German Paul Wegener, it can hardly be claimed as an example of British pagan cinema, despite its British literary origins, but the bacchanal scene presided over by the lissome form of the American dancer Stowitts as Pan certainly foreshadowed the appearance of the Goat of Mendes in Hammer's *The Devil Rides Out*.

Pan made another literary appearance in 1908, featuring as "the Friend and Helper" in Kenneth Grahame's *The Wind in the Willows*. This Piper at the Gates of Dawn may be benign but Mole nonetheless feels "a great Awe fall upon him" when he detects the presence of Pan. What Mole feels is, intriguingly, "no panic terror—indeed he felt wonderfully at peace and happy,"[26] and he is overwhelmed not only by Pan himself but also, and perhaps more powerfully, by what Pan represents: the landscape through which both Mole and Rat have floated on their boat. Grahame's writing is so powerful here and so intense in its description of the affection felt between Mole and Rat, that the passage later informed a similar sculling scene, also set just before dawn, in E.F. Benson's novel, *The Inheritor*.

THE DEVIL HIMSELF! The Goat of Mendes in Hammer's adaptation of Dennis Wheatley's *The Devil Rides Out* (dir. Terence Fisher 1969).

There, as we shall see later, the homosexual subtext is rather more strongly implied. In *The Wind in the Willows*, male friendship is desexualized (after all, this concerns a mole and a rat), but its intensity is not to be mistaken for mere chumminess. There are tears on Rat's cheeks, and the purple flowers that cover the river bank bring with them a powerful connotation of the sacred, due to the ecclesiastical associations of that color. Indeed, Rat calls the riverbank "this holy place,"[27] and exclaims upon the beauty of a singing bird, echoing the opening lines of Keats' "Ode to a

THE FRIEND AND HELPER. Pan graces the cover of Kenneth Grahame's *The Wind in the Willows* (London: Methuen 1908).

Nightingale" ("My heart aches, and a drowsy numbness pains/My sense"). This sound makes him feel that "nothing seems worth while but just to hear that sound once more and go on listening to it for ever."[28] Keats expresses a similar sentiment: "That I might drink, and leave the world unseen/And with thee fade away into the forest dim."[29] (Keats also employs the color purple in "Ode.")

The landscape now becomes almost psychedelic in its intensity. The meadow-grass is of a "greenness unsurpassable," roses seem unusually vivid, willow-herb is "riotous" and meadow-sweet "odorous and pervading."[30] We are transported into the Arcadian opulence of Matthew Arnold's "The Scholar Gypsy" with its overwhelming pastoral imagery—the finery of Pan himself:

> Through the thick corn the scarlet poppies peep,
> And round green roots and yellowing stalks I see
> Pale pink convolvulus in tendrils creep;
> And air-swept lindens yield
> Their scent, and rustle down their perfumed showers
> Of bloom on the bent grass where I am laid,
> And bower me from the August sun with shade.[31]

When Rat and Mole at last encounter Pan, they are afraid and bow their heads in worship. The touching image of "two animals, crouching to the earth"[32] before the "Friend and Helper, with his curved horns, hooked nose, kindly eyes and bearded mouth,"[33] was transmogrified in Hammer's adaptation of Wheatley's *The Devil Rides Out*, when the Satanist, Mocata (Charles Gray), commands Simon Aron (Patrick Mower) and Tanith (Nike Arrighi) to "kneel and face" their Master—the Goat of Mendes: "the Devil himself," as de Richleau helpfully points out. The Goat of Mendes in the film is indeed an impressive sight: half man with a goat's head, shaggy thighs and cloven hooves, inspired by the imagery of Éliphas Lévi but not perhaps as grotesque an image as Wheatley's description of "a gigantic goat, appearing at least three times the size of any other which they had ever seen."

> The two slit-eyes, slanting inwards and down, gave out a red baleful light. Long, pointed ears cocked upwards from the sides of the shaggy head, and from the bald, horrible unnatural bony skull, which was caught by the light of the candles, four enormous curved horns spread out—sideways and up.[34]

Wheatley's Goat of Mendes is not so much an expression of the landscape as of the Satanists who summon him; consequently there is very little description of the setting other than that it is "desolate and remote."[35]

One of the individuals Wheatley interviewed when researching *The Devil Rides Out* was Aleister Crowley, to whom Wheatley was introduced by the socialist MP, MI5 agent and traitor, Tom Driberg. Wheatley invited Crowley to dinner and some time later Driberg asked him what he thought of the Great Beast. Wheatley replied,

> "I found him fascinating to talk to, but I don't believe that he could harm a rabbit."
> "Ah," said my friend, "not now, perhaps. But he had real power before that terrible affair in Paris."
> "What was that?" I asked; and this is what my friend told me:
> "After Crowley left the Abbey of Thelma in Sicily he settled in Paris and formed a coven there. I was one of his disciples and another of them owned a small hotel on the Left Bank. Crowley was very anxious to attempt to raise Pan."

According to this account in Wheatley's introduction to Crowley's novel, *Moonchild* (part of the "Dennis Wheatley Library of the Occult"), one disciple died and Crowley was discovered as "a naked, gibbering idiot in one corner"[36]—a story described as an "extraordinary farrago of nonsense" by Wheatley's biographer, Phil Baker, the truth of the matter being that Driberg had told Wheatley "a fantastically garbled account of 'The Paris Working.'"[37] In fact, no one had died, even though Crowley's magical partner, Victor Neuburg, did suffer a nervous breakdown.

Though "The Paris Working" had been "primarily concerned with invoking Jupiter and Mercury"[38] rather than raising Pan, Crowley was much concerned with the Goat-Foot God: On the back of the copy of *Magick in Theory and Practice* he inscribed for Wheatley, he added some "recommendations," one of which was to "Read 'Hymn to Pan' aloud at midnight when alone with INTENTION to get HIM."[39] Wheatley never tried this himself, but he had the opportunity to do so as Crowley's Hymn, which was originally written in 1913, opens *Magick in Theory and Practice* (the third part of *Book Four*). Unlike Machen or Barrie, Crowley firmly places his image of Pan within a traditionally Arcadian landscape. He mentions "the moon of the woods" and, as in *The Wind in the Willows*, he also indulged in the color purple—"the purple of passionate prayer." There is also "The tangled grove, the gnarled bole/Of the living tree that is spirit and soul,"[40] lines that bring to mind Wheatley's own *Ex Libris* plate, in which Wheatley is depicted sitting in a similar grove with a Tree of Knowledge and a Tree of Life, listening to an extraordinary incarnation of his dubious mentor, Eric Gordon Tombe, as Pan himself, with a bottle of champagne in a cooler and a saxophone at his cloven feet. Tombe's words are printed below the image:

> One admires EVE for having tasted the FORBIDDEN TREE OF KNOWLEDGE:—But what a WONDERFUL EXPERIENCE she missed when she overlooked the TREE OF

Six. The Garden of Pan

LIFE. I should have eaten of not ONE, but ALL the trees in the garden—and THAT; dear boy—is what I hope for YOU!⁴¹

Pan meant different things to different people. Like Machen, Crowley believed that "the Vision of Pan would drive men mad with fear."⁴² He also equated Pan with Bacchus,⁴³ a symbiosis that also appealed to H.H. Munro, better known as "Saki," in his very short, almost anecdotal story, "The Music on the Hill" (1911). Here, the no-nonsense Sylvia Seltoun, who "notwithstanding her name, was accustomed to nothing much more sylvan than 'leafy Kensington,'" finds herself in the depths of the country with her husband, Mortimer, who warns her that "[t]he worship of Pan never has died out."⁴⁴ In the woods, Sylvia later encounters a brown-faced boy, "rather handsome, but a scoundrel to look at. A gipsy lad, I suppose."⁴⁵ She also removes a bunch of grapes from a small bronze figure of Pan that stands on a stone pedestal in the middle of a copse, shut in by yew trees. When she reports her day's adventures to Mortimer, he advises her to avoid the woods and orchards in future. This she fails to do, and she is later gored by the antlers of a deer, shrill pipe music all around her and "the echo of a boy's laughter, golden and equivocal"⁴⁶ ringing in her ears as she expires.

A return to Grahame's more ambivalent image of Pan can be found in Algernon Blackwood's 1917 story, "The Touch of Pan." Like Crowley, Blackwood had once been an Order of the Golden Dawn member, but for him, Pan is less monstrous and more a symbol of sexual freedom and emotional fulfilment. Blackwood contrasts an Edwardian high society house party with a girl of whom her family "did not say that she was imbecile or half-witted, but that she was 'not all there.'" This untidy creature, with torn stockings and mud-spattered skirt, likes climbing trees and riding bareback, and insists, "In the heart of that wood dwell I."⁴⁷ The unnamed man who is attracted to her leaves the vacuous and starchy guests of the house party to be with her. "They were akin, as the birds and animals were akin. They belonged together in some free and open life, natural wild, untamed."⁴⁸ Later the same night, they have another assignation. "Two arms were flung about his neck, a shower of soft hair fell on his cheek with a heady scent of earth and leaves and grass"⁴⁹ They hurry through the park-like grounds of the country house with its gravel paths, well groomed lawn, flowerbeds and ornamental iron railings, their bare feet soaked with the dew—and rush towards the pine wood, which Blackwood compares to the cypress trees associated with Pan in Greece. The girl anoints her lover with the heavy dew and asks him to kiss her. Pan appears, though more in spirit than the flesh:

> With the stupendous Presence there was joy, the joy of abundant, natural life, pure as sunlight and the wind. He passed among them. There was great movement—as of a forest shaking, as of deep water falling, as of a cornfield swaying to the wind, gentle as of harebell shedding its burden of dew that it has held too long because of love.⁵⁰

Pan comes so near that the man feels he can actually touch him, though the ambivalence of the imagery suggests that he is actually touching the body of the girl. Indeed, the man becomes like Pan, even sprouting horns. Blackwood wrote this tale after his collection of nature stories that make up *Pan's Garden* (which begins with "The Man Whom the Trees Loved"), but the general theme is the same: a pantheistic union with nature, the natural landscape being not merely a metaphor for joy but its actual expression.

Lord Dunsany (1878–1957) continued with this approach in his much longer novel, *The Blessing of Pan* (1927). Here, landscape creates both the mood and meaning of the story. A boy called Tommy is drawn to Wold Hill and the Old Stones of Wolding on top of it. The splendidly vivid landscape described by Dunsany "seemed intensely to mean something that had no meaning."⁵¹ Tommy fashions his own Pan pipes from rushes by the river, and "the soft notes of the pipes brought him some consolation for knowing nothing of that solemn purpose with which the evening vibrated and with which Wold Hill seemed to thrill."⁵² One day, Tommy plays his pipes and "nothing seemed strange or perplexed him any more." He feels himself to be "of one fellowship to which the hush of the night, the deep of the woods, or mysteries bold in the moonlight or hidden by mist, reported all their secrets."⁵³

Here, nature is not aggressive, like Wyndham's Triffids, but nonetheless poised to reclaim the earth from humanity. Roses, for example, wait, "perhaps one day to pour in, following the retreat of man."⁵⁴ And this is what happens at the end of the novel. Nature *does* reclaim the village, but not before Tommy has recruited its children to the cause of Pan, summoning them to the stone circle with his pipes. This circle consists of 12 standing stones with a thirteenth lying prone in the center, a formula intriguingly repeated in the ritual at the heart of J. Lee Thompson's *Eye of the Devil*, in which 12 men form a circle around a thirteenth man in the middle. The man in the middle, played in the film by David Niven, is of course the sacrificial victim. No actual sacrifice occurs in Dunsany's novel, though there is a kind of sacrifice at the heart of the story in its rejection of modernity and Christianity in favor of a return to a pagan reconnection with nature. As we shall see, this novel foreshadows several British films based on this general theme, in particular *The Witches* and *Blood on Satan's Claw*.

To symbolize this antagonism, Tommy's main adversary is a kindly, diffident vicar, and it is significant that Tommy's pagan yearnings actually begin on a Sunday. Gradually, his piping lures young girls from their homes, like the children enticed by the Pied Piper (with distant echoes of Peter Pan as well). Later, elderly people join in, and they all meet on the hill, which "seemed all holy, the tall dog-daisies above the shining grass, the old deep hedge below and the woods above, haunted by dark yews, and the low and golden light in which it was all shining."[55] In *Blood on Satan's Claw*, landscape plays a crucial role in the similar, though far more malevolent seventeenth-century tale of Angel (Linda Hayden). Angel forms a group of Satan-worshipping children who gather in a derelict church in the woods. (And, as with Dunsany's tale, a grotesquely old man and woman are also present.) The film opens with shots of archetypal British farmland amid rural Oxfordshire—the county in which Arnold's "The Scholar Gypsy" is also set. While working the fields, a plowman (Barry Andrews), his clogs thick with mud, unearths a skull, thus letting loose powers of evil upon the community. These opening shots, and many others of landscape later in the film, are often filmed from a low angle, the camera resting virtually on the soil to suggest how the evil (and the story) actually emerges from and is part of the landscape itself.

Dunsany employs a similar technique, rooting his story, so to speak, in vivid descriptions of the surroundings in which it takes place. Nature is continually contrasted with civilization. Tommy's pipes, which unnerve the adults and fascinate the children, make "the talk of all seem trivial, or the game [of cards] pointless, till the room felt stuffy and its ornaments mean."[56] Women "threw out antimacassars, or tea-cosies, all in a sudden petulance at their smugness."[57] The call of the pipes is therefore the call of our own inner nature, our natural selves; and here we may make another comparison to children's fiction from the 1970s. Peter Dickinson's *The Changes* was adapted into a successful TV series by the BBC in 1975. In the startling opening scenes, a normal family is shown in their sitting room. The mother is watching television; her daughter is working at her homework, while the father is relaxing. It is very hot and stuffy. Then, for no apparent reason, everyone begins to destroy the technology that surrounds them. They smash the television and destroy everything mechanical and electronic. A post-industrial quasi-rural lifestyle follows, in a story that foreshadowed the later BBC dystopian series, *Survivors* (also 1975), in which civilization is overturned by a plague that kills off the majority of the population.

Dunsany's novel is much less drastic, suggesting that this reaction against civilization is a positive if nonetheless somewhat unnerving development. The poetic descriptions of nature grow in intensity as the novel progresses.

In one page we move from summer, in which the "Brown fields were bare of their sheaves" and the trees offer up "the leaves' last glory before their farewell to the woods," though autumn ("Gold and red in the woods" with "the long grey script of the mist, written on the air") to "the brilliance of stars" in the winter, when the geese, "foreknowing the storms, forsook distant seas, and came over high, a wandering letter V."[58] Dunsany even describes hyacinths as "pieces of sky lured downward by a witch of the deeps of the wood."[59]

Tommy's odd music stirs longings in the dried-up old vicar, longings he had "hoped he would feel no more," and he too feels the urge to "dance fantastic dances to a tune that was unlike anything in all music."[60] Troubled by this, he attempts to talk it over with the bishop of the diocese, but the meeting is unsuccessful. Though this vicar has his doubts about Tommy, the other adults don't suspect the boy at all. Having heard his piping, they look for "somebody leaner and darker" with "olive-brown skin, dark hair and nimble limbs," with "eyes dark and keen and an almost goat-like profile."[61] But Tommy does not at all resemble the traditional figure of Pan.

Tommy's music makes the adults listless, idle and dissipated. Nature now reclaims the village, weeds invading the streets. Events take a more sinister turn with the sacrifice of a bull at the standing stones. Pan himself is

PAGAN SACRIFICE. Linda Hayden as Angel Blake prepares to offer Wendy Padbury's Cathy Vespers to the Devil in *Blood on Satan's Claw* (dir. Piers Haggard, 1971).

suggested as somehow manifesting himself in "a dark shape larger than man's, in the wood above them, playing this music on which the hills and the woods seemed made."[62]

Again, the dénouement of *Blood on Satan's Claw* provides a cinematic parallel to these events, when a girl is sacrificed to a similarly shadowy devil, whom Haggard makes sure we don't see clearly until a brief glimpse at the end when he is destroyed by Patrick Wymark's judge. But in Dunsany's novel, Pan is not defeated. Indeed, the vicar himself is drawn to the hill and feels compelled to sacrifice the bull himself with an old flint that has been in his possession for some years.

Dunsany brings the story to a close with a superb description of the village now almost consumed by triumphant verdure and "mysterious foxgloves."[63] "To such fields the wild clematis came, crawling and clambering, and joining bush to bush, till the place became a thicket too dense for man."[64]

The village now has lusher vegetables and louder birdsong than other places, and, as on Summerisle in *The Wicker Man*, the children of Wolding are taught the old ways of snaring, jam-making, chopping—but not arithmetic! Any stray tourist who finds himself in the vicinity and hears the Pan pipes never returns to London." It is as if Dunsany were deliberately referencing Arnold's "Scholar Gypsy," in which "this strange disease of modern life" is contrasted with all the ravishing pastoral imagery he lavishes on his stanzas.

A version of Dunsany's Tommy features in E.F. Benson's novel, *The Inheritor*, published three years later (1930). Benson's equivalent of Dunsany's Tommy is the distinctly Pan-like Tim, a Cornish yokel who similarly plays pipes, but also eats raw fish whole and generally cavorts around the woods with his handsome friend and "god," Steven Gervase, the novel's amoral hero. Relieved that he has not inherited the family "curse," Steven is nonetheless haunted by the idea that it will eventually return to destroy him: Tradition has it that the firstborn of his family all become satyr-like monsters, complete with horns. Steven once saw his own "cursed" uncle in the suitably sylvan surroundings of the family seat:

> It was spring, and the ground was a carpet of primroses and anemones, with the bluebells just beginning and I remember suddenly realizing that I was I, and that here were trees and flowers, and that they were part of me. And then I heard shouting from the house above me, and somebody screamed, and then there came towards me through the wood the sound of someone running and leaping. The steps came nearer, and the a—a man burst through the thicket of hazel close in front of me. He had a pair of breeches on, shorts, and some sort of wreath on his head, but his chest was naked and covered with thick hair. His face was bearded with a short golden beard, same colour as my hair,

and he had kind merry eyes, and on his forehead, just coming through his hair, two horns, and I don't suppose he was more than four feet tall.[65]

In Benson's hands, this legend is turned into another allegory for the "love that dare not speak its name." The emotionally charged male friendship of Rat and Mole in *The Wind in the Willows* is made overtly homosexual right from the beginning in the scenes set in Cambridge, featuring Steven and his tall, rather dull but muscular friend, the Child. Like Rat and Mole, they take a nocturnal row on the river:

> A barn owl, silent and white and ghostly, was hunting over the open ground to the right, and once or twice, far away, came a blink of lightning, but still no breath ruffled the surface of the river, and no sound ruffled the silence but the cluck of their paddles and the drip of the water off the blades. The Child, heavily weighting one end of the canoe, had stripped to shirt and trousers [...] utterly content with this companionship, absorbed in the sense of friendship; Steven, far more intensely alert, was conscious of the spell of the night itself; it held something for him, something secret and essential, of which the Child knew nothing.[66]

We almost expect the "Friend and Helper" to appear. Indeed, all of Benson's pagan landscapes and references to Pan are clearly metaphors of something else. Even his vocabulary is carefully chosen for *double-entendres*: "It was queer; the night was full of spells,"[67] says Steven at one point. His mother describes a terrible dream she has about him and Tim: "[Y]ou and that mad boy, and there was a wood full of presences, young and gay and antique."[68] "Queer" and "gay" were certainly in use as euphemisms for homosexuality by the 1930s, and Benson's entire novel is a euphemism. Nature, and dancing in nature with Tim, are described as "somehow, for all its infinite grace, terrible."[69] What is "primitive and wild and joyful" is also unnerving, but only to those who are not privy to Benson's jest. Benson plays with the reader, no doubt baffling many who did not understand his intention, but delighting those who know what is really going on. Whenever Benson refers to a male friendship being "sexless," he really means the opposite.

The image of Pan is obviously used as the ultimate symbol of all this:

> Their comradeship had parted there, for this stood outside any relation they held to each other: it reached out into a more primitive love, it was instinct with that knowledge which in Greek fable peopled the woodland with shy presences, with Pan and his fauns, with Dionysus and his maenads.[70]

Steven's young tutor at Cambridge, Maurice, is attracted to Steven and seduced by the pagan environment of Cornwall when he spends the summer with him; but rather like Clive Durham in E.M. Forster's *Maurice* (1971), he retreats from and disapproves of these instincts. Steven himself, in a desperate attempt to do the same, marries the hapless Betty, with disastrous consequences, for Betty does indeed give birth to a deformed stillborn monster—a metaphor if ever there was one, of the disaster that results if a gay man marries a woman and attempts to impose normal family life over his own reality.

Maurice criticizes Steven for lacking normal feelings of remorse or even love—accusing him of being "unmanly." Steven is himself disturbed by his own lack of grief when his mother dies, but this is all really Benson's way of attacking the conventional Christian views of a society that pilloried gayness, with the implication that if one cannot love heterosexually, one cannot really love at all. Steven even explains that attempts were made to build a Wesleyan Chapel in the Cornish village where he lives, but the bricks were found dumped in the sea, and now exotic vines wind themselves around the ruins. Again, Christianity and paganism are vividly contrasted.

Landscape is absolutely central in Benson's method of conveying the erotic nature of a subject he was unable to deal with in more literal terms, and which anyway gains in power and intensity by being approached metaphorically. His descriptions of nature are deeply erotic, to which he here adds an element of the illicit:

> Think of spring nights, Maurice, when the sap hums in the trees; and summer nights—there'll be a beauty tonight—when everything spurring. But the spring nights are the best; I go crazy with joy.... We'll walk all night in the poplar wood, and drink it in, letting ourselves secretly out of the house. Oh, yes at dinner we'll be rather icy to each other, same as we were over bridge the other night, so that my mother thinks we've had what they call a tiff.[71]

Steven wants to be absorbed by nature when he dies, to become bluebells and primroses—imagery which would seem to be coded. He also communes with a squirrel, rather in the manner of Edward Bulwer Lytton's evil magician, Margrave, in *A Strange Story* (1861), though unlike Margrave, Steven doesn't callously kill it.

Time and again, the illicit is linked with the joys of nature: "Something pagan, something to do with woods and wet places."[72] The hazel woods look "like an illustration our of the Dictionary of Mythology."[73] The villagers look like the figures in a classical Greek frieze, while Tim himself is Pan in all but name, except it is he who worships Steven and kneels before him. Described as a beautiful boy of 17 or 18, he is "naked but for a pair of tattered breeches"[74] as he emerges from the sea with his reed pipes. Steven and Tim often disappear together into the woods where Tim has made a shrine. "What have you been up to?" Maurice asks suspiciously.

The reader has no real need of an explanation. Later, Maurice breaks in upon them both, after Steven has made Tim drunk, and is appalled to see Tim dancing to his own "barbarous music."[75] Whereas the Child "didn't know what [his friendship with Steven] meant," Maurice is all too well aware of what is going on, even though he is in denial. "You get glimpses of it, perhaps," Steven snaps, "but then you get frightened, you get genteel."[76] Tim and Steven, however, shamelessly run and dance and "lay on the ground panting for the ecstasy of it; we were the children of the woodland, but also its lords."[77]

Benson includes another Druidical circle of 12 standing stones within which the bodies of previous deformed family members are buried, and this perpetual reminder of his family's "curse" causes Steven in the end to attempt to distance himself from Tim. He is terrified that his happiness with Tim and his longings to be back in the "wet woods" will cause the curse to return in him. Maurice reprimands him for his "indulgence of the craving."[78] And so, Steven marries, with the results already mentioned. Unsurprisingly, Tim hates Steven's wife and wants to poison her. Instead, after the miscarriage of her child, Tim and Steven poison themselves in the ultimate act of defiance against convention.

Dion Fortune, another former member of the Order of the Golden Dawn and one-time associate of Crowley, was obviously well-aware of the previous literature on Pan when writing her own novel, *The Goat-Foot God*, in 1936. She duly includes, perhaps in homage, the phrases "the Great God Pan,"[79] and "the blessing of Pan,"[80] and even includes a poem that echoes Crowley's "Hymn to Pan," with the line, "Come, great Pan, and bless us all"[81]; but her approach takes a more psychological approach to the meaning of Pan as a symbol of the integration of the self and of the self with nature. Like so many characters in Pan fictions, Hugh Paston is a man who is "starved of life." He approaches the subject of magic through decadent estheticism: Following the example of J.K. Huysmans, he attempts to make "every object that surrounded him minister to his moods and have a definite psychological value"[82]—in other words, practicing a form of sympathetic magic. He then encounters a bookseller called Jelkes and an artist called Mona who help him fulfill his quest for Pan, which represents "a hunger for the primitive and vital."[83] Fortune now has Paston imagining a conventional Arcadian landscape:

> The sparse wood of oak and fir; the wine-dark sea beneath; the sound of the bees in the cistuses, the basking lizards, and above all, the flocks of leaping goats springing from rock to rock. He imagined the thin fluting pipe of the goatherd that at any moment might change to the pipes of Pan; he smelt the smell of the pines in the rare

dry air; he felt the sun warm upon his skin; he heard the surf of the loud-sounding sea on the rocks far beneath.[84]

But Fortune does not dwell on this kind of landscape. Her novel is set in 1930s London and, later, in rural England, which she contrasts with the esthetic landscape of interior design. Paston commissions Mona to create a Temple of Pan, suitably "decked-out," in which "every garment one wore, every word one spoke, or that was spoken to one"[85] would create the desired results of union with the Goat-Foot God. It is exactly that kind of sympathetic magic ridiculed by J.G. Frazer in *The Golden Bough* but approximated in the advice of Loyola: "Put yourself in the position of prayer and you will soon feel like praying."[86]

Mona herself has a vision of Pan as "the Shepherd; Pan with his pipes—the Nether Apollo—the harmonizer. She saw him, shaggy and wild and kind,"[87] for Pan is "the keeper of all wild and hunted souls for which no place could be found in a man-made world"[88]; and for Paston, Pan represents "a hunger for the primitive and vital amid all the sophistication and revitalization of his life. Pan was leading him back to the primitive along the path of his own evolution. Provided he had the courage to sink down through his own subconsciousness he would pass through the mediaeval darkness and tragedy and come out into the radiance that was Greece."[89] Fortune comes clean towards the end of the novel, having Paston exclaim that "the whole thing is simply the opening-up of the subconscious."[90] The entire adventure (the building of the temple to Pan, all the occult theorizing, even the ghost of a monk called Ambrosias who had attempted a similar process centuries before) has fundamentally been a psychological process in search of the "Pan within."[91]

Even so, the ritualistic element continues, and Paston eventually leaves the artificial confines of his Pan Temple to discover Ambrosius' altar to Pan in an "open place entirely surrounded by yews."

> The glade was the exact shape of the space made by two intersecting circles, and had evidently been laid out with mathematical precision. In the exact centre of the rabbit-nibbled turf an oblong boulder reclined upon its side.... Ambrosius had chosen his site well. Around the ancient standing-stone he had planted his grove of yew, thus ensuring it being right in the track of one of the lines of force of the ancient worship.[92]

It is here that Paston and his female companion Mona later invoke their rite. A wind stirs, the heat increases and the place begins to fill with light. "Their psychic selves breathed in those bands of light as their physical selves breathed in the atmosphere. And within the earth was the earth-soul, all alive and sentient, and from it they drew their vitality."[93] Out of the landscape, therefore—out of the glade with its standing stone and the newly risen moon, they feel, like Rat and Mole, at one with the earth and at peace with themselves. Fortune's use of the word "dawn" towards the end of her story does strongly suggest a kinship with the title of the chapter in *The Wind in the Willows* in which Rat and Mole encounter Pan: "The Piper at the Gates of Dawn." Ultimately, Paston and Mona realize that what they have experienced was not "the goat-god, crude and earthy. It was the sun!"

> Hugh had not known what Freudian deeps they would work through in the name of the goat-god, and was prepared for anything; but this golden exaltation of high space took him completely by surprise. Then he remembered the favourite phrase of old Jelkes: "All the gods are one god, and all the goddesses are one goddess, and there is one initiator." The All-Father was celestial Zeus—and woodland Pan—and Helios the Life-giver. He was all these things, and having known Pan, a man might pass on to the heavenly gate where Helios waits beside the Dawn.[94]

Seven

Et in Arcadia Ego

There is another kind of British pagan fantasy set more firmly in the ancient world. I have already mentioned the Edwardian musical, *The Arcadians*, which opens with one of the most popular evocations of what Matthew Arnold once characterized as the "sweetness and light" of the ancient world:

> In Arcady life trips along
> As lightsome as the pixy throng
> Who sport beneath the greenwood tree
> In Arcady, in Arcady!
> Drone of bees among the flow'rs,
> Heralding the summer noon,
> Songs of birds amid the bow'rs,
> Litany of joyous June;
> Hush and murmur of the leaves
> As the Zephyr comes and goes;
> Green and gold of ripening sheaves,
> Sailing clouds of pearl and rose;
> The heart to love, the eye to see!—
> These are the joys of Arcady!

This vision of Arcadia, though one unsullied by modern London (which juxtaposition caused the comedy of *The Arcadians*), also attracted composers for the concert hall. Sir Granville Bantock (1868–1946) was once as celebrated as his contemporary, Sir Edward Elgar. He was perhaps the more highly regarded of the two in his time, but Bantock never attained the accolade of having his portrait printed on the back of a British ten pound note as Elgar once did. This is ironic, as Bantock's music is much more *decorative* than Elgar's. Both, however, were indebted to the Germanic models of Wagner and Richard Strauss, and Bantock's orchestration is always inventive and resonant. He excelled in musical narration and was inspired by many different literary interests. Among these were the kind of Celtic subjects I discussed in Chapter Five, and they include a *Hebridean Symphony* in 1913, which has plenty of musical sea imagery as well as quotations from authentic Hebridean folk songs. There is also a *Celtic Symphony* from 1940, with the unusual and thrilling effect of six harps to complement its otherwise purely string orchestra. There are two *Heroic Ballads* from 1944. One of these, "Cuchullan's Lament," was inspired by Marjory Kennedy-Fraser's influential collection of *Songs of the Hebrides*:

> Woe is me! my son a-keening!
> Loud o'er the moor my wail-cry,
> Clanging thy shield and flame-keen sword,
> Who lieth asleep in cold death.

Bantock was equally interested in classical mythology. His *Pagan Symphony* was completed in 1928. Subtitled "Et in Arcadia vixit" ("I too lived in Arcadia"), it is scored for typically inflated, late–Romantic orchestral forces, to which he added a program note, derived from Horace's *Odes*, to what is otherwise an un-signposted, one-movement work. The reference to "far-off rocks" here is significant, as what Bantock achieves in his Symphony is a musical suggestion of Arcadian landscape:

> *Bacchum in remotis carmina rupibus vidi docentum—credite posteri—Nymphasque discentes et aures, capripedum Satyrorum acutas.* (Bacchus I have seen on far-off rocks—if posterity will believe me—teaching his songs divine to the listening Nymphs and to the goat-footed Satyrs with their pointed ears.)

Bantock explains that Bacchus was worshipped as "the bestower of happiness and plenty, the lover of truth and beauty, the victor over the powers of evil." He also refers to Aphrodite, the goddess of Love, who is invoked in the symphony "to remind the world of her supreme power and glorious beauty."[1] Despite the lack of a program, Bantock nonetheless creates a powerful pagan *mood*.

The introduction to the symphony is one of its two major highlights. It features languid solos for flute, oboe and violin, over subdued string chords and horn calls reminiscent of the Tarnhelm motif in Wagner's *Ring*. These are later combined with harp arpeggios, which have the effect of regressing the listener to the mythical past. (As Eero Tarasti informs us, the lyre was the instrument of Apollo and Orpheus, which is why the harp is so often used to represent "a mythical heroic poet or singer."[2])

After many Straussian echoes, *Pagan Symphony*'s other highlight is a "Dance of the Satyrs," which forms the equivalent of the scherzo section of a standard four-movement symphony. It rises through complex contrapuntal writing to a climax of riotous percussion involving timpani, side-drum, snare-drum, cymbals and tambourines, before a "Roman" fanfare of trumpets and trombones leads us into an Oriental "antique dance" with echoes of the Arabian dance from Tchaikovsky's *Nutcracker*. The subsequent invocation to Aphrodite reflects Bantock's earlier settings of poetic fragments by Sappho in his work of that name from 1905. Its prelude also begins with regressive harp arpeggios, followed by a "Hymn to Aphrodite," and then a setting of "The moon has set," which again employs landscape imagery to evoke feelings of loneliness and desire:

> The moon has set, and the Pleiades;
> It is midnight; time is going by,
> And I sleep alone.
> I yearn and seek—
> I know not what to do—
> And I flutter like a child after her mother,
> For Love masters my limbs, and shakes me,
> Fatal creature, bitter-sweet—
> Yea, Eros shakes my soul,
> A wind on the mountain falling on the oaks.
> Alas! I shall be ever maiden:
> Neither honey nor bee for me.[3]

As Lewis Foreman points out, the 86-page vocal score of *Sappho* is framed with an *art nouveau* border, emphasizing that this is very much "a *fin de siècle* score with its vivid invention and true-to-life emotion and storytelling."[4]

Bantock also composed a beautiful *Sapphic Poem* for cello and orchestra in 1906, not to mention a *Pagan Poem* for flute and piano (1930) and another symphony (his third, from 1939) entitled *The Cyprian Goddess*, which is prefaced by two more Odes of Horace in praise of Venus, the goddess in question. In his notes for the Hyperion CD of this work, Foreman quite rightly questions why Bantock was never commissioned to write film music at this time in his long career, as this is really what *The Cyprian Goddess* is, without, alas, a film to accompany it, or even a specific program. But with echoes of the orchestral style of Sibelius, who was a personal friend, along with evocations of the sea and sunsets (important motifs in cinematic evocations of pagan myth), the music then moves into Bantock's characteristically "Orientalist" style, brilliantly creating a musical panorama of the antique world of his dreams—a vision of Arcadia in sound, reborn in Edwardian England.

The gods of Roman mythology who have lent their names to the planets might also qualify Gustav Holst's Symphonic Suite, *The Planets* (first performed in 1918) as another musical depiction of the pagan past, but these pieces were inspired more by astrology than mythology. Holst was a keen amateur astrologer, calling it his "pet vice,"[5] and the associations of five of the seven planets with the gods are often at odds with the original Roman characteristics of the gods themselves. The first movement, "Mars," was completed just as war broke out in 1914 and ruthlessly predicts the mechanized slaughter soon to engulf Europe. Its unstoppable 5/4 rhythm, emphasized by militaristic snare drum, expresses all of Holst's pacifist outrage at armed conflict, but is also a magnificent expression of vital energy and power, which could, if harnessed creatively, achieve great things. It therefore brings a rather more ambivalent and modern perspective to what was once regarded as a heroic figure.

Venus is still recognizable in the Roman goddess of love, but as we move through the subsequent pieces, astrological interpretations predominate. The conflation of Mercury with the Greek Hermes is really an anomaly, popularized by astrology. Mercurius was in fact the Roman god of commerce (hence "mercantile"). Jupiter, the equivalent of Zeus, was never really a "Bringer of Jollity." Saturnus, associated with Cronos by the Romans themselves (and hence with the attribute of being "the Bringer of Old Age"), is again less appropriate than Saturn's more proper association with Demeter, the Greek god of agriculture and the fecundity of the earth. (Saturnus derives his name from the act of sowing seeds [*sero, sevi, satum*]). Uranus was not discovered until 1781 by William Herschel, and thus has no historical connection with the ancient world. Neither does Neptune, which remained unknown until 1846.

If Holst's musical connection with classical paganism was tenuous, that of Cyril Scott (1879–1970) was more secure. The title of his most famous piano work, *Lotus Land* (1904), suggests a *fin de siècle* evocation of that part of the legend of Odysseus, when he and his fellow sailors encounter the lotus eaters, whose food makes them lethargic and uninterested in returning home. Scott would also have been familiar with Tennyson's famous treatment the story in his poem, "The Lotus Eaters," with its effective use of repetition to create a sense of enervation:

> In the afternoon they came unto a land
> In which it seemed always afternoon.
> All round the coast the languid air did swoon,
> Breathing like one that hath a weary dream.[6]

Scott's piece is similarly languid, its repeated perfect cadences in the left hand accompanying a meandering Orientalist melody in the right. The whole thing is punctuated by two gigantic pentatonic glissandi (the black notes of the keyboard), creating an effect of swirling dizziness, entirely worthy of the intoxicating lotus flowers, which caused such enervation and forgetfulness:

> To each, but whoso did receive of them,
> And taste, to him the gushing of the wave
> Far far away did seem to mourn and rave
> On alien shores; and if his fellow spake,
> His voice was thin, as voices from the grave;
> And deep-asleep he seem'd, yet all awake,
> And music in his ears his beating heart did make.[7]

Scott's piece, like all music of course, moves through time but seems not to get anywhere in its exotic languor. Prosaically, he composed the piece in the quintessentially British village of Shere, near Guildford in Surrey: Again, the pagan world made a musical Arcady out of the English fields as it had in *The Wind in the Willows*. Two years later, in 1906, that very different composer, Harry Farjeon, appealed directly to the drawing rooms of Guildford with his charming *Pictures from Greece*, which aspire to being nothing grander than attractive salon music, complete with a cover illustration in the style of Heath-Robinson, The six pieces describe the Dryads, the Fates, Mercury, the Graces, the Naiads and the Muses.

The Muses also inspired and provided the subtitle of Scott's Third Symphony (1937), which suggests, in his idiosyncratic style, four of the nine Greek muses: Melpomene, music of epic poetry and tragedy, Thalia, music of comedy, Erato, music of love and poetry, and Terpsichore, muse of dance and song. Lewis Foreman posits that the example of Stravinsky's *Apollon musagète* (*Apollo and the Muses*, 1928) might have inspired Scott, to whom Stravinsky had inscribed a piano reduction of *The Rite of Spring*.[8] It is scored for immense forces including an orchestral piano, two harps, a great deal of percussion and even a wind machine to suggest the mountainous landscapes of the Greek islands; Scott creates somber and even unnervingly alien musical evocations of the ancient world in the foreground of which are placed the Muses themselves. The effect is often sinister, sometimes frightening, and compliments his lifelong fascination with the occult, which hovers behind much of his work even if it does not often directly inspire it. His "Poem of the Sea," entitled *Neptune* (1933, rev. 1935), began life as a descriptive piece about the sinking of the *Titanic*, but the programmatic elements were criticized after its first performance, causing Scott to recast the work and give it a more "respectable" title. Given its origins, the resonance of the pagan god is really only a spurious connection here, effective though Scott's evocation of the sea and the disaster is.

The classical world continued to have appeal for Benjamin Britten (1913–1976). His suite for solo oboe, *Six Metamorphoses After Ovid*, op. 49, is really a series of variations in which the opening theme is appropriately morphed into character studies of Pan, Phaeton, Niobe, Bacchus, Narcissus and Arethusa. As Michael Kennedy observes, "The obvious is not evaded—a mirror-image for Narcissus, hiccups for Bachus, the cascading fountain for Arethusa," but landscapes these are not. More so is Britten's *Young Apollo*—a kind of extended fanfare for piano and string orchestra, composed virtually on arrival in the U.S. whither he and Peter Pears took refuge from the Second World War in 1939. As a musical depiction of shimmering light, Apollo is appropriately invoked. The shimmering scales and arpeggios in the piano, along with eccentric glissandi in the strings, create a sense of soaring freedom and a vibrant musical sky-scape—comparable to the way in which Lord Leighton alludes to Apollo by means of a flamboyant sunset in his painting, *Clytie*, which I will discuss later.

Gerald Finzi (1901–1956) composed what has become one of the most popular of all examples of English pastoralism, which, through the classical allusion of its title, also has strong Arcadian connotations. This is his unfinished *Eclogue* for piano and orchestra, the title suggesting Virgil's writings in this form, and thus equating the English scene with some kind of pagan serenity. Finzi's biographer Stephen Banfield suggests, however, that the serenity is somewhat troubled, for while it seems as though Finzi aims to pursue it for as long as he can, it in fact eludes him, the recapitulation of the opening motif being "clouded on recapture."[9] This tension, together with its unfinished state, and the fact that its first performance was posthumous, adds to the fragile and elegiac quality of the piece, which, like Vaughan Williams' *Pastoral Symphony*, looks back to a Golden Age, lost forever after the calamity of the First World War.

In striking contrast to the Arcadian allusions in the work of these British composers, British writer, Mary Renault (1905–1983), took a less Romantic approach when recreating the ancient world in her novels, being more interested in character and narrative than in landscape. Her indebtedness to Frazer is evident, however, in such lines as these from *The King Must Die* (1958), her de-mythologizing account of the legend of Theseus and the Minotaur:

> I remembered what I had heard of the old religion. "They care nothing for him," I thought, "though he is going to die for them, or so they hope, and put his life into the corn. He is the scapegoat. Looking at him they see only the year's troubles, the crop that failed, the barren cows, the sickness. They want to kill their troubles with him, and start again."[10]

Renault's aim was not merely to re-tell the myths but to provide a historically plausible explanation of their origin. Hence, the fight with the Minotaur is explained as a ritual dance with a bull. Theseus and the other victims due to be sacrificed, practice with bronze horns, which were said to have been made by Daedalus (or Daidalos, as she spells it), and which are indeed dangerous, but not so dangerous as the bulls themselves. The dance is in honor of Poseidon, to placate him, and before it begins, the "dancers" face Ariadne and swear: "We salute you; we who are going to die." Renault therefore takes an anthropological rather than mythological approach; there are no fabulous creatures in her recreation of the ancient world.

Landscape similarly plays a much-diminished role in the proceedings, as poetic regression is nowhere near as important to her as demystification. The characters may believe in the gods, but the narrator does not and has no interest in supernatural happenings or the suspension of our disbelief. This is even more the case in Robert Graves's *I, Claudius* (1934), which is primarily a study in character and its relation to historical events in the pagan past.

A forerunner of this approach was Walter Pater, in his novel *Marius the Epicurean* (1885); but Pater's aims were more poetic because of his fundamental concern with esthetics. Landscape is hence much more in evidence here. With *Marius*, George Moore believed that Pater had added "an immortal prose masterpiece to the English language,"[11] a judgment with which posterity has unfortunately taken issue, but Moore was right. Pater uses the form of a Bildungsroman to discuss esthetics: Marius, sensitive and literary, is acutely responsive to his surroundings. In Rome, he becomes the amanuensis of Marcus Aurelius, who attempts to convert him to his stoic philosophy; but Marius is repelled by its indifference to suffering, and during walks in the surrounding countryside he resolves to dedicate himself to the *Great Ideal* of intellectual enquiry and esthetic contemplation: what Pater, in his subtitle, terms "his sensations and ideas." The world of sensations is but "an element in the world of thought."

> The purely material world, that close, impassable prison-wall, seemed just then the unreal things, to be actually dissolving away all around him: and he felt a quiet hope, a quiet joy dawning faintly, in the dawning of this doctrine upon him as a really credible opinion. It was like the break of day over some vast prospect with the "new city," as it were some celestial New Rome, in the midst of it.[12]

Landscape, nonetheless, plays an important role in Pater's attempt to summon the atmosphere of the ancient world in which the story is set. Prior to the enlightenment of Marius, the landscape seems to initiate it:

> An air of immense age possessed, above all, the vegetation around—a world of evergreen trees—the olives especially, older than how many generations of men's lives! fretted and twisted by the combining forces of life and death, into every conceivable caprice of form. In the windless weather all seemed to be listening to the roar of the immemorial waterfall, plunging down so unsociably among these human habitations, and with a motion so unchanging from age to age as to count, even in this time-worn place, as an image of unalterable rest. Yet the clear sky all but broke to let through the ray which was silently quickening everything in the late February afternoon, and the unseen violet refined itself through the air.[13]

Earlier in the novel, Pater demonstrates that landscape is an essential element in creating time and place, again emphasizing olive trees, heat effects and mountains:

> In a green meadow at the foot of the steep olive-clad rocks below, the novices were taking their exercise. The softly sloping sides of the vale lay alike in full sunlight; and its distant opening was closed by a beautifully formed mountain, from which the last wreathes of morning mist were rising under the heat.[14]

From the midst of this ancient landscape, Pater even summons Pan, not atavistically in a "contemporary" British setting like so many of his later compatriots, but in a conjured fantasy of the ancient world. While telling the story of Cupid and Psyche in an aside from the main narrative, we are shown Pan in his native surroundings:

> Pan, the rustic god, was sitting just then by the waterside, embracing, in the body of a reed, the goddess Canna; teaching her to respond to him in all varieties of slender sound. Hard by, his flock of goats browsed at will. And the shaggy god called her, wounded and outworn, kindly to him and said, "I am but a rustic herdsman, pretty maiden, yet wise, by favour of my great age and long experience, and if I guess truly by those faltering steps, by thy sorrowful eyes and continual sighing, thou labourest with excess of love. Listen then to me, and seek not death again, in the stream or otherwise. Put aside thy woe, and turn thy prayers to Cupid."[15]

As we have seen, Oscar Wilde had juxtaposed the Arcadian world of Pan with contemporary Victorian Britain in his poems, "Pan" and "Ravenna," but he also couched Pan in the pagan past. Pan appears in his long poem, "Charmides," which scandalized its first readers in 1881 with its imagery of the eponymous hero virtually making love to a statue, caressing the "breasts of polished ivory," "[t]he grand cool flanks, the crescent thighs, the bossy hills of snow."[16] But later, Charmides encounters Pan, and again it is through the carefully arranged associative power of landscape that Wilde creates the appropriate antique mood:

> Down the steep rock with hurried feet and fast
>   Clomb the brave lad, and reached the cave of Pan,
> And heard the goat-foot snoring as he passed,
>   And leapt upon a grassy knoll and ran

> Like a young fawn unto an olive wood
> Which in a shady valley by the well-built city stood.[17]

Landscape is an essential ingredient in Wilde's evocations of the pagan past. In the poem, "The Garden of Eros," landscape opens the narrative:

> It is full summer now, the heart of June;
>   Not yet sunburnt reapers are a-stir
> Upon the upland meadow where too soon
>   Rich autumn time, the season's usurer,
> Will lend his hoarded gold to all the trees,
> And see his treasure scattered by the wild and spendthrift breeze.[18]

The names of flowers punctuate the succeeding stanzas: rose, harebell, narcissus, violets, celandine, lilac, hollyhock, anemone, convolvulus, hyacinths, clematis, fox-gloves, primrose—all are offered as a floral prelude to a poem whose very title is a reference to formal landscape:

> And I will cut a reed by yonder spring
> And make the wood-gods jealous, and old Pan
> Wonder what young intruder dares to sing
> In these still haunts.[19]

Wilde invokes the "Spirit of Beauty" through landscape and flowers, conjuring a fantasy of the pagan past with reference not only to Pan but also to Poserpina, Helena, Cynthia, Endymion, Artemis, Venus, Adonais and Atalanta—all presented as antidotes to the ills of a modern, "scientific age."

> Can it assuage
> One lover's breaking heart? what can it do
> To make one life more beautiful, one day
> More godlike in its period?[20]

Wilde is also keen to observe that English landscape is in many ways more beautiful than ancient Arcady. In "The Burden of Itys," he favorably compares an English field with Grecian meadows:

>   many a rose
>   Which all day long in vales Aeolian
> A lad might seek in vain for over-grows
>   Our hedges like a wanton courtesan
> Unthrifty of its beauty; lilies too
> Ilissos never mirrored star our streams, and cockles blue
>
> Dot the green wheat which, though they are the signs
>   For swallow going south, would never spread
> Their azure tents between the attic vines;
>   Even that little weed of ragged red,

> Which bids the robin pipe, in Arcady
> Would be a trespasser, and many an unsung elegy
>
> Sleeps in the reeds that fringe our winding Thames
> > Which to awake were sweeter ravishment
> Than ever Syrinx wept for...[21]

Wilde thus offers the hope that England might truly become a new Arcady. All that is necessary is freedom from conventional morals and industrial constraints, both of which are symbolized by the "sluggish leadenness"[22] of the Thames.

That great contemporary of Wilde, and president of the Royal Academy Art, Frederic, Lord Leighton (1830–1896), was very much of the opinion that the visual arts, by virtue of being decorative, were also morally uplifting. He too was concerned with the recreation of Arcadia, and many of his paintings depict scenes from classical mythology. Landscapes were again an important element in his most ambitious projects along these lines. Over his long career, he made many informal landscape sketches, which some now regard as examples of his most spirited work; and though he did not think of himself as primarily a landscape artist, he nonetheless recognized the importance of landscape as a means of evoking the classical world. His canvas of *Daedalus and Icarus* (1869) not only gave him the opportunity to contrast the shimmering Apollonian beauty of the young male figure of Icarus with the dark-toned skin of his father, Daedalus, but also to conjure the spirit of the ancient world through setting. As Icarus prepares for his doomed voyage, his wings attached and a blue cloak billowing in the breeze behind him, Leighton presents a backdrop of the sea and rocky coast in a study of contrasting shades of blue—the deep tone of the ocean contrasted against the luminous azure of the sky: "that marvellous blue,"[23] as he described it in his diary, when making sketches of the coastline of Asia Minor on the island of Rhodes.

The classical realism of Leighton's approach foreshadowed the kind of imagery we find in the popular Romanticism of movies featuring the stop-motion effects of Ray Harryhausen (1920–2013), as seen in *Jason and the Argonauts* (dir. Don Chaffey, 1963) and *Clash of the Titans* (dir. Desmond Davis, 1981). Indeed, when we turn our attention to Leighton's magnificent treatment of *Perseus and Andromeda* (1891), we could very well be looking at an admittedly superior movie poster for *Clash of the Titans* itself, as very nearly the same situation that Leighton depicts in his painting occurs in the film. In both instances, Andromeda is bound to a rock, about to be sacrificed to a sea monster, when Perseus, riding winged Pegasus, comes to

Andromeda, Perseus and the Kraken. Film poster for *Clash of the Titans* (dir. Desmond Davis, 1981).

the rescue overhead (the aureole of the sun behind him in Leighton's picture, equating him to an ancient sun god, thus bringing expectations of new hope and fresh life). Leighton's Perseus attacks the monster with a bow and arrow. In Ovid's *Metamorphoses*, he uses a sword, but Harry Hamlin's Perseus in the film is thrown from Pegasus by the Kraken and plunges into the sea. He then swims to Andromeda's rock and uses Medusa's torchlike gaze to petrify the monster. This nicely conflates two strands of the Perseus legend: the story that later developed into the saga of St. George and the Dragon, and Perseus' celebrated decapitation of the Gorgon. In Leighton's companion work, which he completed five years after *Perseus and Andromeda* and entitled *Perseus on Pegasus Hastening to the Rescue of Andromeda*, Perseus is indeed shown carrying the head of Medusa by his side.

Again, landscape plays a crucial role in creating both a sense of drama and the required mythological mood in this painting. We see another of Leighton's views of Asia Minor or of Palestine, with studies of sea and sky made in Donegal in Scotland.[24] In *Perseus and Andromeda*, the rocky crags that surround the unfortunate Andromeda and the fire-breathing sea monster were also based on his sketches of the coast of Donegal, which Leighton described as "quite Dantesque in its grim blackness."[25]

Such landscapes were indeed the forerunners of the varied location work in Harryhausen's cinematic fantasies, which, in their own way, are direct popular descendants of Leighton's elite effusions of academic art. In one painting, Leighton went to the extreme of conveying the meaning of the myth in hand almost entirely by means of landscape. This was *Clytie* (1890–1892), in which Clytie kneels in prayer to the sun god Apollo, imploring him not to desert her. The tiny figure of Clytie is contained in the far right-hand corner of the canvas, the rest of which is devoted to a spectacular and distinctly cinematic sunrise. Far more than his fellow Olympian artist Sir Laurence Alma-Tadema (1836–1912), Leighton valued the emotive power of landscape, employing it to work in a symbolic manner.

Harryhausen also acknowledged his debt to Gustave Doré, who worked in a similar tradition. But even in Pater's *Marius* there is a striking model for the scene in *Clash of the Titans* when Perseus pays Charon the ferryman to take him across the River Styx to the Gorgon's Island of the Dead. Continuing the story of Cupid and Psyche, Pater's narrator explains:

> And soon as thou comest to the river of the dead, Charon, in that crazy bark he hath, will put thee over upon the further side. There is greed even among the dead: and thou shalt deliver to him, for the ferrying, one of those two pieces of money, in such wise that he take it with his hand from between thy lips.[26]

In the film, Tim Piggot-Smith's soldier, Thallo, provides the coin, which Perseus duly offers to the skeletal Charon. Charon then rows them over to the Gorgon's island, which itself bears a striking resemblance to Böcklin's famous painting, *The Isle of the Dead*. Indeed, the island is referred to as such by the Stygian witches from whom Perseus gains knowledge of Medusa. They describe it as "the Isle of the Dead on the very edge of the underworld." In Ovid's *Metamorphoses*, there are only two of these blind "Graiae," the third no doubt added to the film to echo the Shakespearean resonance of the three witches in *Macbeth*. Once arrived at the temple of Medusa, the film carefully stage-manages Ovid's observation of "the statues of men and of beasts transformed to stone at the sight of Medusa."[27]

Beverley Cross's *Clash of the Titans* screenplay conflates and adapts much of the mythic material, re-telling the ancient stories in the populist manner of Charles Kingsley's "Greek Fairy Tales for Children" in *The Heroes* (1855). Lacking cinematic or digital means, Kingsley illustrated these stories himself, increasing their appeal to young readers, amongst whom were his own children, for whom he wrote them. His account of Perseus' encounter with the Gorgon is full of the drama and horror brought to the scene by Harryhausen's inspired animation, with the significant difference that Kingsley's Medusa is chillingly beautiful, with "the face of a nymph, only her eyebrows were knit, and her lips clenched, with everlasting care and pain."

> But as he looked, from among her tresses the vipers' heads awoke, and peeped up with their bright dry eyes, and showed their fangs, and hissed; and Medusa, as she tossed, threw back her wings and showed her brazen claws; and Perseus saw that, for all her beauty, she was as foul and venomous as the rest.
> Then he came down and stepped to her boldly, and looked steadfastly on his mirror, and struck with Herpé [his sword] stoutly once; and he did not need to strike again.
> Then he wrapped the head in the goat-skin, turning away his eyes, and sprang into the air aloft, faster than he ever sprang before.[28]

In the distinctly less poetic remake of *Clash of the Titans* (dir. Louis Leterrier, 2010), a CGI Medusa, half-human, half-reptile, retains the "beautiful" features of Natalia Vodianova who provides her snake-surrounded visage, but she entirely lacks the charm of Harryhausen's more conventionally horrific monster, with its eyes ablaze with beams of petrifying light. These ultimately transform the Kraken into a fractured marble statue, which collapses into a boiling sea. Though described in a less spectacular manner, more in keeping with the Victorian nursery, Kingsley's account of this dénouement is nonetheless powerful and very much in the manner of the climax of the original *Clash of the Titans*:

> On came the great sea-monster, coasting along like a huge black galley, lazily breasting the ripple.... At last he saw Andromeda, and shot forward to take his prey, while the waves foamed white behind him, and before him the fish fled leaping.
>
> Then down from the height of the air fell Perseus like a shooting star; down to the crests of the waves, while Andromeda hid her face as he shouted; and then there was silence for a while.
>
> At last she looked up trembling, and saw Perseus springing toward her and instead of the monster a long black rock, with the sea rippling quietly round it.[29]

The 1981 *Clash of the Titans* begins on a craggy coast, lashed by a stormy sea. These scenes were shot in Cornwall, and depict the incarceration in a casket of Danae and the infant Perseus, her son by Zeus, watched over by her vengeful husband, Acrisius (Donald Houston). But it is not so much the violent events depicted here as the impressive landscape that is the focus of the audience's attention. Pathetic fallacy expresses the emotions of the scene and creates the mythological environment, without which the events themselves would lose much of their resonance and become merely the record of an atrocity. Large rocks loom over the players, suggesting the overpowering force of fate, against which humanity has no control. Harryhausen himself referred to the "unusual rock formations"[30] at Antequera in Spain, which were used as a setting for the shrine of the Stygian witches later in the film. These settings nicely reflect Ovid's description of Perseus' journey "through rocky regions remote and secluded, littered with broken trees."[31] The exteriors of Medusa's temple were shot at Paestum in Southern Italy, while the setting of the walled city of Jaffa, home of Andromeda, made atmospheric use of the Maltese coast. The sea plays an important role in the film, often shown with fiery sunsets over the waves, suggesting the oldest worship of them all, as we witness at the end of *The Wicker Man*.

The gods permeate the landscape, their gifts appearing within it, and Maggie Smith's Thetis is even shown placing Perseus in the amphitheater at Joppa. Her gigantic arm hovers over the prostrate form of the hero, her face looming over the scene before receding and vanishing into the sky. The gods are therefore shown to be part of the landscape, which is also an expression of their power. Even during the main titles we follow a seagull (in fact Poseidon in another form), which flies over cliffs and canyons, some of them snow-covered, taking us to the top of Mount Olympus and the citadel of the gods. Many of the scenes, both in the citadel and in the mythological landscapes of the action below, are shrouded in mist—mist over water, mist over mountains. It is a very Wagnerian effect, Bayreuth once being infamous for its extensive use of steam to cover scene changes and create "mood." Indeed, Bernard Shaw ironically described the effect as giving a flavor of "washing day"[32] to the experience; but there is no denying its mythological power. As we have seen, Terry Jones and Terry Gilliam made equally atmospheric use of mist in *Monty Python and the Holy Grail* to create a very literal sense of "the mists time."

This, however, is not always the case. On their way to find the Stygian witches, Perseus and his companions enter an arid plain, sparsely furnished with two blasted trees (as suggested by Ovid, in the passage above), in a shot that is reminiscent of scenes in Ingmar Bergman's *The Seventh Seal* (1957). Such painterly images raise the film to a poetic level, which, combined with Laurence Rosenthal's Straussian score, demonstrate the popular Romanticism of mainstream cinematic fantasy at its best.

In a reversal of Leighton's Perseus in *Perseus and Andromeda*, the *Clash of the Titans* Gorgon supplements her ghastly gaze with the more conventional armory of a bow and arrow. With her hideous features, lobster body and rattlesnake tail, she also echoes Wilde's description of her "leaden eyeballs," "snaky horrors" and "bloodless lips" in "Charmides."[33] She is certainly a much more grisly apparition than the Gorgon of Hammer Films' 1964 adventure, directed by Terence Fisher and starring Peter Cushing and Christopher Lee. Hammer's Gorgon is called Megaera, which is actually the name of one of the Greek Furies, a confusion that permeates the rest of the film, conflating, as it does, the traditional Gothic environment of a ruined castle in Central Europe with a Greek legend. The confusion pays dividends, however, as the film is powerfully melancholic in its mood, the only real disappointment being Megaera herself, who is nowhere near as effective as Harryhausen's monstrosity. But this lack is more than made up for by the elaborate sets of Bernard Robinson, which are more eloquent at conveying mood than any monster. The ruins of Castle Borski, wherein Megaera dwells, are one of Hammer's finest Gothic achievements, perhaps excelling the impressive, though far from ruinous castle of Dracula in the company's first film about that character from 1958. The fact that the spirit of Megaera intermittently inhabits the beautiful body of a young woman called Carla Hoffman (played by Barbara Shelley), echos Charles Kingsley's version of the story, where the Gorgon is still beautiful. In Hammer's version, Carla is transformed into a monstrosity when Megaera's spirit possesses her, though her hideous alter ego is in fact played by another actress (Prudence Hyman).

Hammer's version of the tale, like that of Perseus and Andromeda, is a curiously haunting love story, with Carla as a kind of Andromeda, who is sacrificed to two monsters—the Gorgon herself, and her possessive employer and repressed lover, Dr. Namaroff (Cushing), who runs the Vandorff Medical Institute and suspects the truth about her. The Perseus character is

Richard Pasco's Paul Heintz, who has arrived in Vandorff to investigate the death of his father from the Gorgon's gaze. Alas, the story does not have a happy ending. Paul's attempts to take Carla away from the influence of the Gorgon and Dr. Namaroff fail and Megaera is beheaded by Christopher Lee's Prof. Meister, the suitably named academic who works out what is actually going on.

The Gorgon inhabits the world of Dracula, and Megaera is a kind of Countess Dracula; but the special manner with which she dispatches her victims is nowhere near as significant as the location in which she does it. The landscape of the Gothic castle is the film's justification, almost as though Hammer were looking for a new monster to move into the space vacated by Dracula. Nonetheless, the conflation of ancient Greece with nineteenth-century Gothic does provide us with the opportunity to pursue a psychological interpretation: Carla wears close-fitting, buttoned-up gowns and is reluctant to elope with Paul. Unable to release herself from the father figure of Cushing's Namaroff, her pent-up sexual frustration erupts in the form of phallic snakes. She turns men to stone, and if, as Freud suggests, decapitation is a psychological metaphor for castration, her own demise suggests a female equivalent.

Eight

The Golden Bough

Sir James Frazer's much-harried study of magic and religion, first published in 1890, may have fallen foul of later anthropologists but, like Freud's similarly controversial psychoanalytical theories, its impact on the arts has been considerable. T.S. Eliot acknowledged, in his later explanatory notes to *The Wasteland*, that anyone familiar with *The Golden Bough* "will immediately recognize in the poem certain references to vegetation ceremonies," adding that the reference to the Hanged Man in the first section the poem, "The Burial of the Dead," "is associated in my mind with the Hanged God of Frazer"[1]—a reference to Frazer's chapter on "Human Representatives of Attis":

> We may conjecture that in old days the priest who bore the name and played the part of Attis at the spring festival of Cybele was regularly hanged or otherwise slain upon the sacred tree, and that this barbarous custom was afterwards mitigated into the form which it is known to us in later times, when the priest merely drew blood from his body under the tree and attached an effigy instead of himself to its trunk. In the holy grove at Upsala men and animals were sacrificed by being hanged upon the sacred trees. The human victims dedicated to Odin were regularly put to death by hanging or by a combination of hanging and stabbing, the man being strung up to a tree or a gallows and then wounded with a spear. Hence Odin was called the Lord of the Gallows or the God of the Hanged and he is represented sitting under a gallows tree.[2]

Right at the beginning of *The Wasteland*, Eliot refers to "the dead land,"[3] which requires the rejuvenating sacrifice of a god-king. This dead land is that of modern civilization, still reeling from the devastating impact of the First World War, but it also refers to ancient myths, such as that of Osiris, who was slain and dismembered by his brother Set. Isis, the consort of Osiris, gathered the pieces together, missing only the phallus, which Set retained (the infamous "Talisman of Set" mentioned by Wheatley in *The Devil Rides Out*). Frazer identified that the Osiris myth was not only the origin of the myth of Dionysus and Attis, who were similarly dismembered and resurrected for the good of the land, but also of the redemptive myth of Christ.

Updated to an early twentieth-century London canal behind a gasworks, the Osiris myth is given Eliot's modernist treatment. He refers to "the king" suggesting the hope of renewal even out of the demoralized and disorientated environment of postwar Europe. *The Wasteland* also references the grail legend of the Fisher King, who similarly presided over a wasteland, thus linking his vision to Arthurian romance. The poem is therefore in many respects a companion piece to the kind of fantasy we have been exploring so far. As a hallucinatory vision of modern sensibility, it has rarely been surpassed, but it is also a kind a psycho-geography, with its many references to London and the River Thames, which is now inhabited by Wagner's Rhine-maidens, who have strayed from their traditional setting to this oily, tarry, sweating metropolitan artery. Mixing modern shipping with memories of Queen Elizabeth I and her entourage sailing down the river in gilded barges, Eliot creates a kaleidoscopic, time-shifting landscape of urban associations.

This patterning of literary, historical and geographical associations is one of the hallmarks of modernist literature in general, but on a more popular level, the subject of ritual sacrifice lies at the heart of Evelyn Eaton's historical novel, *The King Is a Witch*, which concerns King Edward III and his "Substitute Victim," Roger Mortimer, Earl of March:

> Edward the Third was 14 when he ascended the throne, after the murder of his father, King Edward the Second, when no man had been found to die in his stead. If the Royal Victim were still strong and lusty at the appointed time, a Substitute Victim was usually killed, but King Edward the Second had been 49, the seven times seven fatal climacteric after which a man's powers decline ... there were no more Substitute Victims for him.[4]

The Golden Bough also inspired Aleister Crowley's collection of stories in *Golden Twigs*. He wrote these entertaining and eloquent tales in 1916; not published for over 60 years, they demonstrate Crowley's close reading of Frazer's text, ironizing it to some extent, but for the most part taking it very seriously indeed. He even referred to Frazer on his dedicatory page as "Master of Gods," and it is to this collection, as well as various British films rooted in Frazer's work, that I will concentrate here.

Crowley dedicated *Golden Twigs* to D.H. Lawrence, whom he regarded as a fellow worker for "the restoration of true magic."[5] Lawrence read and admired Frazer, and though professing not to like mysticism,[6] he did equate science with magic:

> I honestly believe that the great pagan world of which Egypt and Greece were the last living terms, the great pagan world which preceded our own era once, had a vast and perhaps perfect science of its own, a science in terms of life. In our era this science crumbled into magic and charlatanry. But even wisdom crumbles.

> I believe that this great science previous to ours and quite different in constitution and nature from our science once was universal, established all over from the then-existing globe. I believe it was esoteric, invested in a large priesthood.[7]

Thus do Crowley, Lawrence and Frazer perhaps uncomfortably rub shoulders with one another; but Crowley admired Frazer far more than Lawrence, referring to the academic's "magical prose," to which a large element of Frazer's success is due. The descriptive passages in particular were bound to appeal to imaginative writers by the sheer power of their diction.

Crowley opens *Golden Twigs* with "The King of the Wood," a satire on the story that is central to Frazer's argument. The high priest of Nemi guards the grove of Diana and carries a drawn sword, "peering warily about him as if at every instant he expects to be set upon by an enemy," as Frazer describes it. "He was a priest and a murderer; and the man for whom he looked was sooner or later to murder him and hold the priesthood in his stead."[8] Such is the legend that inspired Frazer's series of comparisons to reveal the kinship of so many myths of sacrifice and renewal. Frazer's poetic imagination was certainly stimulated by both the story and the setting:

> Italian pilgrims turned to the quarter where, standing sharply out against the faint blue line of the Apennines or the deeper blue of the distant sea, the Alban Mountain rose before them, the home of the mysterious priest of Nemi, the King of the Wood. There, among the green woods and beside the still waters of the lonely hills, the ancient Aryan worship of the god of the oak, the tender and the dripping sky lingered in its early, almost Druidical form, long after a great political and intellectual revolution had shifted the capital of Latin religion from the forest to the city, from Nemi to Rome.[9]

Crowley was also keen to recreate this scene in "The King of the Wood," with its moonlit glade, the "stealth and vigilance" of the priest's manner, the shrine itself "set in a great mass of woodland, absolutely still on that windless night save where, bubbling from the basalt, a spring ran over the pebbles and fell in a series of cascades into the lake."[10]

Crowley's priest kills a woman who gasps for "Sanctuary" and another who lurks in the shadows behind her. The scene then changes to a villa within sight of the grove and the temple, where Titus, a burly slave, follows a beckoning figure clad in a dark robe. This mysterious person, who lures him to (of course!) a statue of Pan in the middle of a fountain, is the wife of Titus' master, and Titus is smitten. She encourages him to kill the priest, promising him that when he is King of the Wood, they will live gloriously in the grove together. This eventually comes to pass, though in the end both the slave and the wife are slain in their turn. Throughout, Crowley demonstrates his ability to evoke landscape in passages such as this: "The trees were sombre and spectral, black and jagged against a lowering and stormy sky; the rising wind made melancholy music in the branches, its own howl like a wolf's."[11]

The next story, "The Old Man of the Peepul Tree," continues the arboreal themes from the Nemi story, but in a modern setting. The action takes place in New York and its heroine rejoices in the distinctly Wagnerian name of Sieglinde. This brings to mind that other tree, growing in the middle of Hunding's hut in Act I of *Die Walküre*. As we might expect, Crowley's Sieglinde has a brother called Siegmund, as in Wagner's opera, but this Siegmund is an unsuccessful composer. One day, Sieglinde sits beneath a peepul tree ("the sacred fig of India") which grows in the Bronx Park, and a tree elf whispers a tune in her ear. When she whistles this back to her brother, he writes it down and subsequently makes a fortune out of it. In gratitude, Sieglinde clasps the trunk of this tree and kisses it "madly."[12] Such an action also derives from Frazer, who mentions the ancient Lithuanians and their "remarkable oaks and other great shady trees, from which they received oracular responses."[13] The King of the Wood worshipped the sacred tree which he guarded with his own life, and also "embraced it as his wife."[14]

Crowley was also obviously very impressed by Frazer's splendid description of the Mass of Saint Sécaire:

> The Mass of Saint Sécaire may be said only in a ruined or deserted church, where owls mope and hoot, where bats flit in the gloaming, where gypsies lodge of nights, and where toads squat under the desecrated altar. Thither the bad priest comes by night with his light o' love, and at the first stroke of 11 he begins to mumble the mass backwards, and ends just as the clocks are knelling the midnight hour.[15]

Crowley quotes this passage in his own account of "The Mass of Saint Sécaire," in which a character called Dufour, like Crowley himself, "was squandering his father's millions on an attempt to learn black magic."[16] Dufour uses the Mass of Saint Sécaire to remove his rival in love. Frazer adds that the man for whom this mass is said apparently soon withers away, "and nobody can say what is the matter with him," which is exactly what happens to the unfortunate victim of Crowley's protagonist.

Frazer has some interesting things to say about what he calls "Imitative Magic" ("the attempt ... to injure or destroy an enemy by injuring or destroying an image of him, in the belief that, just as the image suffers, so does the man and that when he perishes he must die"[17]). He adds, "imagination acts upon man as really as does gravitation, and may kill him as certainly as a dose of prussic acid."[18] This is a subject to which we will return later.

Other stories in Crowley's collection were inspired by this impressive passage from Frazer:

> A reminiscence of the manner in which these old representatives of the deity were put to death is perhaps preserved in the famous story of Marsyas. He was said to be a Phrygian satyr or Silenus, according to others a shepherd or herdsman, who played sweetly on the flute. A friend of Cybele, he roamed the country with the disconsolate goddess to soothe her grief for the death of Attis. The composition of the Mother's Air, a tune played on the flute in honour of the Great Mother Goddess, was attributed to him by the people of Celaenae in Phyrgia. Vain of his skill, he challenged Apollo to a musical contest, he to play the flute and Apollo the lyre. Being vanquished, Marsyas was tied up to a pine tree and flayed or cut limb from limb either by the victorious Apollo or by a Scythian slave. His skin was shown at Celaenae in historical times. It hung at the foot of the citadel in a cave from which the river Marsyas rushed with an impetuous and noisy tide to join the Maeander. So Adonis bursts full-born from the precipices of the Lebanon; so the blue river of Ibreez leaps in a crystal jet from the red rocks of the Taurus; so the stream, which now rumbles deep underground, used to gleam for a moment on its passage from darkness to darkness in the dim light of the Corsican cave. In all these copious fountains, with their glad promise of fertility and life, men of old saw the hand of God and worshipped him beside the rushing river with the music of its tumbling waters in their ears.[19]

Crowley responded to this passage with three stories: "The Stone of Cybele," "The Oracle of the Corycian Cave" and "The God of Ibreez." The first of these is set during the first World War, when it was written. The eponymous Stone of Cybele is inherited by the daughter of Colonel Flack, who has died in action. This girl, Cotys, has a deformed, ugly and unsporty cousin called Claude, whose only friend is blind Hughes, who plays the flute and is nicknamed Marsyas. Claude encourages Cotys to regress back to her former life as a priestess of Cybele, using the stone as a psychometric porthole and intending to revive paganism in the present day: "There were hopes of a pagan Pope before the century was over."[20] Having revived the rites, Cotys and Claude are married and they name their child Atys.

We are compensated for the lack of landscape in this tale by "The Oracle of the Corycian Cave," which describes the eponymous Cave itself:

> Myrtles and carobs and pomegranates and many another miracle of flower and leaf shadow the way; rivulets trickle and swell the brooks that purl over the pebbles.... Here the cave ends with wonder, for from the rock a column of living water is hurled forth and vanishes again into an invisible abyss.... Such then is the shrine of the god to whom Corycus and its neighbourhood paid full allegiance.[21]

Crowley also includes a passage on how to make rain. The advice is to prophesy it when you can smell it in the air: "Thus shall you have power over them."[22] This ties in with Frazer's observation that "the sorcerer who sincerely believes in his own extravagant pretensions is in far greater peril and is much more likely to be cut short in his career than the deliberate imposter."[23] It also foreshadows the celebrated scene in *Night of the Demon* (dir. Jacques Tourneur, 1957) in which Niall MacGinnis' magician, Julian Carswell, conjures up a storm to demonstrate his power; and in his chapter on "The Magical Control of the Weather," Frazer observes that "in rude society there is hardly a person who does not dabble in magic,"[24] which is very much the situation in *The Witches*, in which an entire rural community is involved in witchcraft.

Crowley's response to the story of Ibreez contains another fine water landscape:

> The morning dawned. Krasota found herself looking up into the mountain; giant precipices, red as blood, towered on each side of her, and from the western cliff a river burst in one magnificent jet, a crystal arch of water that matched the sky for azure.... The grassy plateau on which she stood was smooth and green, shadowed by ancient walnut trees.[25]

In accordance with the theme of sacrifice in all these stories, Crowley writes, "there shall be a perfectly black bull with a white star upon his forehead as the god in whom the life of the nation is concealed. We will assure his continual vigour by killing him every year on the day of spring and his life shall pass into that of his successor."[26] This description also derives from Frazer, who explains that when "a bullock was sacrificed for the good of the kingdom, the king stood over the sacrifice to offer prayer and thanksgiving."[27]

Sometimes the sacrifice was a man rather than a bull, and such rural rituals formed the basis of James MacTaggart's BBC Play for Today, *Robin Redbreast* (1970). In this story, TV script editor, Norah Palmer (Anna Cropper), has broken up with her partner and takes refuge in an isolated English village. This environment has much in common with Hammer's *The Witches*, and I will return to this aspect of the production in the next chapter; but here is the place to discuss *Robin Redbreast*'s debt to Frazer, who is acknowledged in the dialogue at the end of the play. Norah is groomed by the villagers to serve as the mating partner of a young Edgar (Andrew Bradford), whom the villagers refer to as Rob. An innocent, somewhat gauche orphan, Rob has been cared for by the sinister Mrs. Vigo (Freda Bamford), who is also Norah's self-appointed housekeeper. Together with the equally sinister leader of the local community, Fisher (Bernard Hepton), they arrange to have Norah impregnated by Rob, who is then slain, so that his blood may fertilize the fields and ensure a successful harvest the following year. At first, Norah thinks it is her they wish to sacrifice, but Mrs. Vigo explains, "What good would a woman's blood be for the land? It takes a man's for that." However, the villagers do want Norah's child, so that in 20 years they will be able to repeat the ritual for the benefit of future generations. ("There's always one young man who answers to the name of Robin in these parts. Has to be," says Mrs. Vigo.) Norah manages to escape with her unborn baby, but glancing back as she drives away, she experiences a vision of Mrs. Vigo dressed in black witch's weeds, with Fisher wearing the horns of Herne the Hunter. By contrasting the regressive world of village paganism with the weary cynicism of Norah's city life, MacTaggart and his screenwriter, James Bowen, are able to question just how far humanity, with its superficial advances in technology, has progressed away from its instinctual, magical past. Vic Pratt has written eloquently about *Robin Redbreast*'s sociological implications in his essay for the BFI DVD release of the play, pointing out, "[W]e're reminded once more that if ignored, if forgotten, if concreted over, the countryside, its traditions and its ostracised peoples, may well return with a vengeance, one of these days, to wreak havoc on those too-clever city folk."[28]

Though inspired by a real-life example of this kind of ritual killing in Warwickshire, the drama's closing dialogue explains the connection *Robin Redbreast* has with Frazer's magnum opus:

> FISHER: The goddess of fertility in the old legends was in some ways like yourself, Miss Palmer—not a married lady, but nevertheless, if you'll excuse the freedom, not a virgin either. In the autumn, she would couple with the young king. He'd be treated like a king, served and pampered, you might say, and then, of course…
> NORAH: Killed!
> FISHER: … he would pass away, yes, assisted to it, you might say. And from his blood, the crops would spring.
> NORAH: A Greek legend, Mr. Fisher…
> FISHER: And Egyptian, Mexican—many places. You must read a book by Sir James Frazer. The *Golden Bough* in seven volumes.
> NORAH: But not an English legend!
> FISHER: Robin Hood. Robin-of-the-Dale. Even Robin Redbreast—one of the very birds in your garden. A male robin only lives a year, you know. The female has many partners. Always Robin. Such a bounty there was, such fruitfulness, Miss Palmer, from the blood that drained from Robin Hood, so the old stories say. But they are only stories, of course.

Thomas Keightley usefully explains the etymology of the name Robin in his *Fairy Mythology*. Having established Robin's connection with Puck (celebrated by Shakespeare in *A Midsummer Night's Dream*), he adds:

> Robin Goodfellow … is evidently a domestic spirit, answering in name and character to the Nisse God-dreng of Scandinavia, the Knecht Ruprecht, *i.e.*, Robin of Germany. He seems to unite in his person the Boggard and Barguest of Yorkshire.
> Hob-goblin is, as we have seen, another name of the same spirit. Goblin is the French *gobelin*, German Kobold; Hob is Rob, Robin, Bob; just as Hodge is Roger. We still have the proper names Hobbs, Hobson [and thus the connection with the Devil in the name of the fictional tube station of Hobbs Lane in *Quatermass and the Pit*].

Robin Hood, though we can produce no instance of it, must, we think, also have been an appellation of this spirit, and been given to the famed outlaw of merry Sherwood from his sportive character and his abiding in the recesses of the greenwood. The hood is a usual appendage of the domestic spirit.[29]

Though *Robin Redbreast* is set largely in and around Norah's farmhouse, MacTaggart inserts footage of the surrounding landscape—the woods and trees, which are Robin's proper environment. The dénouement, however, takes place in Norah's living room, the axe-wielding executioner coming down the chimney like a psychopathic Santa Claus, and dragging Rob outside to be killed.

We first encounter Edgar/Rob when he is practicing his martial arts, stripped to the waist in the woods. These are pine woods, but as Fisher later explains, "It used to be all oak round here; but the forestry commission don't like the old ways." As Norah walks through these lonely woods, we hear Rob's shrieks forming an eerie counterpoint to the wind as he practices his moves. One particularly impressive shot has the camera looking directly

WIND IN THE WOODS. An atmospheric shot from *Robin Redbreast* (dir. James MacTaggart, 1970)

up at the swaying canopy of trees against the sky. Zoom shots of trees punctuate the action later on, to particularly powerful effect during Norah's dream in which they are juxtaposed with images of Cyril Cross's halfwit, Peter, wielding his sacrificial axe, of Rob advancing through the dark holding a knife and of Fisher frighteningly staring out through his pebble glasses. Again, landscape, though used sparingly, is an essential element in a story about the inter-relation of natural rhythms with ancient beliefs and rituals.

The play's theme of pagan sacrifice is markedly contrasted with a supposedly Christian harvest festival (though this one is replete with corn dollies, eggs and slaughtered rabbits). All this foreshadowed the similar juxtaposition in *The Wicker Man*. In *Robin Redbreast*, the local vicar is held in contempt by the villagers, who have their own, older religion. In *The Wicker Man*, the situation is even more drastic, for the church itself is in ruins and all traces of Christianity have been swept aside. Many of the rituals in that film also derive from Frazer's masterpiece, not least the notorious Druidical practice of the title itself:

> Colossal images of wicker-work or of wood and grass were constructed; these were filled with live men, cattle and animals of other kinds; fire was then applied to the images, and they were burned with their living contents.
> ... These wicker giants of the Druids seem to have had till lately, if not down to the present time, their representatives at the spring and midsummer festivals of modern Europe. At Douay, down at least to the early part of the nineteenth century, a procession took place annually on the Sunday nearest to the seventh of July. The great feature of the procession was a colossal figure, some 20 or 30 high, made of osiers, and called "the giant," which was moved through the streets by means of rollers and ropes worked by men who were enclosed within the effigy. The figure was armed as a knight with lance and sword, helmet and shield.[30]

Frazer also discusses the significance of the Maypole as another element of tree worship:

> In spring or early summer or even on Midsummer Day, it was and still is in many parts of Europe the custom to go out to the woods, cut down a tree and bring it to the village, where it is set up amid general rejoicings, or the people cut branches in the woods, and fasten them on every house. The intention of these customs is to bring home to the village, and to each house, the blessings which the tree-spirit has in its power to bestow. Hence the custom in some places of planting a May-tree before every house, or of carrying the village May-tree from door to door, that every household may receive its blessing.... [T]he raising of the May-pole, the decoration of which is done by the village maidens, is an affair of much ceremony; the people flock to it from all quarters, and dance round it in a great ring.[31]

The Wicker Man is somewhat more explicit in its explanation of this ceremony: Miss Rose describes the phallic nature of the pole to her pupils in the schoolroom, while an appalled Sergeant Howie looks on. Later, Howie experiences (very briefly) a Hand of Glory, which as Frazer explains "was the dried and pickled hand of a man who had been hanged":

> If a candle made of the fat of a malefactor who had also died on the gallows was lighted and placed in the Hand of Glory as in a candlestick, it rendered motionless all persons to whom it was presented; they could not stir a finger any more than if they were dead. Sometimes the dead man's hand is itself the candle, or rather bunch of candles, all its withered fingers being set on fire; but should any member of the household be awake, one of the fingers will not kindle. Such nefarious lights can only be extinguished with milk.[32]

No milk being to hand, Howie merely sweeps the Hand of Glory aside and is soon back on his feet. Indeed, the audience barely catches a glimpse of this gruesome sight, which is revealed to be remarkably convincing in the famous film still of the scene. *The Wicker Man* also references the many corn rituals explored by Frazer. In his search for the missing Rowan Morrison, Howie visits a bakery and is shown a large loaf of bread called "The Life of the Fields" and a smaller round loaf in the form of a solar disc with the features of a man known as "John Barleycorn." Frazer, in turn, quoted Robert Burns' poem on this particular subject:

> They wasted o'er a scorching flame
> The marrow of his bones;
> But a miller us'd him worst of all,
> For he crush'd him between two stones.

> This concentration, so to say, of the nature of Adonis upon the cereal crops is characteristic of the stage of culture reached by his worshippers in historical times [...] The berries and roots of the wilderness, the grass of the pastures, which had been matters of vital importance to their ruder forefathers, were now of little moment to them: more and more their thoughts and energies were engrossed by the staple of their life, the corn; more and more accordingly the propitiation of the deities of fertility in general and of the corn-spirit in particular tended to become the central feature of their religion.[33]

The Wicker Man's later procession of children, who "carry death out of the village" (symbolized by a doll), also directly echoes a ritual recorded in its various guises by Frazer when discussing the bringing in of summer. Among the alternatives he mentions is this version from Bohemia:

> Now carry we Death out of the village,
> The new Summer into the village,
> Welcome, dear Summer,
> Green little corn.
>
> We carry Death out of the village,
> And the New Year into the village,

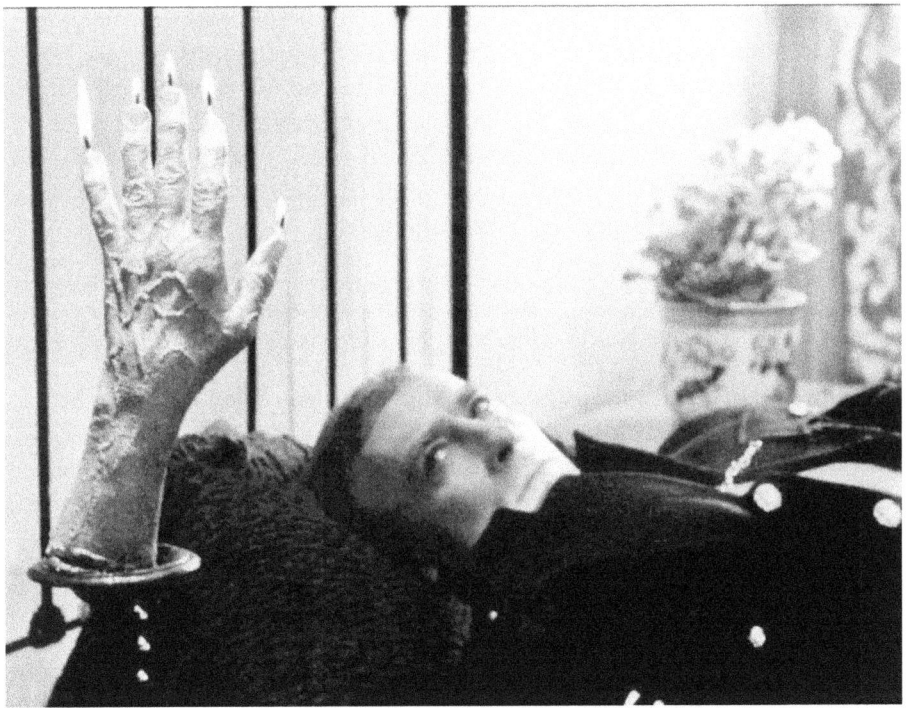

HAND OF GLORY. Edward Woodward manages to stay awake in *The Wicker Man* (dir. Robin Hardy, 1973).

> Dear Spring, we bid you welcome,
> Green grass, we bid you welcome.
>
> We have carried away Death
> And brought life back.
> He has taken up his quarters in the village,
> Therefore sing joyous songs.[34]

Frazer's description of a Whit-Monday ceremony in Wurmligen in Swabia, also lies behind the famous procession towards the end of *The Wicker Man*, in which Lord Summerisle leads his people in fancy dress:

> Amongst the personages who figure in the procession are a Moorish king with a sooty face and a crown on his head, a Dr. Iron-Beard, a corporal, and an executioner. They halt on the village green, and each of the characters makes a speech in rhythm. The executioner announces that the leaf-clad man has been condemned to death, and cuts off his false head.[35]

Much the same occurs in the film, with an ordeal by interlocking swords, through which the villagers must pass their heads. One head is indeed cut off—but it is, as in Frazer's account, a false head. The Swabian ceremony is yet another variant of the King of the Wood, which forms the core idea of *The Wicker Man*. To ensure a successful harvest of apples, after several years of failed crops, Lord Summerisle organizes the ritual sacrifice of a perfect fool in the shape of Edward Woodward's "Christian copper"—a devout, puritanical policeman. Lord Summerisle is not only the head of a tribe but also a magician, as Frazer makes clear:

> For when the welfare of the tribe is supposed to depend on the performance of these magical rites, the magician rises into a position of much influence and repute, and many readily acquire the rank and authority of a chief or king.[36]

However, as Sergeant Howie points out to Summerisle just before he is taken away for the sacrifice, if the crops fail again next year, only Summerisle himself will be a suitable sacrifice. Summerisle's expression clouds momentarily at this unwelcome news, the surf roaring against the headland behind him, but he soon dismisses any anxiety by assuring Howie that the apples will not fail. The scene again derives from Frazer's belief that it is "divine kings on whose life the fertility of men, of cattle, and of vegetation is believed to depend, and who are put to death, whether in single combat or otherwise, in order that their divine spirit may be transmitted to their successors in full vigour, uncontaminated by the weakness and decay of sickness or old age, because any such degeneration on the part of the king would, in the opinion of his worshippers, entail a corresponding degeneration on mankind, on cattle, and on the crops."[37]

Lord Summerisle, we assume, manages to escape being sacrificed, but David Niven's Philippe de Montfaucon in *Eye of the Devil* does not. Here, Frazer is even more in evidence as Montfaucon returns to his ancestral Franch home to be ritually slain by an arrow from the bow of David Hemmings' Christian de Caray. Frazer includes various village rituals in his section on "Burying the Carnival," which resemble the film's festival of *Les Trieze Jours*, which is eerily accompanied by bells and percussion. It gives the semblance of being a Christian ceremony but it is, as Deborah Kerr's character observes, "much more than that." Silent villagers gather around the church in which an occult ritual is performed, anointing Montfaucon's son as the next in line to be sacrificed. Montfaucon lifts his son and exclaims, "Let the earth bring forth vines, yielding fruit after its kind, whose seed is in itself upon the earth. And the word was God." He then kisses the child. The image of a sacrificial object (the son) being displayed to the community during a festival or carnival is present in all of Frazer's examples: the effigy, Caramantran, in Provence which is "stoned to death" by the populace on Ash Wednesday,[38] the Burial of Shrove Tuesday in Normandy in which another effigy is burned,[39] the straw Shrovetide Bear of Tübingen in Germany that is buried,[40] etc. Though nothing so dramatic actually occurs during the creepily quiet *Treize Jours* festival in *Eye of the Devil*, Flora Robson's Countess Estelle knows exactly what Montfaucon's anointing kiss implies and screams accordingly: The boy's fate is consequently sealed if the crops fail after his father's own forthcoming sacrifice.

NINE

Witchcraft in the Village

Villages both create and persecute witchcraft. Indeed, the word "pagan" derives from the Latin "pagus" meaning "rural" or "of the village." Neither entirely natural nor entirely man-made, villages are places where civilization interacts with the forces of nature in a way that is denied to towns and cities, and this is why films such as *The Witches*, *Eye of the Devil*, *The Wicker Man* and even *Night of the Eagle* are all set in small rural communities.

In his sociological study *Akenfield* (1969), Ronald Blythe describes pretty much the typical layout of a standard British village:

> In Akenfield, evidence of the good life, a tall old church on the hillside, a pub selling the local brew, a pretty stream, a football pitch, a handsome square vicarage with a cedar of Lebanon shading it, a school with jars of tadpoles in the window, three shops with doorbells, a Tudor mansion, half a dozen farms and a lot of quaint cottages.[1]

Blythe could almost have been describing the fictional village of Hedderby in *The Witches*, the Nigel Kneale–scripted Hammer film. He also acknowledges that village life can be "suffocating and inhibiting" and accurately captures the kind of resistance and taciturn behavior experienced by Joan Fontaine's character Miss Mayfield, as an outsider in a closed rural community:

> They are not loquacious people. The old ones have emerged from indignities and sufferings which taught a man how to hold his tongue, and a guarded note marks much of their conversation. On the whole, they will admit certain information about their lives during the "bad days" and will courteously rake up a few old customs as makeweight, but they remain intrinsically private folk and their characters cannot be termed open.[2]

Miss Mayfield is made apparently welcome in the close-knit community of Hedderby, but there are plenty of sidelong glances and suggestions of what Stella Gibbons, in her satire on rural life, *Cold Comfort Farm* (1932), called "something nasty in the woodshed." The nasty thing in Hedderby's woodshed resides in the kind of mansion mentioned by Blythe, and takes the form of Kay Walsh's Stephanie Bax, a writer, along with her somewhat odd brother, Alan (Alec McCowen). Alan, a failed priest who wears a dog collar while listening to tape recordings of organ music in his statue-filled bedroom, is a red herring. The real villain is Stephanie, who has formed a coven from the villagers over whom she presides, with the intention of transferring her own intelligence into the body of a girl who happens to be one of Miss Mayfield's pupils. Now a liability, Miss Mayfield is reminded of her traumatic experiences with witchcraft in Africa, with the desired effect of inducing a nervous breakdown. She is packed off to a nursing home, but soon escapes and returns to the village only to find herself involved in the long-planned occult ritual. This she subverts at the last moment, however, causing Stephanie's death.

The film's strength lies in its vivid portrayal of village life, in particular that element of suspicion towards newcomers and the privacy referred to by Blythe, which can often seem sinister to outsiders, as though the villagers have something to hide. In this case, they do, but *The Witches* grows out of perceptions in real life, no matter how misguided they may be.

Excessive conformity, sunny days and rural tranquility can indeed seem oppressive. I have felt it myself in the immaculate village of Eccleston in Cheshire, which forms part of the estate of the Duke of Westminster, whose ancestors fill the graveyard around the church like so many vampires waiting for sunset. Everywhere is perfectly maintained and consequently a little too good to be true. I left a somewhat subversive poem in the empty church and was startled out of my skin by the church clock, which chimed sonorously as I left, fully expecting a hand on my shoulder—or perhaps a fang in my neck. Hedderby, in fact the village of Hambledon in Buckinghamshire and only a few miles from Henley-on-Thames, has less aristocratic pretensions, but is nonetheless very well-manicured, suitably self-contained, and has consequently been much-used as a film location over the years as a representative example of what the rest of the word thinks of as the quintessential British village.

Location is all-important in this witchcraft film, the irony here being that the entire community is involved in the practice, rather than the usual state of affairs in which the community unites *against* an individual witch. Robin Briggs, in his study of European witchcraft, identifies the norm as "communal solidarity, with everyone united in demanding persecution."[3] He cites "the special village committee, elected at a general meeting of the community to take charge of action against suspected witches,"[4] but *The Witches* inverts this, placing innocent victim, Gwen Mayfield, in the role of the persecuted witch instead. It was therefore necessary to create a supernormal, ideal and idyllic image of village life, with the sun perpetually shining during a seemingly endless summer, into which unnerving elements could be gradually introduced. Thus, a black cat walks into Miss Mayfield's flower-adorned, grace-and-favor home; her housekeeper (Michelle Dotrice) looks worried when the Baxes are mentioned; Gwen Ffrangcon-Davies exploits her slight astigmatism to sinister effect as Grannie Rigg; the butcher Bob Curd (Duncan Lamont) sharpens his knives with frightening implication; a voodoo doll is discovered in a tree. Little by little the secret is whittled out of the village, leading to Stephanie's revelation as the mastermind.

Against this self-contained and apparently bucolic haven, director Cyril Frankel is careful to contrast the surrounding roads and traffic. When Miss Mayfield eventually escapes from her enforced idleness in the nursing home, she is given a lift by Bob Curd, who whisks her back to Hedderby, which is now revealed as a quite undesirable alternative to the urban world of freedom and reason, for all of that urban world's unattractive modernity. As Blythe points out, village life can become "suffocating and inhibiting" because there used to be no way of even occasionally getting away from it.[5] It is the claustrophobia of Hedderby that is the real subject of *The Witches*, and consequently its locations and landscapes are crucial. Frankel shows us the old mansion, the village green with a stream running through it, the fields, the school, the shops with their suspicious female customers, and country lanes leading to and away from the village. As the story develops, Hedderby does indeed become suffocating and inhibiting.

There is also a sexual element at work: Stephanie is clearly attracted to Miss Mayfield in a distinctly predatory manner. Her implied lesbianism is consequently interpreted as another aspect of the village's malaise. The disturbingly homophobic implication is that Hedderby's corruption stems from the so-called sexual perversion of Stephanie, and only Miss Mayfield's resistance to such "unnatural" emotions can restore true normality to the environment, which is exactly what happens in the end, with the added implication that Alan, now free from his baleful sister, will eventually marry Miss Mayfield. Thus is the audience allowed to breath a conventional sigh of relief.

Nigel Kneale returned to the subject of witchcraft within an introverted rural community with an episode of ATV's television series, *Against the Crowd*: "Murrain" (1975) concerns a group of surly pig farmers (led by Beeley, played by Bernard Lee) who believe that a lonely old woman (Una Brandon-Jones) living in a nearby house is a witch and has vindictively caused the "murrain" sickness in their pigs. They are also convinced that

Nine. Witchcraft in the Village　　　161

she is responsible for the mysterious illness of one of their children, along with other misfortunes such as lameness in a farmer. A visiting vet (David Simeon) accuses them all of "going on a witch hunt":

> So let's talk about the witch—the poor old biddy you've got lined up for the part. What's her name—oh, if it's safe to say it out loud.... Mrs. Clemson? ... For a start, she is old, right? And ugly? Wrinkles and wens you get when you're old—even a wart or two. All helps, doesn't it? Makes her nasty to look at. A bit odd too. Talks to herself—shouts at people. Nobody goes near. On her own over there, is she? Nothing but a cat or a bird. So, she talks to that.... You're trying to justify the persecution of some poor half-witted old biddy. And how do you do that? Kill her cat in the name of magic and then go home and watch your color telly.

But Beeley counters this with a different kind of observation: "Magic's a dirty word? Scrying is magic. In the olden times, they took a picture miles away, then it come before them on a bit of glass. Scrying it was called. Now they've got another name."

Kneale's conclusion is cunningly ambivalent. Beeley and the others charge up to the woman's house intent on murdering her. She appears and gesticulates at Beeley, who promptly falls dead from a massive heart attack. We are left to ponder if the cause was natural or supernatural. Crucially, all this takes place in a somewhat sullen and muddy area of Derbyshire, the uncomfortable rural landscape appropriately reflecting the mean attitudes of the farmers, the poverty of the so-called witch and the introverted isolation that causes both.

A similarly remote location provided the setting of James MacTaggart's *Robin Redbreast*, which appeared only one year after Blythe's *Akenfield*. It not only seems to have been responding to Blythe's sociological perspective on village life, but also to the rural superstition and conspiracy of Kneale's *The Witches* four years before. The rural context of *Robin Redbreast*'s pagan sacrifice story is mostly implied: We are in fact shown only one or two shots of the village itself, the rest being played out on studio sets or in the immediate vicinity of the grounds of the house in which most of the action takes place. The inhabitants speak with archaic diction ("This am your place") and repeated, consequently unnerving phrases such as "Known for it." Rob himself says, "There's nobody educated around here. It's all inbreeding and intermarriage." As will happen to Howie in *The Wicker Man*, Norah finds herself trapped in the village. Her car is sabotaged, her phone cut off, her letters intercepted, and when she tries to take a bus out of the village, it drives past her without stopping. She is being "watched" until Easter, when Rob will be killed. The fact that the villagers allow her to drive away at the end does not necessarily mean they will allow her to keep her child when it is born, having marked it as the next one to be sacrificed, much as young Jacques de Montfaucon is marked at the end of *Eye of the Devil*.

Many British witchcraft films exploit this kind of claustrophobia, though most less successfully than *The Witches*. Based on Fritz Leiber's novel, *Conjure Wife*, Sidney Hayers' *Night of the Eagle* replaces a tight-knit village environment with an incestuous academic one. Here, the landscape is not one of rural lanes and village greens, though the community seems that of a leafy provincial town rather than a metropolis. Instead, we are confronted with the confining corridors of a medical college where Peter Wyngarde's lecturer, Norman Taylor, suffers the destructive anima of principal, Flora Carr (played with a squint and a limp by Margaret Johnston). Jealous Flora is a witch and does her best to remove Norman from her establishment. The action is mostly divided between Norman's place of work and his cottage, where his wife, Tansy (Janet Blair), has also been

BELIEVE IT OR NOT. Peter Wyngarde makes up his mind at the end of *Night of the Eagle* (dir. Sidney Hayers, 1962).

Nine. Witchcraft in the Village

STAY MISTY FOR ME. Dry ice swathes the set of *The City of the Dead* (dir. John Moxey, 1960)

using witchcraft to protect him; but halfway through the film, Tansy decides that the only way to save her husband is to sacrifice herself. She plans to drown herself, forcing Norman to follow her to their holiday beach cottage, and thus provides Hayers with a splendid opportunity to evoke the seashore by moonlight in a sequence of eerie, oceanic beauty.

However, the film's main power comes from the claustrophobic exploitation of its domestic interiors. (Hayers dwells on close-ups of Norman and Tansy searching through drawers and cupboards, Tansy irrationally trying to hide her magical charms, while Norman rationally tries to destroy them.)

There are also the aforementioned corridors, which form a suitably dream-like setting for the climax, in which Flora uses a form of audio-hypnosis via a tape recording to persuade Norman (or is it really the case?— the film retains some ambivalence over the matter) that a huge stone eagle over the entrance to the college has come to life to pursue him. The outsize eagle flaps menacingly down the corridors, far more convincingly (and consequently to much more disturbing effect) than the animated creatures in Ray Harryhausen's fantasy adventure films; Norman is ultimately convinced that witchcraft is a reality. To emphasize the point, he accidentally smudges the word "Not" in the sentence he wrote on the blackboard at the beginning of the film for the edification of his students and the audience: "I do NOT believe." For a story about mind-control, the architectural setting provides a successful metaphor for the mind itself, houses being a well-known motif of the unconscious in Jungian psychoanalysis.

The City of the Dead was British-made but set in America, with Christopher Lee impersonating an American academic-cum-devil-worshipper in the "city" of the title, the village of Whitewood, Massachusetts. Never has a village been shrouded in quite so much mist as in this film, which is certainly atmospheric, but which also immediately gives the game away as being a location for what we expect: the tale of a resurrected witch from Puritan days, who runs the local hotel and sacrifices young women to the demonic cause. As in *The Witches,* the church is derelict and deserted (save for a blind priest) and the action contrasts the claustrophobia and antiquity of the village with the normality of 1960s modernity outside.

More interesting is Don Sharp's *Witchcraft,* in which a striking witch (Yvette Rees as Vanessa Whitlock) is raised from her tomb in protest against the activities of a property developer (Jack Hedley). The concept of a property developer causing havoc with the past was certainly pertinent in the 1960s, when traditional rural life and the architecture of so many provincial British towns were suffering from "progress" in ways that were far more destructive than Hitler's Luftwaffe had been during the Blitz. When Lon Chaney's devil worshipper Morgan Whitlock accuses the developer of ruining the countryside with "trash," he spoke for many people who had experienced just that in reality. Here, however, it is not the village but rather a house that provides the landscape of claustrophobia. Once again Oakley Court on the banks of the Thames provided a suitably oppressive environment, its exterior imaginatively filmed from many different angles by Sharp, along with complementary shots of mist-shrouded graveyards. The whole culminates in a witchcraft ceremony whose participants closely resemble *City of the Dead*'s robed and hooded worshippers. The situation of *Romeo and Juliet* is also echoed in the plot's antagonism between two rival families, the young leads representing the star-crossed lovers, though Shakespeare this most definitely is not.

A house also features as the setting of the "Sweets to the Sweet" story in *The House That Dripped Blood,* though the real landscapes at work here are the faces of the actors. Being a low-budget film, close-ups and tight shots inevitably prevailed, but here all we really need to see are the faces, particularly the angelic features of Chloe Franks who plays Jane, the oppressed daughter of Christopher Lee's terrified John Reid. Franks is the personification of Hedderby: apparently sweet, seemingly normal, delightfully innocent, but in fact the daughter of a witch, and she uses sympathetic magic to kill her own father. There is also another schoolmistress in the form of Nyree Dawn Porter's Ann Norton who, like Miss Mayfield, gradually grows to understand the true nature of the situation. Mr. Reid and Jane move into their new home in the summer with birdsong fluting outside, but the weather degenerates into a thunderstorm during the film's climax. Ann says the house "is so cozy and cheerful" but the house too is playing a game of illusion and reality, as the Gothic traceries in the windows might lead us to believe. Having pierced the wax image of her father with a hat pin, Jane throws the doll on the fire, giving Christopher Lee another opportunity to let out one of his famously blood-curdling screams.

The witchcraft film that most brilliantly understood the significance of landscape is surely Michael Reeves' *Witchfinder General*. This is more about the persecution of innocent women than their demonic power, but much of the film's tension similarly depends on the contrast between the glories of the British countryside and the depravity of its inhabitants.

The film opens with just such a juxtaposition: sunlight glitters through a screen of trees, while sheep safely graze in the field. Simultaneously, the sound of a mallet building a gallows is heard, and through the village streets lined with charming cottages, a procession of townspeople drag a woman accused of witchcraft to her death. Rolling fields and magnificent English skies accompany this brutal murder, while Paul Ferris' Main Title music picks up on this juxtaposition, contrasting the threatening motif with which

CALM BEFORE THE STORM. An example of the rural tranquility that director Michael Reeves contrasts with scenes of brutal horror in *Witchfinder General* (1968).

he begins with a sweeping pastoral melody comparable to "Greensleeves." Later, we see Hilary Dwyer's Sara sitting beside a river lit by golden light in another idyllic image, while her father, the priest, John Lowes (Rupert Davies), is being violently interrogated by Matthew Hopkins (Vincent Price) and his assistant, John Sterne (Robert Russell).

Whenever he can, Reeves includes painterly shots of British landscape. After the Main Title, the action begins with a long tracking shot of foliage and forests. Later there is a magnificent shot of Hopkins on horseback riding along a path flanked by trees, which Vincent Price the art historian would surely have appreciated. Ian Ogilvy's soldier, Richard Marshall, also rides to the rescue through another poetic landscape with another noble tree and lots of sheep.

The climax is set in the picturesque Suffolk village of Lavenham, with its famous sixteenth-century Guildhall now owned and sanitized by the National Trust, which seems reluctant to exploit or even mention its connection with the film. Here, among frighteningly passive villagers and children, a witch is solemnly burned on Hopkins' orders in the center of the community. It is a scene that sums up the oppressive conformity of village life, which is the ultimate danger of all closed and hierarchical communities. The landscape surrounding them and the structures that define them lend a powerful sense of identity and authority to those who work on the land and impose the law. As with racism, witch hunts were a particularly nasty

THE PRICE OF FEAR. Vincent Price as Matthew Hopkins riding through woodland in *Witchfinder General* **(dir. Michael Reeves, 1968).**

example of how communities reinforce their identities by defining and rejecting what they perceive to be different. The "other" is exorcised to maintain conformity: "Identity" is the key to all our atrocities.

Some of Reeves' imagery of juxtaposition was paralleled by Lawrence Gordon Clarke's BBC adaptation of M.R. James' witchcraft story "The Ash Tree" (1975). Barbara Ewing, having been vampirised by Christopher Lee in *Dracula Has Risen From the Grave* and defenestrated by a jealous piano in *Torture Garden* (dir. Freddie Francis, 1968), here plays Anne Mothersole, a witch with real demonic powers. She curses the man who presides over her hanging on a bleak moorland hill; but, as Clarke explains in his introduction to the DVD release of this Ghost Story for Christmas, the character of the witch here is more complex. James' conception of Mothersole is not that of an innocent woman, unjustly accused of crimes she did not commit; she is a "malign and evil woman"—a real witch indeed, who can bring "huge spiders out of trees and kill people." She might also be regarded as "a personification of fertility," for when she is killed, her death causes animals and crops to die and wither away. Clarke believes that he and screenwriter, David Rudkin, presented her rather too much as a victim, which she no doubt would have been in reality, but she is not presented as such in the original story. Landscape plays a major role in Rudkin's adaptation, as it did in his earlier *Penda's Fen*, rooting the magical powers of the witch in equally magical powers of nature.

One of the most interesting literary precedents for these films can be found in Elizabeth Gaskell's novella, *Lois the Witch*. Gaskell based her story on the Salem witch trials, using Charles Upham's *Lectures on Witchcraft* as her source material. Her aim was obviously more of a moral than sensational one, aiming to expose the truth behind such mass hysteria, and accurately identify that it is petty jealousy and erotic frustration within the confines of an introverted and confined environment that is responsible for such appalling atrocities as the public hanging of innocent women. No era is immune from such mass hysteria. In our own time, fear and resentment, magnified by exploitative politicians, the internet and the mass media, would find an invaluable corrective in Gaskell's tale. Though set in 1691, it is just as relevant now as it was when it was first published in Charles Dickens' magazine *All the Year Round* in 1858.

Gaskell's heroine, orphaned Lois, hails from the small English village of Barford, three miles from Warwick, where her father had been a preacher. Gaskell emphasizes the narrow confines of her life there: "Barford Parsonage at that time scarcely exceeded in size and dignity the cottages by which it was surrounded: it only contained three rooms on a floor, and

WITCHERY. Illuminated title page of the manuscript of Elizabeth Gaskell's *Lois the Witch* (1860).

was but two stories high." Barford is as confined as Salem. Indeed, as Lois herself recalls: "They are fearful creatures, the witches! and yet I am sorry for the poor old women, whilst I dread them. We had one in Barford, when I was a little child. No-one knew whence she came, but she settled herself down in a mud hut by the common side; and there she lived, she and her cat." This witch was drowned in the river Avon: "I saw old Hannah in the water, her grey hair all streaming down her shoulders, and her face bloody and black with the stones and the mud they had been throwing at her and her cat tied round her neck."[6] This terrible memory unfortunately foreshadows Lois' own fate. From this small community, Lois is sent out to the even more irrational confines of Salem, where conditions are primitive:

> English roads were bad enough at that period and for long after, but in America the way was simply the cleared ground of the forest; the stumps of the felled trees still remaining in the direct line, forming obstacles, which it required the most careful driving to avoid; and in the hollows, where the ground was swampy, the pulpy nature of it was obviated by logs of wood laid across the boggy part. The deep tree forest, tangled into heavy darkness even thus early in the year, came within a few yards of the road all the way, though efforts were regularly made by the inhabitants of the neighbouring settlements to keep a certain space clear on each side, for fear of the lurking Indians, who might otherwise come upon them unawares.... But at last they drew near to Salem, which rivaled Boston in size in those days, and boasted the name of one or two streets, although to an English eye they looked rather more like irregularly built houses clustered round the meeting-house, or rather one of the meeting-houses, for a second was in process of building; between the two were the gardens and grazing group for those who dreaded their cattle straying into the woods and the consequent danger of reclaiming them.[7]

This is very much the environment of *The City of the Dead* (though without *City*'s swirling fog). In fact, Lois's "sarcastic," "contemptuous" and coldly dutiful aunt resembles Patricia Jessel's portrayal of Elizabeth Selwyn aka Mrs. Newless in that film, but the subsequent action of *Lois the Witch* more closely anticipates what happens in *Witchfinder General*. Indeed, Gaskell makes a direct reference to Matthew Hopkins in her story. "Oh, Faith!" Lois confides to her new American cousin. "This country is worse than ever England was, even in the days of Master Matthew Hopkins, the witch-finder. I grow frightened of everyone, I think."[8]

Like Reeves, Gaskell understands that "cowardice makes us all cruel," and fear surrounds the people of this prayer-ridden backwater:

> The gravest divines not only believed stories similar to that of the double-headed serpent, and other tales of witchcraft, but they made such narrations the subjects of preaching and prayer. They showed "no mercy towards anyone whom they believed to be in league with the Evil One."[9]

The innocent, well-meaning but hapless Lois gradually finds herself confronting just such an accusation. A stern old minister, Mr. Tappau, accuses her of bringing the errors of England to Salem "as a seed with her, even across the great ocean."[10] It is not long before jealousy and resentment cause Lois' cousins to start calling her a witch. Trying to cheer one of them up, Lois talks about British Hallowe'en customs, and this unintentionally begins the process. Local troubles, which have nothing to do with Lois, lead to an environment of escalating paranoia. Mr. Tappau's daughters feed on this and suffer from convulsions and contortions, causing Mr. Tappau to exclaim, "Satan is of a truth let loose amongst us."[11]

Lois is then subjected to the attentions of her mentally ill male cousin, Manasseh, who has visions that tell him he must marry her. Lois is understandably reluctant, especially as she has a betrothed in England. As if this is not awkward enough, Lois' cousin Flora is enamored of another cleric, Pastor Nolan, and she fears that Lois has beguiled him. Metaphorically speaking, Lois' funeral pyre now only requires an igniting spark of hysteria to consume her, and this is exactly what happens. Gaskell eloquently outlines the dangers of such a situation, and how easily it can provoke catastrophe:

> "The sin of witchcraft." We read about it, we look on it from the outside; but we can hardly realise the terror it induced. Every impulsive or unaccustomed action, every little nervous affection, every ache or pain was noticed, not merely by those around the sufferer, but by the person himself, whoever he might be, that was acting, or being acted upon, in any but the most simple and ordinary manner. He or she (for it was most frequently a woman or girl that was the supposed subject) felt a desire for some unusual kind of food—some unusual motion or rest—her hand twitched, her foot was asleep, or her leg had a cramp; and the dreadful question immediately suggested itself, "Is anyone possessing an evil power over me, by the help of Satan?"[12]

The first victim of this state of affairs is Hota, the Indian servant of Lois' aunt. Hota is accused of witchcraft and hanged. Trusting Lois is taken in by the propaganda that justifies this atrocity, at which she shudders accordingly, but not with the "intellectual shuddering at the folly and superstition of the people, but tender moral shuddering at the sight of guilt which she believed in, and at the evidence of men's hatred and abhorrence, which when shown even to the guilty, troubled and distressed her merciful heart."[13]

Faith, who is now "at enmity with all the world in her bitter jealousy of heart,"[14] and her sister Prudence, who is angry at Lois' refusal to lend her her coat so that she might attend another hanging ("I never yet saw a woman hanged, and I see not why I should not go"[15]), now turn on Lois, childishly taunting her with "Witch Lois! Witch Lois!"[16] Alas, from such petty emotions, Lois, who even worries that the accusations against her might be true, is eventually tried and condemned by the community. A later apology from them cannot wipe out the power of Gaskell's warning about the fragility of civilized behavior when threatened by "malice, distinct, unmistakable personal malice."

> Such a taint did witchcraft bring upon a whole family, that generations of blameless life were not at that day esteemed sufficient to wash it out.[17]

A comparable visualization of such hysterical delusion can be found in Ken Russell's cinematic response to Aldous Huxley's *The Devils of Loudon* (1952). Russell's lurid depiction of the "possessed" nuns in *The Devils* (1971) is a parallel example of the psychological processes Gaskell describes, which take place within a similarly guilt-ridden, paranoid and claustrophobic environment. In the case of *The Devils*, it just happens to be a Catholic rather than a Puritanical one.

There are other evocations of witchcraft in British fiction. In Benson's equally rural *Raven's Brood* (1934), witches are blamed for sick cattle and hailstorms. Young lads and lasses dance around a circle of standing stones and leap over bonfires to ensure fertility, just as they do in *The Wicker Man*. An old woman, Sally Anstell, is said to be a witch, and no one would want to meet her by the big stone in the woods, which Benson describes when the young woman, Mollie, who is barren, sacrifices a cat in another kind of fertility rite:

> There were legends about it, similar to those attached to the circle. It had been made an altar according to tradition, and blood-sacrifices were made on it, and magic dances done round it, and women who performed such rites got their heart's desire if it was a child they wanted.
> ... Mollie picked up that which was lying on the altar, and Dennis saw that it was a cat. The fur was soaked in blood, and she squeezed the twitching body with both hands, as if squeezing a sponge to wring the water from it. She dipped her fingers in the blood that lay in a pool on the stone, and opening her dress smeared her breast with it.[18]

As in *Blood on Satan's Claw,* Benson carefully describes Dennis plowing the land, for it is out of the landscape itself that this community and its beliefs have emerged. There is no evil to be dug up here, as is the case with Haggard's film, but the sense of place is equally important:

> Dennis walked by the side of the beasts, with a rein in his hand and a backward eye to see that the harrow kept a straight course, for the cross-grained bitch like to go askew if she wasn't watched, and close behind it there hopped a robin, the bold thing, with beady eye alert for a breakfast from the broken clods. Primroses were a-bloom in the banks and wild violets, and at the far corner, where he must turn his harrow, was a gorse bush in full flower, and now the sun was warm enough to speak the honey-sweetness of it on the air.[19]

The writer who revived interest in the subject of witchcraft in the twentieth century was without doubt Montague Summers (1880–1948), who caused controversy from the start by professing his strong belief that witches were in actual communion with the devil:

> I have endeavored to show the witch as she really was—an evil liver; a social pest and parasite; the devotee of a loathly and obscene creed; an adept at poisoning, blackmail, and other creeping crimes; a member of a powerful secret organization inimical to Church and State; a blasphemer in word and deed; swaying the villagers by terror and superstition; a charlatan and a quack sometimes; a bawd; an abortionist; the dark counselor of lewd court ladies and adulterous gallants; a minister to vice and inconceivable corruption; battening upon the filth and foulest passions of the age.[20]

When Summers' *The History of Witchcraft and Demonology* first appeared in 1926, H.G. Wells, "frantic with rage" that such a subject should be taken seriously by a scientific publisher such as Kegan Paul, Trench, Trubner & Co., published what Summers called "a futile and flaming article" attacking it. Summers stood firm in his cool conviction, arguing that "spiritualism, so vaunted, so advertised, so mysteriously attractive, so praised and advertised by such highly placed writers as Sir Oliver Lodge and Sir Arthur Conan Doyle, was nothing else than demoniality in masquerade." He continued:

> In *the Freethinker* and *The Literary Guide* vulgarians snapped and snarled. One was reminded of the lady, upon being introduced to a Prince of the Church, impudently burst out with: "I am a free-thinker." "Free, madame, I doubt not," replied His Eminence with a courtly bow, "but a thinker, no."[21]

The first edition of *The History of Witchcraft and Demonology* sold out in two or three days, anticipating the popularity of the occult thrillers by Dennis Wheatley, whom Summers incidentally helped to inspire. (Wheatley based the character of Canon Copely-Style in *To the Devil a Daughter* on Summers, whom he once met and felt to be "positively demoniac" when Wheatley failed to buy a proffered book from him.[22])

"The evil which many had hardly suspected," Summers insisted, in response to his critics, "deeming it either a mere historical question, long dead and gone, of no interest save to the antiquarian, or else altogether fabled, was shown to be very much alive, potent in politics, potent in society, corrupting the arts, a festering, leprous disease and decay."[23] This is exactly what the public has always wanted to hear, and Summers' apparently complete conviction that witchcraft was a real and ongoing demonic problem was what made his books on the subject so popular. The scholarly footnotes and evidence of his wide and abstruse reading on the subject also helped persuade the willing reader that he was not a crackpot. Needless to say, this

Nine. Witchcraft in the Village

EXTREME PREJUDICE. The title page of Montague Summers' reissue of Guazzo's *Compendium Maleficarum* (London: John Rodker, 1929).

is one of the reasons why Summers has been sidelined if not entirely discredited by the considerable academic industry of sociological and psychological witchcraft studies in our own time. (Robin Briggs, for example, makes no mention of Summers in his 450-page *Witches & Neighbours*.) This is hardly surprising for, as Phil Baker puts it, Summers' book "set the subject back 400 years."[24] However, where popularity is concerned, objectivity is not always the name of the game. Between 1928 and 1930, Summers went on to edit the classic medieval witch-hunting "manuals" of Heinrich Kramer and Jacob Sprenger (*Malleus Maleficarum*), Francesco Maria Guazzo (*Compendium Maleficarum*) and Nicolas Remy (*Demonalatry*). Just a few years after this flurry of erudition, Wheatley began to make an impact with his occult novels, starting in 1934 with *The Devil Rides Out*. Both authors had apparently caught the mood of the moment.

It is particularly appropriate from our point of view that Summers' second book on witchcraft was entitled *The Geography of Witchcraft* (1927), for he not only takes a country-by-country approach to the subject but also includes in it some strikingly imaginative descriptions of landscape. When Summers deals with Scotland, he points out, in a distinctly Wheatley-esque manner, far removed from the sober style of the academy, that the landscape of that country greatly assisted the spread of witchcraft there: "The lonely hills and wild untrod moors, the echoing glens and remote glades, seemed the very places for the hauntings of mysterious powers influences which were, however, in popular lore always ranged on the side of evil, harbingers of death and destruction and hell." He continues to speak of Scotland as "a fearful country ruled over by the Devil, who is actually spoken of as a fairy-man, inhabited by malignant fiends, where the revels of elves and pretty pixies dancing their graceful rounds in the silvery moonlight, are a foul Sabbat of demons, hideous carlines and their dark familiars."[25] In the chapter on France, we learn:

> At the dead of night a harshly creaking wain may be heard on the silent road. It halts before some door. A soul quits the doomed house and the cart passes on its way. It is the Ankou, the spirit of death, who travels in the darkness, calling to those who are about to die, summoning them to take their place beside her. It is said that in some churches a figure of the Ankou may be seen, a grisly skeleton.[26]

Summers mentions "ancient dolmens, relics of a vanished race" around which the Nain, a spirit with the legs and hoofs of a goat, dances in the pale starlight[27]; and in Germany we are taken to the Rhine,

> the river of the undine and the lorelei; along its banks are countless haunted castles, in the romantic woods innumerable phantoms and unearthly visitants. The Brocken was the rendezvous of witches the whole world over; in the Harz Mountains you may meet the Black Huntsman; and amid the glades of the Black Forest the werewolf yet prowls for his prey.[28]

This mixture of atmospheric landscape and credulity, linked to many salacious accounts of torture and Summers' moral indignation with regard to what he finds so fascinating, is very much the mixture Wheatley distilled in his black magic novels, beginning with the disclaimer to *The Devil Rides Out*, in which, like Summers, he declares his belief in the real dangers of the occult, dissuades the reader from indulging in it and then parades before him an exciting panoply of all that he has just so fascinatingly forbidden.

The Geography of Witchcraft also informs us about Matthew Hopkins' abuse of John Lowes, which director Michael Reeves dramatizes so brutally in *Witchfinder General*:

> In Suffolk, Hopkins caused an immense sensation by discovering that John Lowes, minister of Brandeston, an old man of 80 [Robin Briggs suggests Lowes was actually in his seventies] who had occupied the living for half a century since the days of Elizabeth, was a foul witch. He had been a quarrelsome old fellow, it appears, misliked by many in his parish, and although at first he stoutly denied his guilt, when thoroughly taken in hand by the most approved methods, "till he was weary of his life and scarce sensible of what he said or did," he confessed his sorceries and went to the gallows at Bury.[29]

Summers' seeming acceptance of confession extracted under torture is worrying to say the least; as Briggs points out, it was hardly surprising that a man Lowes' age broke down under such appalling treatment.[30] However, both Summers and Briggs agree that Hopkins most probably died at home from consumption rather than meeting his end with an axe in his back as portrayed in *Witchfinder General*; though Summers also considers the possibility of Bishop Francis Hutchinson's opinion that Hopkins was lynched by an irate mob and drowned after being put to the ordeal by water, adding that this "is commonly accepted."[31]

The key to Summers' fascination with the subject might well be found in the final chapter of his *History of Witchcraft and Demonology*, which is devoted to his other consuming passion, the stage. Here he catalogs the many theatrical representations of witchcraft through the ages, though from a strictly British point of view. And what emerges, alongside his immense knowledge of the subject, is his endearing love of theatrical effect—the *scenery* of witchcraft, so to speak. He suggests that the success of Thomas Shadwell's *The Lancashire Witches and Teague o Divelly, the Irish Priest* (1681) "was wholly due to the mechanist and the scenic effects, the 'flyings' of the witches, and the music, this last so prominent a feature that Downes does not hesitate to call it 'a kind of Opera.'"[32] He also mentions another kind of opera, Henry Purcell's *Dido and Aeneas* (1680), which also features witches and one of the most celebrated choral numbers in all of opera, "In Our Deep Vaulted Cell"—an echo chorus sung by demons:

> In our deep vaulted cell the charm we'll prepare,
> Too dreadful a practice for this open air.

Summers also devotes a paragraph to Sir Henry Irving's celebrated production of W.G. Wills' *Faust*, which received its première at London's Lyceum Theater in 1885, praising it as "a superb pantomime, a thing helped out by a witches' kitchen, by a bacchanalia of demons, by chromo-lithographic effects, by the mechanist and the brushes of Telbin and Hawes Craven [Irving's principal set designer, along with Joseph Harker, who later lent his initial and surname to the solicitor in Bram Stoker's *Dracula*]."[33] He also describes "the wild overture to *Macbeth*" with equal relish: "In storm and wilderness we are suddenly brought face to face with three mysterious phantasms that ride on the wind and mingle with the mist in thunder, lightning, and in rain."[34] He adds that Macbeth was immensely popular throughout the Restoration period when "the witch scenes were elaborated and presented with every resource of scenery, mechanism, dance, song and meretricious ornament."[35]

Another play on the subject of the Pendle witches, *The Lancashire Witches, a Romance of Pendle Forest* by Edward Fitzball, was first performed at the Adelphi Theater in 1848. Again, Summers raves over the stagecraft of this production:

> The fourth scene of the second act presents the ruins of Whalley Abbey by moonlight. During an incantation the picture gradually changes; the broken arches form themselves into perfect masonry; the ivy disappears from the windows to show the ruby and gold of coloured glass; the decaying altar glitters with piled plate and the gleam of myriad tapers. A choir of nuns rises from the grave to dance with spectral gallants. Among the votaries are Nutter, Demdike and Chattox, "Three Weird Sisters, doomed for their frailties to become Witches." But they utter no word, and have no part save this in the action. The scene must have proved extraordinarily effective upon the stage. It owes much to the haunted convent in Meyerbeer's *Robert le diable*, produced at the Académie Royale in November 1831, and given in a piratical form both at Drury Lane and Covent Garden within a few weeks.[36]

Theatrical witches like these also appeared in a scene from Sam Gallu's efficient little horror film, *Theatre of Death* (1967), in which Christopher Lee plays Philippe Darvas, the tyrannical director of a Parisian Grand Guignol theater. At a party in his home, Darvas presents a preview of one of the sketches for the new season, calling upon two of his young actresses to play the parts to his guests. Having tied Lelia Goldoni's Dani Gireaux to a pillar, hypnotized Jenny Till's Nicole Chapel, thrust a poker into the fire and turned down the lights, he treats the viewer to one of the few occasions in cinema when stage directions are actually read out.

Opposite: STAGE DIRECTIONS. A page from the script of *Theatre of Death* (dir. Sam Gallu, 1967) (author's collection).

47 CONTD.

                    DARVAS
               (announces theatrically)
          Time: Sixteen hundred and ninety-
          two, a spring night. Place:
          Salem, Massachusetts - the town
          square, immediately prior to the
          burning of Miss Sarah Fletcher as
          a witch.

     He nods for NICOLE to approach the tied DANI. DARVAS'
     voice lowers to a stage whisper....

                    DARVAS
          In the background - the sound
          of the approaching townspeople.
          The wood is piled high around
          the elder sister's stake. The
          younger sister - Prudence -
          approaches.

48 CLOSER SHOT - THE ACTION ON THE IMPROMPTU STAGE

     NICOLE, walking in a trance, moves to the defenceless
     DANI. She doesn't even glance at the script in her hand.

                    NICOLE
               (softly)
          Sarah? Sarah?

                    DANI
          Prudence. For the love of
          God. Help me. Quickly, undo
          the chains.

                    NICOLE
          Sarah, I don't love God - that's
          why I can't help. But, did you
          think I'd let _them_ burn you?

                    DANI
          No, no. I knew you wouldn't.
          But hurry. I can hear
          their footsteps. They'll soon
          be here.

                    NICOLE
          Don't be frightened, Sister.
          Did you think - even for an
          instant - that I'd let their rough
          hands set light to that raven
          hair.

CONTINUED

"What you are about to see," Darvas explains, "is a scene from a sketch entitled *The Witches of Salem*. The story concerns two sisters. When the older of the two has misguidedly caused the death of the younger's lover, the vengeful, half-crazed girl has the elder sister proclaimed and tried as a witch. Time: 1692, Salem, Massachusetts. Spring night. Place: the darkened town square prior to the burning of Sarah Fletcher as a witch. In the background, the sound of the approaching townspeople. The wood is piled high round the stake. In the foreground, Prudence Fletcher approaches…"

"Did you think—even for an instant—that I'd have let their rough hands set light to that raven hair?" Nicole asks, as she advances on Dani with the red-hot poker, "When *I*… and *only I* have that right!"

The tension is broken by Dani's boyfriend (played by Julian Glover), and Dani survives to perform the sketch in costume later on where it has even more impact.

Like Wheatley, Christopher Lee also felt that there are very real and "sinister dangers implicit in dabbling with black magic." It didn't stop him making films about the subject, but he justified them by believing they might help put people off such dabbling.[37] This is hardly a very convincing moral stance, but if cinema is anything, it is a kind of witchcraft, a summoning of visions, an aphrodisiac, a magic potion that can make us believe anything (even if only for the time we spend in our cinema seat). It is therefore quite appropriate that British films should so enthusiastically have embraced the subject—and not just British cinema, of course: Benjamin Christensen's *Häxen* (*Witchcraft Through the Ages*, 1921) shows us witches flying through the air on their broomsticks. Atmospheric landscapes about in Mario Bava's *La Maschera del Demonio* (*Black Sunday*, 1960). That ultimate Hollywood fantasy, *The Wizard of Oz* (dir. Victor Fleming, 1939) created the most enduring modern archetype of what a witch should look like, but all that, as they say, is another story…

Ten

The Road to Penda's Fen

Landscape can function as a time machine, inspiring regressions. Perhaps one of the reasons why this is the case is that, seasonal transformations notwithstanding, landscape, if left alone, endures. It is easier to access the past in a place that ancient peoples might still recognize if they were here to see it. If you have lived in the same house since you were small, your childhood might seem less remote at 55 than if you have moved on. Psychics would have more to say on this subject, perhaps feeling a sense of unease in certain places due to what happened there in the past. I recall my parents telling me a story about driving out into the countryside around the Nottinghamshire village in which we lived during the 1960s. It was a sparkling summer morning and they were looking for a suitable place to picnic. Having found a spot that looked promising, they stopped their car, collected the hamper from the trunk and set off over a stile; but as soon as they crossed it, a sudden and unexpected feeling of leaden gloom came down upon both of them like a curtain. They pressed on, however, and headed for a mound in the distance. It was marked out with chains but had no explanatory notice or danger sign. Eventually, neither of them felt able to continue; the atmosphere of the place was too unnerving. They later discovered that they had stumbled on a site where mustard gas had been buried during the Second World War.

I find such stories intriguing, especially as I have never remotely experienced anything like this myself. My own response to landscape is imaginative and esthetic, certainly, but not regressive in the sense of my being able intuitively to access its history, no matter how vaguely. My impercipience seems to be at odds with the experiences of many and of much fiction too. Stone circles, as we have seen, also suggest this kind of portal, either literal or metaphoric, and Stonehenge in particular has often been used as a symbol of a pagan past that is somehow more powerful or more desirable than the present.

Thomas Hardy featured Stonehenge in this manner at the end of his novel, *Tess of the d'Urbervilles* (1891). Tess has made the mistake of confessing to her husband Angel that she had a brief affair with the landowner, Alec d'Urberville. Offending Angel's rigid moral code (despite his confession to her of a similar kind of dalliance), they separate immediately after their wedding and, years later, Tess reluctantly marries and later murders Alec d'Urberville, who has in effect ruined her life. At the end of the story, when Tess is finally arrested for her crime, Hardy exploits Stonehenge's popular associations with sacrifice. He presents Tess as a sacrificial victim on the altar of social inequality, male hypocrisy, sexual double standards and prudery—not to mention the novel's other targets of urban modernity and industrialism. The landscape of Stonehenge lends a pagan force to Tess' tragic demise, investing a modern tale of love and loss with a resonance it would struggle to find in an entirely modern setting:

> She ceased, and he fell into thought. In the far northeast sky he could see between the pillars a level streak of light. The uniform concavity of black cloud was lifting bodily like the lid of a pot, letting in at the earth's edge the coming day, against which the towering monoliths and trilithons began to be blackly defined.
> "Did they sacrifice to God here?" asked she.
> "No," said he.
> "Who to?"
> "I believe to the sun. That lofty stone set away by itself is in the direction of the sun, which will presently rise behind it."
> ... The band of silver paleness along the east horizon made even the distant parts of the Great Plain appear dark and near; and the whole enormous landscape bore that impress of reserve, taciturnity and hesitation which is usual just before day. The eastward pillars and their architraves stood up blackly against the light, and the great flame-shaped Sun-stone beyond them; and the Stone of Sacrifice midway.[1]

It is amid this setting, and not in the seedy boarding house in which she committed her crime, that the police arrest Tess: The landscape makes all the difference. Films too have exploited Stonehenge for its pagan resonance and authority. Accompanied by Clifton Parker's sombre and menacing music, the opening shots of *Night of the Demon* feature evocative shots of Stonehenge, and a portentous narration about the powers of the old gods:

> It has been written, since the beginning of time, even unto these ancient stones, that evil, supernatural beings exist in a world of darkness. And it is also said, man using the magic power of the ancient runic symbols can call forth these powers of darkness—the demons of Hell.

Stonehenge also appears in the middle of Roger Corman's Poe adaptation, *The Tomb of Ligeia* (1964), as a brief honeymoon location for Verden

Ten. The Road to *Penda's Fen*

RUINS AND RUNES. Dana Andrews examines the runes at Stonehenge in *Night of the Demon* (dir. Jacques Tourneur, 1957).

Fell (Vincent Price) and his new bride, Rowena (Elizabeth Shepherd). "In Celtic religions," Price explains in voiceover, "Stonehenge was a temple to the god of healing. It was built more than 3000 years ago; and do you know why it remains today, Rowena? Because it was built with a sense of purpose. Stone by stone, like the pyramids in Egypt or like the Aztec towers in Mexico." None of this really means very much, but the shots of Stonehenge itself are what count, suggesting that this marriage is not a conventional affair but something rather more metaphysically complex—the reanimation of Fell's former wife, no less.

The sublimity of Stonehenge had been discussed much earlier by Edmund Burke in his treatise on the Sublime and the Beautiful (1757), where he placed its effect under the category of "Difficulty":

> Another source of greatness is *Difficulty*. When any work seems to have required immense force and labour to effect it, the idea is grand. Stonehenge, neither for disposition nor ornament, has any thing admirable; but those huge rude masses of stone, set on end, and piled each on other, turn the mind on the immense force necessary for

such a work. Nay, the rudeness of the work increases this cause of grandeur, as it excludes the idea of art and contrivance; for dexterity produces another sort of effect, which is different enough from this.[2]

It was this sublimity that inspired landscape artists such as Turner and Constable to paint their famous views of Stonehenge. When Constable's watercolor of it was first exhibited at the Royal Academy in 1836, he attached to it an evocative caption:

> The mysterious monument of Stonehenge, standing remote on a bare and boundless heath, as much unconnected with the events of past ages as it is with the uses of the present, carries you back beyond all historical record into the obscurity of a totally unknown period.[3]

To suggest these references to past ages and the present day, he included figures and the meteorological effects of two rainbows, metaphoric of the tension between transience and eternity. Turner, in his 1827 watercolor, went further, having a thunderstorm strike down a flock of sheep in the foreground, along with a howling dog, which the critic John Ruskin sug-

IT'S MUCH TOO DANGEROUS TO JUMP THROUGH THE FIRE WITH YOUR CLOTHES ON. The parthenogenesis scene from *The Wicker Man* (dir. Robin Hardy, 1973).

gested might indicate a subtext concerning God's vengeance on the pagans.[4] But Turner was really more interested in creating a sublime effect than an accurate record, and added extra stones, as well as distorting the perspective, to make his image even more impressive. John William Inchbold, a follower of the Pre-Raphaelites and much admired by Tennyson, also painted "this strange weird ruin," as he called it. His 1869 oil painting of Stonehenge aimed "to secure architectural grandeur and natural sublimity, especially that religiousness by the introduction of the sun setting in the very centre of the altar-like portal, whilst the clouds are meant to suggest what is at once fiery and spiritual, the forms being (as often in nature) scarcely draped in cloudy matter."[5] Again, one is tempted to draw a comparison between Inchbold's use of the setting sun here with the miraculous final frames of *The Wicker Man*, where the sun is also used to evoke the film's deeply pagan power. *The Wicker Man* also features standing stones of its own, which provide the setting for the parthenogenesis scene in which naked women leap over the flames. Countering Sergeant Howie's outrage that they are naked, Lord Summerisle explains that it is much too dangerous to jump through the fire with your clothes on.

In 1977, Stonehenge's rival circles at Avebury in Wiltshire inspired the British children's TV series *Children of the Stones*, which regards the stones as transmitters of occult "magnetic" power. This power has the ability to brainwash the inhabitants of the fictional village they surround (nearly all of whom greet each other with the increasingly unnerving phrase "Happy Day"). The story is based on the idea of both recurrence and regression, with past events continually repeating themselves; hence Iain Cuthbertson's astronomer Rafael Hendrick repeats, like others before him, an ancient Druid priest's summoning of these powers to maintain control of the village. His toast, when drinking, is to "Old Times—and New." His mission is to "make us as one with nature and the elements."

The power takes the form of a bright column of light descending into the center of the stone circle—an image that returned in Nigel Kneale's fourth and final Quatermass television drama in 1979, starring John Mills in the title role. This dystopian story continued Kneale's interest in the association of pagan motifs with science fiction. Young people from all over the world are influenced by an organization calling itself the Planet People. They gather at megalithic sites where they believe they will be transported to a better world; but the truth of the matter is rather more sinister: The prehistoric stone circles are explained as markers left by aliens, who then harvest young people by means a blinding light that leaves nothing of their victims but ashes.

Simon Marsden experienced something comparably strange when, after photographing the Rollright Stones on the Cotswold Hills in Oxfordshire, he drove to the nearby village of Long Compton. Noticing a mound, he crossed a field to photograph it and was "suddenly hurled backwards by a great force, like a thunderbolt." A dark bruise later developed, from his shoulder down the length of his arm, stopping at his wrist:

> It was some months later that I learnt of an ancient legend that tells of a young man of Long Compton who succeeded in summoning up the Devil at a Bronze Age earthwork in what was then known as the Close Field, adjacent to the church.[6]

Fictional standing stones also feature in one of the most eccentric but intriguing of British horror films. Don Sharp's *Psychomania* (1971) is compelling in many ways: as a record of early '70s Britain with its bleak concrete shopping precincts, of consumer inflation in later years in its advertising signs, not to mention its orange-themed interior design. (The film is carefully composed around various shades of that once fashionable color.) *Psychomania* commemorates the dying embers of the summer of love represented by David Whitaker and John Worth's song "Riding Free" (sung in Donovan-style by a guitar-strumming biker), and the film also forms a kind of epitaph for George Sanders, who committed suicide after filming his last scene. Sanders plays an incarnation of the Devil, dressed up as

PETRIFIED WITCHES. The standing stones of *Psychomania* (dir. Don Sharp, 1973).

Beryl Reid's butler. Reid plays Mrs. Latham, a psychic who has sold her soul (and that of her son, Tom, played by Nicky Henson) to the forces of darkness, in return for advantages the film only suggests rather than fully reveals: perhaps her psychic abilities and her luxuriously appointed home. Tom leads a biker gang called The Living Dead, and he later learns how to become just that: The way to achieve immortality is to commit suicide and believe, while you are dying, that you will return from the dead. Once reinstated, such suicides are naturally invincible and capable of anything. Perhaps Sanders might have smiled in recollection of the plot of his last film as his overdose began to take effect; but he had no intention of coming back, even if that was possible.

The bikers' meeting place is an area of open ground on which stand "The Seven Witches." These standing stones were apparently once witches who failed to keep their bargain with the Devil and were consequently punished with petrification. The same fate awaits the bikers at the end of what is really a witchcraft film in biker dress. The bikes they ride might very well be regarded as internal combustion broomsticks, they wear leathers and skull-decorated helmets rather than cloaks and pointed hats, and their aim is to cause havoc and mayhem: "Teach him a lesson," one of the only two female members of the gang says, before causing a fatal traffic accident.

Sharp also deliberately has his bikers drive through tree-lined roads, surrounded by wood-clad hills, bringing with them their pagan associations even in this bizarre context; and the film opens with highly atmospheric shots of the bikers weaving their way around the mist-shrouded stone circle, echoing the kind of ceremonies popularly imagined to have been performed by witches and druids at such places. During a dream sequence, in which the heroine, Abby (played by Mary Larkin), imagines her lover (Henson) back from the dead, Sharp films from the ground up, framing slow-motion shots of the lovers through a screen of dead vegetation, seed heads and teasels. In this, his approach parallels that of Piers Haggard, who created similar imagery in the opening titles of *Blood on Satan's Claw*. Like that film, *Psychomania* rises out of the earth, just as Tom later drives from his grave on the bike with which he was buried. It is perhaps the most startling of all resurrection scenes in British horror films, and the painterly photography of *Psychomania*, along with its surreal imagery and social comment, raises what was originally conceived as a piece of low-budget exploitation to the level of popular art. Appropriately for a film about a cult, it has become a cult film itself, like *The Wicker Man*.

Catherine Storr's novel, *Marianne Dreams* (1958), was made into the British television series, *Escape into Night*, in 1972, and this also featured the power of standing stones. More psychological than pagan, these stones surround an imaginary house, which has been drawn by a convalescent child, Marianne, and she visits it in her dreams. Omitted in the novel's film adaptation, *Paperhouse* (dir. Bernard Rose, 1988), these sinister stones unnervingly evoke their pagan counterparts, but *Marianne Dreams* is fundamentally a psychological tale concerned with regression into the subconscious.

In her waking life, Marianne's doctor is also treating a seriously ill boy called Mark. Marianne consequently imagines Mark in her dream house, and the stones thus represent Mark's illness. The stones have eyes and voices reminiscent of Doctor Who's robotic Daleks, along with a disturbing sound effect (the scraping of piano strings after the manner of Henry Cowell's avant garde masterpiece, *Banshee*). As they move closer to the house, they shout, "We're coming!" through the loudspeaker of the radio Marianne has also drawn. Since they cannot abide light, Marianne and Mark use a lighthouse, also drawn by Marianne, to defeat them and thus do they make their escape. Marianne thwarts the stones in her dream world and helps Mark to the safety of the imaginary lighthouse, the real Mark is also cured of his illness and the story ends back in waking reality with the two children reunited outside a real lighthouse.

The use of a deserted house as a way of charting the landscape of the unconscious is profoundly Jungian. Jung made the same equation in his autobiography:

> I was in a house I did not know, which had two storeys. It was my house. I found myself in the upper story, where there was a kind of salon furnished with fine old pieces in rococo style. On the walls hung a number of precious old paintings. I wondered that this should be my house, and thought, "Not bad." But then it occurred to me that I did not know what the lower floor looked like. Descending the stairs, I reached the ground floor. There everything was much older, and I realized that this part of the house must date from about the fifteenth or sixteenth century. The furnishings were medieval; the floors were of red brick. Everywhere it was rather dark. I went from one room to another, thinking, "Now I really must explore the whole house." I came upon a heavy door, and opened it. Beyond it, I discovered a stone stairway that led down into the cellar. Descending again, I found myself in a beautifully vaulted room which looked exceedingly ancient. Examining the walls, I discovered layers of brick among the ordinary stone blocks, and chips of brick in the mortar. As soon as I saw this I knew that the walls dated from Roman times. My interest by now was intense. I looked more closely at the floor. It was on stone slabs, and in one of these I discovered a ring. When I pulled it, the stone slab lifted, and again I saw a stairway of narrow stone steps, leading down into the depths. These, too, I descended, and entered a low cave cut into the rock. Thick dust lay on the floor, and in the dust were scattered bones and broken pottery, like remains of a primitive culture. I discovered two human skulls, obviously very old and half disintegrated. Then I awoke.[7]

Ten. The Road to *Penda's Fen*

Landscape, even the landscape of a house or of the unconscious, may act as a gateway to a past that in turn affects the present. Time, like the stones of Avebury or Stonehenge, is circular. This kind of historical regression through landscape was also employed by Alan Garner in his 1973 novel, *Red Shift*, which became a TV drama in 1978. The action moves back and forth through time with three different stories united by a particular place (Mow Cop Hill on the Cheshire-Staffordshire border) and by an artifact from that place—an axe-head once used as a weapon in Roman times. This axe-head is subsequently thought of as a talisman during the English Civil War, and finally as a symbol of the troubled love affair between two teenagers in the 1970s. The past thus fertilizes the present through the interdependence of different periods on landscape. The presence of landscape in the story was made more powerful when the novel was dramatized, creating a visual presence which Garner's stichomythic, rather than descriptive approach in the novel only suggested.

Similarly, in Garner's *The Moon of Gomrath* (1963), the world of pagan magic emerges from the natural landscape of Alderley Edge. Young protagonists, Susan and Colin, "found it unbearable that the woods for them should be empty of anything but loveliness, that the boulder that hid the iron gates should remain a boulder, that the cliff above the Holywell should be just a cliff."[8] This yearning for an extra dimension to landscape is obviously Garner's own, hence his imaginative response to it as a gateway to the past and the imagination. Susan and Colin find themselves entering this imaginative world as they run through the landscape:

> Whether the change was in themselves or in the wood, Colin and Susan felt it. The Edge had suddenly become, not quite malevolent, but alien, unsafe. And they longed to be clear of the trees: for either the light, or nerves, or both, seemed to be playing still further tricks on them. They kept imagining that there was white movement among the tree tops—nothing clear, but suggested, and elusive.[9]

Out of this mood and terrain emerges Uthecar Hornskin, the dwarf, who leads them to their adventures in the parallel landscape of magic.

The time-slip device exploited by Garner had been used many times before, notably by Rudyard Kipling (1865–1936) in his poem "Merrow Down" (1922), in which he too commemorates a particular place, "an hour out of Guildford town" in Surrey. The text regresses back to the time when "dark Phoenicians" traded their wares along the Western Road, then "long and long before that time"[10] when bison roamed and beavers built in Broadstonebrook in prehistoric times. Edward German's setting of this text in his *Just-So Songbook* of 1924 effectively captures the melancholy nature of lost time and the resilience of landscape by means of a recurring motif, which conveys the quality of a sigh and yet also simultaneously an acceptance of the inevitable. (This is perhaps due to the circularity of German's motif, which falls and then rises, like an ever-turning wheel.) A.E. Housman (1859–1936) also used landscape as a fulcrum by which to evoke ancient times. In *A Shropshire Lad* (1887), later set to music by that master of English "pastoral" style Ralph Vaughan Williams, the landscape of Wedlock Edge, along with an atmospheric dose of bad weather, inspire a regression to the time of the Roman conquest of Britain:

> On Wenlock Edge the wood's in trouble;
> His forest fleece the Wrekin heaves;
> The gale, it plies the saplings double,
> And thick on Severn snow the leaves.
>
> 'Twould blow like this through holt and hanger
> When Uricon the city stood:
> 'Tis the old wind in the old anger,
> But then it threshed another wood.
>
> Then, 'twas before my time, the Roman
> At yonder heaving hill would stare:
> The blood that warms an English yeoman,
> The thoughts that hurt him, they were there.
>
> There, like the wind through woods in riot,
> Through him the gale of life blew high;
> The tree of man was never quiet:
> Then 'twas the Roman, now 'tis I.
>
> The gale, it plies the saplings double,
> It blows so hard, 'twill soon be gone:
> To-day the Roman and his trouble
> Are ashes under Uricon.[11]

Arthur Machen also experimented with time-slip techniques in his first novel, *The Hill of Dreams* (1907). The narrator, Lucian Taylor, is an aspiring writer who enjoys wandering around the Roman ruins at Caermaen on the Welsh borders, where the surroundings inspire a powerfully imaginative regression:

> Thin and strange, mingled together, the voices came up to him on the hill; it was as if an outland race inhabited the ruined city and talked in a strange language of strange and terrible things.
> The sun had slid down the sky, and hung quivering over the huge dark dome of the mountain like a burnt sacrifice, and then suddenly vanished.... In his imagination he saw the earthen gates of the tombs broken open, and the serried legion swarming to the eagles. Century by century they passed up; they rose, dripping, from the river bed,

they rose from the level, their armour shone in the quiet orchard, they gathered in ranks and companies from the cemetery, and as the trumpet sounded, the hill fort above the town gave up its dead.[12]

The power of the landscape eventually convinces Lucien that "two unknown beings stood together there in the darkness and tried the balance of his life, and spoke his doom."[13] Later, he wanders through the Caermaen ruins with the aim of "gradually levelling to the dust the squalid kraals of modern times, and rebuilding the splendid and golden city of Siluria," with its tessellated pavements and luxurious hangings. "The dull modern life was far away, and people who saw him at this period wondered what was amiss; the abstraction of his glance was obvious even to eyes not over-sharp."[14] Having reconstructed the Roman settlement in his mind's eye, he wanders through the past he has constructed for himself out of the landscape and its archeological remains:

> He knew perfectly well that for his present purpose the tawny sheen and shimmer of the tide was the only fact of importance about the river, and so he regarded the city as a curious work of jewelry. Its radiant marble porticoes, the white walls of the villas, a dome of burning copper, the flash and scintillation of tiled roofs, the quiet red of brickwork, dark groves of ilex, and cypress, and laurel, glowing rose-gardens, and here and there the silver fountain, seemed arranged and contrasted with wonderful art, and the town appeared a delicious ornament, every cube of colour owing its place to the thought and inspiration of the artificer.[15]

Lucien's Caermaen regressions are reminiscent of Guido von List's fantasies on Carnumtum, the site of an ancient Roman settlement on the banks of the Danube in Austria. In 1875, List (1848–1919) camped in the ruins of Carnumtum where he experienced a vision of the victory of the Germans over the Roman occupiers, an event that transpired 1500 years before. According to Nicholas Goodrich-Clarke, List celebrated "with a fire and the burial of eight wine bottles in the shape of a swastika beneath the arch of the Pagan Gate."[16] This proved prophetic given List's influence on the occult, Ariosophist and nationalist fringe groups that contributed to the emergence of National Socialism 60 years later. In 1875, List published the two-volume novel, *Carnumtum*, in which a romance takes place amid his imaginative reconstruction of the buildings of the ruined town. "To List," Goodrich-Clarke observes, "the very word Carnumtum evoked the hazy aura of olden Germanic valour, a signal motto recalling the event that put the ancient Germans back on the stage of world history."[17]

A more wholesome approach to living history had been essayed in England 16 years earlier by Thomas Hughes, famous for his novel, *Tom Brown's Schooldays*. Hughes' *The Scouring of the White Horse* (1859) is rather different, however, and in its construction does indeed anticipate the "wandering" style of Machen's *London Adventure* and thus ultimately becomes one of the literary foundation stones for the psycho-geographic approach of W.S. Sebald's *The Rings of Saturn* (1995). Hughes' mixture of traditional songs, the story of his own love for a farmer's daughter, the events during "Scouring" or maintenance of the White Horse of Uffington in Berkshire, and its accompanying games and rituals, is a mixture of reportage, romance and folklore.

Leaving London, Hughes discusses the possible origins of the famous White Horse, which is cut from the chalk hills. Legends claim it as the site for the slaying of the Dragon by St. George: "And this bare place is where his blood ran out, and nothing'll grow on it since, not so much as a thistle."[18] There are also connections with King Arthur and Pendragon, one of the mounds being called Pendragon's Hill, but as Hughes' guide points out, "Pendragon, you know, is only a name common to those of the

CHALKING HORSE. A Richard Doyle illustration for Thomas Hughes' *The Scouring of the White Horse* (London: Macmillan, 1859).

kings of the ancient Britons, who were chosen leaders in the time of national distress, and means nothing more than "caput regum, the chief of kings." According to some, "Arthur" is the same or a like word, being

> "Ardh-reg" or "Ard-heer," and meaning "summus Rex" (whence the "Arviragus" of Juvenal; but I lay no stress on this). Now we know of at least three Pendragons.... And if Arthur and Pendragon are the same words, doubtless (as has been well supposed) there were many Arthurs at this time, one of whom was probably slain in battle and buried here.[19]

Approaching the White Horse itself ("a colossal figure cut out in the turf, and giving the name to a whole district"), Hughes' guide points out the Manger—a hole in the hillside, so called because it lies directly under the Horse's nose. Locals like to claim the Horse was made "by the Saxons and their great king. The Druids don't seem akin to us somehow; and then one would lose all about the great battle, which was certainly fought up here."[20] Chapter Three accordingly records a local man's account of the battle of Ashdown in 871, for which the White Horse is said to have been created as a commemoration of King Alfred's victory over the Danish:

> The Pagan occupied the higher ground, and the Christians came up from below. There was also in that place a single stunted thorn-tree, which I myself have seen with my own eyes. Around this tree the opposing hosts came together with loud shouts from all sides, the one to pursue their wicked course, the other to fight for their lives, their dearest ties, and their country.... This year, AD 871, is a year for Berkshire men to be proud of, for on them fell the brunt of that fiery trial; and their gallant stand probably saved England a hundred years of Paganism.[21]

Hughes admits that "the story of the battle, and all the talk about Pendragon and Arthur, coming upon the back of the famous, and the out of the way country life, which was so strange to me, had carried me into a sort of new world; and I shouldn't have been much surprised to see a dragon running about the hill, though I should have been horribly frightened."[22] This is not quite the decadence of Lucien's regressions, but it certainly demonstrates the power of landscape to stimulate the imagination.

Which brings me to the goal of my journey, *Penda's Fen*. This television play by David Rudkin, directed by Alan Clarke for the BBC in 1974, is in many ways a culmination of the British pagan fantasy tradition I have been exploring, equipping it with a clear political and cultural mission to revitalize a society threatened by military danger, oppressive ideologies and commercial forces. All these aspects are filtered through the personal odyssey of its leading character, Stephen Franklin (Spencer Banks), whom we first see as a neat and tidy, prudish and certainly conventional schoolboy, smart in his CCF army uniform, critical of subversive television plays (ironically rather like the one in which he finds himself), which he regards as representative of the "modern wilderness of immorality," and consequently an upholder of traditional religious values. Things begin to change when sexual impulses suggest he might be homosexual, or at least bisexual, that he is in fact an adopted child, and that Honeybone, the boy at school about whom he sexually fantasizes, is in fact a bully who humiliates him in front of the other boys. As Rudkin puts it, *Penda's Fen* is about "the lies that a society will tell in order to force people to identify themselves very narrowly and very shallowly, and what a struggle it is to burst through these lies and to shove them to one side and stand up and start to be your true, difficult, contradictory, bloody self."[23]

Having undergone this baptism by fire (fire, indeed, flickers around his dream of Honeybone's naked body), Stephen begins to change his ideas. At the local church hall, Arne (Ian Hogg), a playwright, gives a speech during an "Any Questions" meeting. He argues that governments hold the population to ransom, along with the "manipulators, fixers and psychopaths" who have the real power in the land. "Is it the strikers who play *Monopoly* for real with our countryside and cities?" he asks. "Is it strikers who pillage our earth, ransack it, drain it dry for quick gain to hand on nothing but dust to the children of tomorrow?"

Alan Clarke majestically juxtaposes the remainder of Arne's speech with breathtaking shots of idyllic British rural landscape that would have been well-known to Sir Edward Elgar, whom Stephen much admires, but has yet fully to understand. "Not far from here is an expanse of country," Arne continues. "You all know it well. Brummies drive out of a Sunday to leave their litter there." He points out that Elgar enshrined this farmland and pasture and ancient fen in his music. "The earth beneath your feet feels solid there. It is not. Somewhere there the land is hollow. Somewhere beneath is being constructed something we are not supposed to know." And now we see sinister radio telescope dishes amid this rolling landscape. "A top secret. We locals are not supposed to know it's even there. And you accept it. What is it then? An air raid shelter to shift the population of Birmingham to, in all of four minutes? What is it hidden beneath this shell of lovely earth? Some hideous angel of technocratic death?"

Now, Clarke shows us three noble trees standing in a cornfield, rather like sentinels or angels themselves). "An alternative city for government from beneath?" Another shot of a field with trees. "Motorways there? Offices? Control suites? Silent and empty, waiting for the day"—followed by a cut to haystacks arranged in a row, again implying something distinctly sinister.

Ten. The Road to *Penda's Fen*

Rudkin and Clarke use landscape throughout *Penda's Fen* as a symbol of what is most valuable about England. Cities and factories are definitely not what Rudkin is fighting for—quite the opposite. Factories are later shown as places of servitude—"conveyor belts," as Stephen's mother puts it. The landscape—the "beautiful world" so much loved by the ghost of Elgar, whom Stephen also encounters one thundery afternoon—is what makes life worth living, and the pagan history of Britain is offered by Rudkin as an alternative to the exploitative, commercial and industrial forces that are destroying Britain's cultural and spiritual heritage—one in which angels and demons are quite capable of appearing as they do in the poetry of William Blake. Indeed, the film specifically references Blake's *Jerusalem*, which suggests that Blake's paean to England's Green and Pleasant Land has been hijacked by the forces of a reactionary society. That society is represented by Stephen's very traditional public school. I myself attended just this kind of educational establishment when this film was first screened, so I can vouch for its authentic portrayal here. Rather than a Green and Pleasant Land, Rudkin seems to be suggesting that there is much to recommend in a Green and Pagan one.

Rudkin had a penchant for Hammer horror films, which his later drama, *Artemis '81*, references in several scenes. In *Penda's Fen*, one scene resembles Hammer's *Quatermass 2* (dir. Val Guest, 1957). On Penda's Fen at night, a man stumbles back to his car with a grotesquely burned and corrupted face and arm. The following day, Arne responds to the newspaper report by arguing that secret government military research establishments are so often built beneath ancient, sacred sites, like Los Alamos in America, "as though thereby to bottle the primal genie of the earth and to pervert it."

We then cut to an elegiac sunset over summer fields, through which Stephen and his clerical father walk while discussing the Manichaean heresy of the struggle between light and darkness. That night, Stephen wakes from a nightmare to discover a demon, or some kind of incubus, sitting on his chest. Behind the grotesque mask it wears are the eyes of the local milkman to whom Stephen is also attracted. The demon therefore represents his freedom, sexual and otherwise, and, from then on, Stephen's life begins to change. He resigns from the CCF as a "non-cooperative." His schoolmaster begins to wonder "if you want to be a man at all," to which Stephen returns the rather back-handed compliment that he has always admired his teacher as being a representative of "an English norm."

Now, Stephen cycles through the landscape, free of his school and military uniforms, and his sense of freedom seems to echo Ken Russell's shots of the young Elgar riding through the Malvern Hills on his white pony in *Elgar* (1962), his early TV documentary for the BBC. But Stephen falls off his bike, and his concussion causes him to hallucinate a strange ritual in the gardens of a manor house in which young people willingly have their hands chopped off, again allegorizing our willingness to submit to oppression. Rescued by the milkman he finds so sexually attractive, Stephen's next shock is to learn that his father holds highly unorthodox religious views: "Jesus," his father once wrote, "is dangled over a sick culture centred on authority and death."

Again, the pagan landscape that surrounds Stephen is claimed to be an antidote to the ills of urban, commercial culture railed against by Arne, who subversively advocates the need for "Disobedience. Chaos. Out of those alone can some new experiment in human living be born." His father agrees that pagans practiced human sacrifice, "but do we not?" He too believes we should "revolt from the monolith" and "come back to the village." The sun glows as it does at the end of *The Wicker Man*, as the Reverend Franklin dreams of "some second coming, through some last disobedience and last resurrection."

Benediction. **King Penda (Geoffrey Staines) blesses Stephen (Spencer Banks) at the end of *Penda's Fen* (dir. Alan Clarke, 1974).**

Ten. The Road to *Penda's Fen*

Having finally rejected the forces of convention and corruption, King Penda appears to Stephen, enthroned on the top of Penda's Fen overlooking a panorama of the landscape below. Penda, the last pagan king in England, versus the new machine, as the Reverend Franklin puts it. "What mystery went down with him?" he had wondered earlier. But now, Penda anoints Stephen as his successor: "Our land must live," he decrees. "Cherish our flame." And with that, Stephen walks back down to civilization, the sounds of which gradually accompany the end credits, symbolizing that Stephen is indeed taking that flame, that message, and that pagan hope back to the sick world, as a new messiah for a new kingdom.

Chapter Notes

Preface

1. Charles Reade, *It's Never Too Late to Mend*, http://www.gutenberg.org/files/4606/4606.txt

Introduction

1. Algernon Blackwood *Ancient Sorceries and Other Weird Tales*, ed. S.T. Joshi (London: Penguin, 2002), 258.
2. J. R. R. Tolkien, *The Fellowship of the Ring* (London: George Allen & Unwin, 1974), 123.
3. Sir James Frazer, *The Golden Bough—A Study in Magic and Religion* (Abridged Edition) (London: Macmillan, 1950), 1.
4. George MacDonald, *Phantastes—A Faerie Romance* (London: J. M. Dent, 1940), 9–10.
5. Leonard Forster (ed.), *The Penguin Book of German Verse* (Harmondsworth: Penguin, 1961), 208.
6. Richard Wagner (trans. Lionel Salter), CD booklet for *Götterdämmerung* (Hamburg: Deutsche Grammophon, 1998), 61.
7. Sheridan Le Fanu, *The Wyvern Mystery* (Thrupp: Alan Sutton, 2000), 6.
8. Sir James Frazer, *The Golden Bough—A Study in Magic and Religion* (Abridged Edition), 109–110. (Note 3).
9. George MacDonald, *Phantastes—A Faerie Romance*, 8–9. (Note 4).
10. J. R. R. Tolkien, *The Fellowship of the Ring*, 121. (Note 2).
11. Dante, *The Divine Comedy*, trans. Francis Cary (London: Bibliophile Books, 1988), 11.
12. Sir James Frazer, *The Golden Bough—A Study in Magic and Religion* (Abridged Edition), 110. (Note 3).
13. Alexander Macbain, *Celtic Mythology and Religion* (Sterling: Eneas Mackay, 1917), 75.
14. *Ibid.*, 75–76.
15. "Edmund Blyth-Visions of a Cathedral." *National Trust*. https://www.nationaltrust.org.uk/whipsnade-tree-cathedral/features/edmund-blyth---visions-of-a-cathedral.
16. Richard Fricke, "Impressions and experience of Bayreuth in 1876," trans. Stewart Spencer, *Wagner* Vol. 12, no. 1 (1991), 44.
17. Cosima Wagner (trans. Geoffrey Skelton), "Diaries," Vol. 2, *(London: Collins, 1980)* (1878), 154.
18. Octave Mirbeau, *Torture Garden*, trans. Alvah C. Bessie (New York: Juno Books, 2000), 77.
19. *Ibid.*, 79.
20. Kenneth Grahame, *The Golden Age* (London: Thomas Nelson & Sons, 1927), 12.

Chapter One

1. Evelyn Eaton, *The King Is a Witch* (The Dennis Wheatley Library of the Occult) (London: Sphere, 1976), 147.
2. *Ibid.*, 148.
3. Alfred Lord Tennyson, *Poetical Works of Alfred Lord Tennyson, Poet Laureate* (London: Macmillan, 1911), 249.
4. *Ibid.*, 261.
5. W. Y. Evans-Wentz, *The Fairy Faith in Celtic Countries* (Oxford: Henry Frowde, 1911), 320–321.
6. *Ibid.*, 71 ("Morte d'Arthur").
7. *Ibid.*, 67 ("Morte d'Arthur").
8. *Ibid.*, 68–69 ("Morte d'Arthur").
9. *Ibid.*, 72 ("Morte d'Arthur").
10. Hallam Tennyson, *Alfred Lord Tennyson—A Memoir by His Son*, Vol. 2 (London: Macmillan, 1897), 90.
11. Alfred Lord Tennyson, *Poetical Works of Alfred Lord Tennyson, Poet Laureate* 463. (Note 3) ("Guinevere").
12. *Ibid.*, 465. ("Guinevere").
13. Thomas Keightley, *The Fairy Mythology*

(London: G. Bell, 1878), 322. (Chaucer's "Wife of Bath's Tale" quoted).
14. Hallam Tennyson, *Alfred Lord Tennyson—A Memoir by His Son*, vol. 2, 314–315. (Note 10).
15. Alfred Lord Tennyson, *Poetical Works of Alfred Lord Tennyson, Poet Laureate*, 314–315. (Note 3) ("The Coming of Arthur").
16. *Ibid.*
17. Thomas Gray, *The Poems of Thomas Gray with a Selection of Letters & Essays* (London: J. M. Dent, n.d.), 12 ("The Bard").
18. Alfred Lord Tennyson, *Poetical Works of Alfred Lord Tennyson, Poet Laureate*, 462. (Note 3) ("Guinevere").
19. *Ibid.*, 422. ("The Holy Grail").
20. *Ibid.*, 396. ("Lancelot and Elaine").
21. *Ibid.*, 402. ("Lancelot and Elaine").
22. *Ibid.*
23. *Ibid.*, 404. ("Lancelot and Elaine").
24. *Ibid.*, 384. ("Merlin and Vivien").
25. *Ibid.*, 385. ("Merlin and Vivien").
26. *Ibid.*, 386. ("Merlin and Vivien").
27. *Ibid.*, 389. ("Merlin and Vivien").
28. *Ibid.*, 356. ("Geraint and Enid").
29. *Ibid.*, 354. ("Geraint and Enid").
30. *Ibid.*, 357. ("Geraint and Enid").
31. *Ibid.*, 360. ("Geraint and Enid").
32. *Ibid.*, 356–357. ("Geraint and Enid").
33. *Ibid.*, 361. ("Geraint and Enid").
34. *Ibid.*, 395. ("Merlin and Vivien")
35. *Ibid.*, 380. ("Merlin and Vivien").
36. *Ibid.*, 424. ("The Holy Grail").
37. *Ibid.*, 468. ("The Passing of Arthur").
38. *Ibid.*, 470. ("The Passing of Arthur").
39. *Ibid.*, 472. ("The Passing of Arthur").
40. *Ibid.*, 472. ("The Passing of Arthur").
41. *Ibid.*, 474. ("The Passing of Arthur").
42. Matthew Arnold, *The Poems of Matthew Arnold 1840–1869* (Oxford: Henry Froud/Oxford University Press, 1909), 259. ("Balder Dead").
43. Dion Fortune, *The Goat-Foot God* (Wellingborough: Aquarian Press, 1989), 61–62.
44. W. Y. Evans-Wentz, *The Fairy Faith in Celtic Countries*, 353. (Note 5).
45. Alfred Lord Tennyson, *Poetical Works of Alfred Lord Tennyson, Poet Laureate*, 383. (Note 3) ("Merlin and Vivien").
46. *Ibid.*, 390. ("Merlin and Vivien").
47. *Ibid.*
48. *Ibid.*, 313. ("The Coming of Arthur").
49. *Ibid.*, 321. ("Gareth and Lynette").
50. *Ibid.*, 321–322. ("Gareth and Lynette").
51. *Ibid.*, 459. ("Guinevere").
52. *Ibid.*, 460. ("Guinevere").
53. Michael Hurd, *Rutland Boughton and the Glastonbury Festivals* (Oxford: Oxford University Press, 1993), 39.
54. *Ibid.*, 40.
55. *Ibid.*, 43.
56. *Ibid.*, 302.
57. *Ibid.*, 40.
58. George Bernard Shaw, *Major Critical Essays* (London: Constable, 1932), 276. ("The Perfect Wagnerite").
59. Michael Hurd, *Rutland Boughton and the Glastonbury Festivals*, 309 (Note 53).
60. *Ibid.*, 41.
61. *Ibid.*, 315.
62. William Morris, *Prose and Poetry* (Oxford: Oxford University Press, 1913), 198.
63. Martin Harrison and Bill Waters, *Burne-Jones* (London: Barrie and Jenkins, 1973), 153.
64. Bram Stoker, *Personal Reminiscences of Henry Irving* (London: William Heinemann, 1907), 165.
65. Laurence Irving, *Henry Irving* (London: Faber and Faber, 1951), 567.
66. *Ibid.*, 567–568.
67. George Bernard Shaw, *Our Theatres in the Nineties* Vol. 1, (London: Constable, 1932, pp. 14–15.

Chapter Two

1. Hallam Tennyson, *Alfred Lord Tennyson—A Memoir by His Son*, Vol. 2 (London: Macmillan, 1897), 90.
2. John Matthews, *The Grail—Quest for the Eternal* (London: Thames and Hudson, 1981), 17.
3. C. G. Jung (ed.), *Man and His Symbols* (London: Aldus Books, 1964), 210. ("The process of individuation" by M.-L. von Franz).
4. Alfred Lord Tennyson, *Poetical Works of Alfred Lord Tennyson, Poet Laureate* (London: Macmillan, 1911), 419. ("The Holy Grail").
5. *Ibid.*, 432. ("The Holy Grail").
6. Karl Marx, *Capital*, ed. David McLellan (Oxford: Oxford University Press, 1995), 86–87.
7. William Morris, *Prose and Poetry of William Morris* (Oxford: Humphrey Milford/Oxford University Press, 1913), 211–212. ("Sir Galahad, a Christmas Mystery").

8. Roger Sherman Loomis, *The Development of Arthurian Romance* (New York: Dover, 2000), 105.
9. William Morris, *Prose and Poetry of William Morris*, 213. (Note 7) ("Sir Galahad, A Christmas Mystery").
10. John Golby (ed.), *Culture and Society in Britain (1850–1890)* (Oxford: Oxford University Press, 1986), 147. (William Morris, "How I Became a Socialist").
11. Georgiana Burne-Jones, *Memorials of Edward Burne-Jones*, vol. 2, (London: Macmillan, 1906), 208–209.
12. *Ibid.*, 79.
13. Cosima Wagner, *Diaries*, trans. Geoffrey Skelton, vol. I 1869–1877, (London: Collins, 1978), 964. (Entry for Monday May 14, 1877).
14. Georgiana Burne-Jones, *Memorials of Edward Burne-Jones*, vol 2, 43. (Note 11).
15. Stewart Spencer (ed.), *Wagner* Vol. 11, no. 3 (1990): 110–111. (Richard Wagner, "Prelude ['The holy Grail']").
16. Alfred Lord Tennyson, *Poetical Works of Alfred Lord Tennyson, Poet Laureate*, 424. (Note 4) ("The Holy Grail").
17. *Ibid.*, 435. ("The Holy Grail").
18. *Ibid.*, 425. ("The Holy Grail").
19. *Ibid.*, 426. ("The Holy Grail").
20. *Ibid.*
21. *Ibid.* 421. ("The Holy Grail").
22. Dion Fortune, *The Goat-Foot God* (Wellingborough: Aquarian Press, 1989), 61–62.
23. John Cowper Powys, *A Glastonbury Romance* (London: Pan Books, 1975), xi.
24. *Ibid.*, 255.
25. *Ibid.*, 746.
26. *Ibid.*, 614.
27. *Ibid.*, 757.
28. *Ibid.*, 939.
29. *Ibid.*, 807.
30. *Ibid.*, 756.
31. *Ibid.*, 122.
32. *Ibid.*, 125.
33. *Ibid.*, 214.
34. *Ibid.*, 285.
35. *Ibid.*, 159.
36. *Ibid.*, 707.
37. *Ibid.*, 259.
38. *Ibid.*, 709.
39. *Ibid.*, 260.
40. Charles Williams, *War in Heaven* (London: Sphere, 1976), 196.
41. Mary Anne Atwood, *A Suggestive Inquiry into Hermetic Mystery, 1850*, 146.
42. Lindsay Clarke, *Parzival and the Stone from Heaven* (London: HarpurCollins, 2001), 205.
43. *Ibid.*, 226.
44. Lindsay Clarke, *The Chymical Wedding* (London: Pan Books, 1990), 166.
45. *Ibid.*, 69.
46. *Ibid.*, 49.
47. Bram Stoker, *The Lair of the White Worm* (London: Arrow Books, 1975), 24.
48. *Ibid.*, 157.
49. *Ibid.*, 189.
50. Charlotte Guest (trans.), *The Mabinogion* (London: Bernard Quarritch, 1877), 426.
51. *Ibid.*, 432.
52. Alan Garner, *The Owl Service* (Lions/Collins, 1987), 11.
53. *Ibid.*, 29.
54. *Ibid.*, 30.

Chapter Three

1. W. B. Yeats, *The Green Helmet and Other Poems* (London: Macmillain, 1912), 90–91.
2. Charles Dickens, *A Tale of Two Cities* and *A Christmas Carol* (London: Hazel, Watson & Viney, n.d.), 378 ("A Christmas Carol").
3. Sir James Frazer, *The Golden Bough—A Study in Magic and Religion* (Abridged Edition) (London: Macmillan and Co., 1950), 126.
4. Lindsay Clarke, *The Chymical Wedding* (London: Pan Books, 1990), 13.
5. J. R. R. Tolkein, *The Two Towers* (London: George Allen & Unwin, 1974), 66.
6. Algernon Blackwood, *Ancient Sorceries and Other Weird Stories* (London: Penguin, 2002), 237 ("The Man Whom the Trees Loved").
7. *Ibid.*, 259. ("The Man Whom the Trees Loved").
8. William Anderson, *Green Man* (London: HarpurCollins, 1990), 115.
9. Algernon Blackwood, *Ancient Sorceries and Other Weird Stories*, 254. (Note 6) ("The Man Whom the Trees Loved").
10. *Ibid.*, 273. ("The Man Whom The Trees Loved").
11. *Ibid.*, 54. ("The Willows").
12. *Ibid.*, 17. ("The Willows").
13. *Ibid.*, 32. ("The Willows").

14. *Ibid.*, 36. ("The Willows").
15. *Ibid.*, 15. ("The Willows").
16. John Wyndham, *The Day of the Triffids* (London: Book Club Associates, 1981), 38.
17. D. H. Lawrence, *Women in Love* (London: Book Club Associates, 1980), 85.
18. E. F. Benson, *Raven's Brood* (Brighton: Millivres Books, 1993), 117.

Chapter Four

1. Richard Wagner, *Selected Letters of Richard Wagner*, trans. Stewart Spencer (London: Dent, 1987), 452. (Letter to Mathilde Wesendonck, mid April 1859).
2. Matthew Arnold, *The Poems of Matthew Arnold* (Oxford: Henry Frowde/Oxford University Press, 1909), 141. ("Tristan and Iseult").
3. Donald Thomas, *Swinburne—The Poet in his World* (London: Weidenfeld & Nicolson, 1979), 178.
4. *Ibid.*, 213.
5. Algernon Charles Swinburne, *Tristram of Lyonesse* (London: William Heinemann, 1917), 120–121.
6. J. Comyns Carr, *Tristram & Iseult* (London: Duckworth, 1906), 1.
7. *Ibid.*, 58.
8. *Ibid.*, 70.
9. Arthur Symons, *Tristan and Iseult* (London: William Heinemann, 1917), 22.
10. *Ibid.*, 49–50.
11. *Ibid.*, 94.
12. Thomas Hardy, *The Famous Tragedy of the the Queen of Cornwall at Tintagel in Lyonnesse—A New Version of an Old Story, Arranged as a play for Mummers* (London: Macmillan, 1923), 4.
13. Michael Hurd, *Rutland Boughton and the Glastonbury Festivals* (Oxford, Oxford University Press, 1993), 161.
14. *Ibid.*, 163.
15. *Ibid.*, 164.
16. *Ibid.*
17. John Masefield, *Tristan and Isolt* (London: William Heinemann, 1927), 11.
18. *Ibid.*, 21.
19. *Ibid.*, 47.
20. *Ibid.*, 126–127.
21. Matthew Arnold, *The Poems of Matthew Arnold*, 259. (Note 2).
22. Oliver Strunk (ed.), *Source Readings in Music History*, Vol. 5 "The Romantic Era," (London: Faber and Faber, 1981), 144. (Richard Wagner: "The Artwork of the Future").

Chapter Five

1. Frank Delaney, *The Celts* (London: BBC/Hodder and Stoughton, 1986), 150.
2. Stephen Wischhusen (ed.), *The Hour of One—Six Gothic Melodramas* (London: Gordon Frazer, 1975), 85.
3. Frank Delaney, *The Celts*, 213. (Note 1).
4. Ossian, *Fingal*, http://www.sacred-texts.com/neu/ossian/oss24.htm.
5. *Ibid.*, 312.
6. *Ibid.*, 325.
7. *Ibid.*, 347.
8. Richard Ellmann, *Yeats—The Man and the Masks* (London: Penguin, 1987),115.
9. W. B. Yeats, *Collected Poems of W. B. Yeats* (London: Macmillan, 1950), 441. ("The Wanderings of Oisin").
10. W. B. Yeats, *The Trembling of the Veil* (London, privately printed by T. W. Laurie, 1922), 135–136.
11. Jeremy Maas and others, *Victorian Fairy Painting* (London: Royal Academy of Arts/Merrell Holberton, 1997), 11. (Jeremy Maas, "Victorian Fairy Painting").
12. Alexander Pope, *The Poetical Works of Alexander Pope* (London: Macmillan, 1927), 76. ("The Rape of the Lock").
13. William Shakespeare, *Shakespeare Complete Works*, ed. W. J. Craig (Oxford, Oxford University Press, 1974), 175. ("A Midsummer Night's Dream").
14. W. Y. Evans-Wentz, *The Fairy Faith in Celtic Countries* (Oxford: Henry Frowde, 1911), 291.
15. Richard Ellmann, *Yeats—The Man and the Masks*, 125. (Note 8).
16. *Ibid.*, 126.
17. W. Y. Evans-Wentz *The Fairy Faith in Celtic Countries*, 376. (Note 14).
18. Fiona Macleod, *Pharais and The Mountain Lovers* (London: William Heinemann, 1927), xi. ("Pharais").
19. Richard Ellmann, *Yeats—The Man and the Masks*, 128. (Note 8).
20. *Ibid.*, 132.
21. Fiona Macleod, *Poems and Dramas* (London: William Heinemann, 1927), 311. ("The Immortal Hour").

22. *Ibid.*, 312. ("The Immortal Hour").
23. J. R. R. Tolkein, *The Fellowship of the Ring* (London: George Allen & Unwin, 1974), 369.
24. Fiona Macleod, *Poems and Dramas*, 344 ("The Immortal Hour") (Note 21).
25. *Ibid.* 378–379.
26. John Kemplay, *The Paintings of John Duncan—A Scottish Symbolist* (San Francisco: Pomegranate Books, 1994), 17.
27. *Ibid.*, 105.
28. *Ibid.*, 51.
29. Fiona Macleod, *Poem and Dramas*, 111. ("Heart o' Beauty") (Note 21).
30. *Ibid.*, 237. ("Dim Face of Beauty").
31. W. B. Yeats, *The Collected Poems of W. B. Yeats* (London: Macmillan, 1950), 41. ("The Rose of the World").
32. *Ibid.*, 56. ("To Ireland in the Coming Times")
33. A. E. George Russell, *Collected Poems* (London: Macmillan, 1935), 9. ("The Great Breath").
34. Fiona Macleod, *Poems and Dramas*, 379. ("The Immortal Hour") (Note 21).
35. *Ibid.*, 243. ("Flame on the Wind").
36. Fiona Macleod, *Pharais and The Mountain Lovers*, 254. ("The Mountain Lovers") (Note 18).
37. Fiona Macleod, *The Silence of Amor/ Where the Forest Murmurs* (London: William Heinemann, 1927), 107–108. ("The Hill-Tarn").
38. Edgar Allan Poe, *The Complete Illustrated Stories and Poems of Edgar Allan Poe* (London: Chancellor Press, 1988), 133. ("Landor's Cottage").
39. M. R. James, *Collected Ghost Stories* (Ware: Wordsworth Classics, 1994), 308. ("A Warning to the Curious").
40. *Ibid.*, 317. ("A Warning to the Curious").
41. Alexander Macbain, *Celtic Mythology and Religion* (Sterling: Eneas Mackay, 1917), 96.
42. Iain Sinclair, *Lud Heat* (Cheltenham: Skylight Press, 2012), 6.
43. *Ibid.*, 23.
44. *Ibid.*
45. Arthur Machen, *The London Adventure—or The Art of Wandering* (London: Village Press, 1974), 14.
46. An email to the author from Markus Wallasvaara, 15th November 2016.
47. Allan Brown, *Inside The Wicker Man* (London: Sidgwick and Jackson, 2000), 167.
48. *Ibid.*, 168
49. http://www.fifetoday.co.uk/news/local-headlines/brussels-beckons-as-lord-of-tears-earns-prestige-invitation-1-3261474.

Chapter Six

1. W. Somerset Maugham, *Cakes and Ale* (London: Heron Books, n. d.), 122.
2. Fiona Macleod, *The Dominion of Dreams/Under the Dark Star* (London: William Heinemann, 1927), 4–9. ("Dalua").
3. Oscar Wilde, *Complete Works of Oscar Wilde* (London: Collins, 1977), 812. ("Pan").
4. *Ibid.*, 828–829. ("Ravenna").
5. Aubrey Beardsley, *Venus and Tannhäuser* (London: Bracken Books, 1985), 29.
6. D. H. Lawrence, *Lady Chatterley's Lover* (London: Guild Publishing, 1981), 362.
7. W. B. Yeats, *The Collected Poems of W. B. Yeats* (London: Macmillan, 1950), 20. ("The Stolen Child").
8. Karen McGavock, *J. M. Barrie's Peter Pan In and Out of Time* (London: Rowman and Littlefield, 2006), 206.
9. J. M. Barrie, *Peter Pan in Kensington Gardens* (New York: Calla Editions, 2013), 31–32.
10. *Ibid.*, 19.
11. *Ibid.*, 27.
12. Matthew Arnold, *The Poems of Matthew Arnold* (Oxford: Henry Frowde/Oxford University Press, 1909), 182–183. ("Lines Written in Kensington Gardens").
13. Thomas Tickell, "Kensington Gardens," http://spenserians.cath.vt.edu/TextRecord.php?action=GET&textoid=33916.
14. Dennis Wheatley (ed.), *Uncanny Tales 2* (London: Sphere, 1974), 15–16. (Arthur Machen, "The Great-God Pan").
15. *Ibid.*, 16. (Arthur Machen, "The Great-God Pan").
16. *Ibid.*, 17. (Arthur Machen, "The Great-God Pan").
17. *Ibid.*, 24. (Arthur Machen, "The Great-God Pan").
18. *Ibid.*, 49. (Arthur Machen, "The Great-God Pan").
19. *Ibid.*, 54. (Arthur Machen, "The Great-God Pan").

20. *Ibid.*, 60. (Arthur Machen, "The Great-God Pan").
21. *Ibid.*, 62. (Arthur Machen, "The Great-God Pan").
22. E, M. Forster, *The Longest Journey* (Harmondsworth: Penguin, 1978), 77.
23. W. Somerset Maugham, *The Magician* (Geneva: Edito-Service S. A., 1968), 112.
24. *Ibid.* 112–113.
25. *Ibid.* 114.
26. Kenneth Grahame, *The Wind in the Willows* (London, Methuen, 1950), 92.
27. *Ibid.*
28. *Ibid.*, 90.
29. John Keats, *Poetical Works*, ed. H. W. Garrod (London: Oxford University Press, 1973), 207. ("Ode to a Nightingale").
30. Kenneth Grahame, *The Wind in the Willows*, 91. (Note 26).
31. Matthew Arnold, *The Poems of Matthew Arnold*, 231. (Note 12).
32. Kenneth Grahame, *The Wind in the Willows*, 93. (Note 26).
33. *Ibid.*, 92.
34. Dennis Wheatley, *The Devil Rides Out* (London: Heron, 1972), 109–110.
35. *Ibid.*, 108.
36. Aleister Crowley, *Moonchild* (London: Sphere, 1972), 9–10. (Dennis Wheatley's introduction).
37. Phil Baker, *The Devil Is a Gentleman—The Life and Times of Dennis Wheatley* (Sawtry: Dedalus, 2009), 302.
38. *Ibid.*, 303.
39. *Ibid.*, 301.
40. Aleister Crowley, *Magick Liber Aba—Book 4, Parts I–IV* (San Francisco: Weiser Books, 1997), 121. ("Magic in Theory and Practice").
41. Phil Baker, *The Devil Is a Gentleman—The Life and Times of Dennis Wheatley*, 7. (Note 37).
42. Aleister Crowley, *Magick Liber Aba—Book 4, Parts I–IV*, 164. (Note 40) ("Magic in Theory and Practice").
43. *Ibid.*, 523.
44. Saki (H. H. Munro), *The Short Stories of Saki* (London: John Lane/The Bodley Head, 1942), 180. ("The Music on the Hill").
45. *Ibid.*, 182.
46. *Ibid.*, 185.
47. Algernon Blackwood, *Tales of Terror and Darkness* (London: Spring Books, 1977), 195. ("The Touch of Pan").
48. *Ibid.*, 296. ("The Touch of Pan").
49. *Ibid.*, 299. ("The Touch of Pan").
50. *Ibid.*, 304. ("The Touch of Pan").
51. Lord Dunsany, *The Blessing of Pan* (Holicong: Wildside Press, 2003), 39.
52. *Ibid.*, 44.
53. *Ibid.*, 48.
54. *Ibid.*, 46.
55. *Ibid.*, 124–125.
56. *Ibid.*, 53.
57. *Ibid.*, 58.
58. *Ibid.*, 56.
59. *Ibid.*, 60.
60. *Ibid.*, 85.
61. *Ibid.*, 59–60.
62. *Ibid.*, 256.
63. *Ibid.*, 274.
64. *Ibid.*, 267.
65. E. F. Benson, *The Inheritor* (Brighton: Millivres Books, 1992), 87–88.
66. *Ibid.*, 29.
67. *Ibid.*, 31.
68. *Ibid.*, 291.
69. *Ibid.*, 51.
70. *Ibid.*, 78.
71. *Ibid.*, 90.
72. *Ibid.*, 124.
73. *Ibid.*, 154.
74. *Ibid.*, 156.
75. *Ibid.*, 192.
76. *Ibid.*, 205.
77. *Ibid.*, 230.
78. *Ibid.*, 237.
79. Dion Fortune, *The Goat-Foot God* (Wellingborough: Aquarian Press, 1989), 231.
80. *Ibid.*, 230.
81. *Ibid.*, 6.
82. *Ibid.*, 57.
83. *Ibid.*, 275.
84. *Ibid.*, 67.
85. *Ibid.*, 66.
86. *Ibid.*, 65.
87. *Ibid.*, 265.
88. *Ibid.*, 266.
89. *Ibid.*, 275.
90. *Ibid.*, 290.
91. *Ibid.*, 302.
92. *Ibid.*, 325–326.
93. *Ibid.*, 343.
94. *Ibid.* 344.

Chapter Seven

1. Sir Granville Bantock, *Pagan Symphony/Fifine at the Fair/Two Heroic Ballads*/Royal Philharmonic Orchestra, cond. Vernon Handley. Hyperion CD, CDA66630, 1992 (CD booklet, 3)
2. Eero Tarasti *Myth and Music* (Helsinki, Suomen Musiikkitieteellinen Seura, 1978), 77.
3. Sir Granville Bantock, *Sappho/Sappic Poem*/Royal Philharmonic Orchestra, cond. Vernon Handley, Hyperion CD, CDA66899, 1997 (CD booklet, 19–20).
4. *Ibid.* (CD booklet, 11).
5. Imogen Holst, *Gustav Holst* (London: Oxford University Press, 1938), 43.
6. Alfred Lord Tennyson, *Poetical Works of Alfred Lord Tennyson, Poet Laureate* (London: Macmillan, 1911), 54. ("The Lotus Eaters").
7. *Ibid.*, 54. ("The Lotus Eaters").
8. Cyril Scott, *Symphony No 3 "The Muses"/Piano Concerto No. 2/Neptune*/BBC Philharmonic, cond. Martyn Brabbins, Chandos CD CHAN 10211, 2004 (CD booklet, 9).
9. Stephen Banfield, *Gerald Finzi—An English Composer* (London: Faber and Faber, 1997), 451.
10. Mary Renault, *The King Must Die* (London: Longmans, 1958), 75.
11. George Moore, *Avowals* (London: William Heinemann, 1924), 172.
12. Walter Pater, *Marius the Epicurian—His Sensations and Ideas* (London: Macmillan, 1924), 236.
13. *Ibid.*, 233.
14. *Ibid.*, 29.
15. *Ibid.*, 56.
16. Oscar Wilde, *Complete Works of Oscar Wilde* (London: Collins, 1977), 755. ("Charmides").
17. *Ibid.*, 756. ("Charmides").
18. *Ibid.*, 717. ("The Garden of Eros").
19. *Ibid.*, 719. ("The Garden of Eros").
20. *Ibid.*, 722. ("The Garden of Eros").
21. *Ibid.*, 738. ("The Burden of Itys").
22. *Ibid.*, 743. ("The Burden of Itys").
23. Stephen Jones et al., *Frederic Leighton 1830–1896* (*London:* Royal Academy of Arts/Harry N. Abrams, 1996), 165.
24. *Ibid.*, 239.
25. *Ibid.*, 220.
26. Walter Pater, *Marius the Epicurian—His Sensations and Ideas*, 64. (Note 12).
27. Ovid, *Metamorphoses*, trans. David Raeburn (London: Penguin, 2004), 170.
28. Charles Kingsley, *The Heroes, or Greek Fairy Tales for My Children* (London: Macmillan, 1898), 32–33.
29. *Ibid.*, 48.
30. Ray Harryhausen in "A Conversation with Ray Harryhausen" a special feature on the DVD release of *Clash of the Titans*, Warner Bros./Turner Entertainment, Z1 65137, 2002.
31. Ovid *Metamorphoses*, trans. David Raeburn 169–170. (Note 27).
32. Robert Hartford (ed.), *Bayreuth—The Early Years* (London: Victor Gollancz, 1980), 227. (Bernard Shaw quoted).
33. Oscar Wilde, *Complete Works of Oscar Wilde*, 754. (Note 16) ("Charmides").

Chapter Eight

1. T. S. Eliot, *Collected Poems 1909–1962* (London: Faber and Faber, 1974), 80. ("Notes on 'The Wasteland'").
2. Sir James Frazer, *The Golden Bough—A Study in Magic and Religion* (Abridged Edition) (London: Macmillan, 1950), 354–355.
3. T. S. Eliot, *Collected Poems 1909–1962*, 63. ("The Wasteland").
4. Evelyn Eaton, *The King Is a Witch* (The Dennis Wheatley Library of the Occult) (London: Sphere, 1976), 25–26.
5. Aleister Crowley, *The Simon Iff Stories & Other Works* (Ware: Wordsworth Editions, 2012), 424. ("Golden Twigs").
6. D. H. Lawrence, *Studies in Classic American Literature/Fantasia of the Unconscious/Psychoanalysis and the Unconscious* (Geneva: Edito-Service S.A., 1969), 189. ("Fantasia of the Unconscious").
7. *Ibid.*, 178. ("Fantasia of the Unconscious").
8. Sir James Frazer, *The Golden Bough—A Study in Magic and Religion* (Abridged Edition) 1. (Note 2).
9. *Ibid.*, 167.
10. Aleister Crowley, *The Simon Iff Stories & Other Works*, 426. (Note 5) ("Golden Twigs").
11. *Ibid.*, 431. ("Golden Twigs").
12. *Ibid.*, 491. ("Golden Twigs").
13. Sir James Frazer, *The Golden Bough—A Study in Magic and Religion* (Abridged Edition), 110. (Note 2).

14. *Ibid.*, 8.
15. *Ibid.*, 54.
16. Aleister Crowley, *The Simon Iff Stories & Other Works,* 497. (Note 5) ("Golden Twigs").
17. Sir James Frazer, *The Golden Bough—A Study in Magic and Religion* (Abridged Edition, 12–13. (Note 2)
18. *Ibid.*, 223.
19. *Ibid.*, 354.
20. Aleister Crowley, *The Simon Iff Stories & Other Works,* 446. (Note 5) ("Golden Twigs").
21. *Ibid.*, 455–456. ("Golden Twigs").
22. *Ibid.*, 454. ("Golden Twigs").
23. Sir James Frazer, *The Golden Bough—A Study in Magic and Religion* (Abridged Edition), 46. (Note 2).
24. *Ibid.*, 60.
25. Aleister Crowley, *The Simon Iff Stories & Other Works,* 515. (Note 5) ("Golden Twigs").
26. *Ibid.*, 514. ("Golden Twigs").
27. Sir James Frazer, *The Golden Bough—A Study in Magic and Religion* (Abridged Edition), 10. (Note 2).
28. *Robin Redbreast,* BFI/DVD, BFIVD997, 2013 (Vic Pratt, "Hunting for sherds: Robin Redbreast," in accompanying booklet, 3).
29. Thomas Keightley, *The Fairy Mythology* (London: G. Bell, 1878), 317–318.
30. *Ibid.*, 654.
31. *Ibid.*, 120–122.
32. *Ibid.*, 30–31.
33. *Ibid.*, 338.
34. *Ibid.*, 309–310.
35. *Ibid.*, 297.
36. *Ibid.*, 45.
37. *Ibid.*, 269.
38. *Ibid.*, 304–305.
39. *Ibid.*, 305.
40. *Ibid.*, 306.

Chapter Nine

1. Ronald Blythe, *Akenfield* (London: Guild Publishing, 1980), 16–17.
2. *Ibid.*, 17.
3. Robin Briggs, *Witches and Neighbours* (London: HarpurCollins, 1996), 341.
4. *Ibid.*, 341.
5. Ronald Blythe, *Akenfield,* 16. (Note 1).
6. Elizabeth Gaskell, *Tales of Mystery & the Macabre* (Ware: Wordsworth Editions, 2008), 94. ("Lois the Witch").
7. *Ibid.*, 96. ("Lois the Witch").
8. *Ibid.*, 125. ("Lois the Witch").
9. *Ibid.*, 104. ("Lois the Witch").
10. *Ibid.*, 105. ("Lois the Witch").
11. *Ibid.*, 123. ("Lois the Witch").
12. *Ibid.*, 125–126. ("Lois the Witch").
13. *Ibid.*, 129. ("Lois the Witch").
14. *Ibid.*, 140. ("Lois the Witch").
15. *Ibid.*, 139. ("Lois the Witch").
16. *Ibid.*, 140. ("Lois the Witch").
17. *Ibid.*, 155. ("Lois the Witch").
18. E. F. Benson, *Ravens' Brood* (Brighton: Millivres Books, 1993), 166.
19. *Ibid.*, 70.
20. Montague Summers, *The History of Witchcraft and Demonology* (London: Routledge & Kegan Paul, 1973), xiv.
21. Montague Summers, *The Galanty Show* (London: Cecil Woolf, 1980), 157–158.
22. Phil Baker, *The Devil Is a Gentleman—The Life and Times of Dennis Wheatley* (Sawtry: Dedalus. 2009), 316.
23. Montague Summers, *The Galanty Show,* 156–157. (Note 21).
24. Phil Baker, *The Devil Is a Gentleman—The Life and Times of Dennis Wheatley,* 306. (Note 22).
25. Montague Summers, *The Geography of Witchcraft* (London: Routledge & Kegan Paul, 1978), 201.
26. *Ibid.*, 388.
27. *Ibid.*, 389.
28. *Ibid.*, 519.
29. *Ibid.*, 142–143.
30. Robin Briggs, *Witches and Neighbours,* 54. (Note 3).
31. Montague Summers, *The Geography of Witchcraft,* 144. (Note 25).
32. Montague Summers, *The History of Witchcraft and Demonology,* 299. (Note 20).
33. *Ibid.*, 284.
34. *Ibid.*, 289.
35. *Ibid.*, 302.
36. *Ibid.*, 309–310.
37. Christopher Lee, *Lord of Misrule—The Autobiography of Christopher Lee* (London: Orion, 2003), 227.

Chapter Ten

1. Thomas Hardy, *Tess of the d'Ubervilles* (London: Folio, 1988), 414–415.
2. Edmund Burke, *A Philosophical Enquiry into the Origin of Our Ideas of the Sublime*

and Beautiful (Oxford: Oxford University Press, 1990), 71.

3. *Making History—Antiquaries in Britain 1707–2007* (London: Royal Academy of Art, 2007), 244.

4. *Ibid.*, 242.

5. *Ibid.*, 246.

6. Simon Marsden, *The Haunted Realm* (London: Little Brown, 1998), 106.

7. C. G. Jung, *Memories, Dreams, Reflections* (Fontana, 1989), 182–183.

8. Alan Garner, *The Moon of Gomrath* (Lions/Collins, 1988), 15.

9. *Ibid.*, 17.

10. Rudyard Kipling, "Merrow Down," http://www.kiplingsociety.co.uk/poems_merrow.htm.

11. A. E. Houseman, *A Shropshire Lad*, http://www.chiark.greenend.org.uk/~martinh/poems/housman.html#ASLxxxi. ("On Wenlock Edge the wood's in trouble").

12. Arthur Machen, *The Hill of Dreams* (New York: Dover, 1986), 54–55.

13. *Ibid.*, 57.

14. *Ibid.*, 112–113.

15. *Ibid.*, 120.

16. Nicholas Goodrick-Clarke, *The Occult Roots of Nazism* (Wellingborough: Aquarian, 1985), 35.

17. *Ibid.*, 36.

18. Thomas Hughes, *The Scouring of the White Horse* (Gloucester: Alan Sutton, 1989), 18.

19. *Ibid.*, 23.

20. *Ibid.*, vii.

21. *Ibid.*, 21.

22. *Ibid.*, 35–36.

23. *Ibid.*, 42; *Penda's Fen*, BFI/BBC DVD, BFIV2070, 2016 ("The Landscape of Feelings" documentary).

Bibliography

Anderson, William. *Green Man*. London: HarperCollins, 1990.
Arnold, Matthew. *The Poems of Matthew Arnold 1840–1869*. Oxford: Henry Froud/Oxford University Press, 1909.
Atwood, Mary Anne. *A Suggestive Inquiry into Hermetic Mystery*. Published anonymously,1850.
Baker, Phil. *The Devil Is a Gentleman—The Life and Times of Dennis Wheatley*. Sawtry: Dedalus, 2009.
Banfield, Stephen. *Gerald Finzi—An English Composer*. London: Faber and Faber, 1997.
Barrie, J. M. *Peter Pan in Kensington Gardens*. New York: Calla Editions, 2013.
Beardsley, Aubrey. *Venus and Tannhäuser*. London: Bracken Books, 1985.
Benson, E. F. *The Inheritor*. Brighton: Millivres Books, 1992.
———. *Raven's Brood*. Brighton: Millivres Books, 1993.
Blackwood, Algernon. *Ancient Sorceries and Other Weird Tales*, Edited by S.T. Joshi. London: Penguin, 2002.
———. *Tales of Terror and Darkness*. London: Spring Books, 1977.
Blythe, Ronald. *Akenfield*. London: Guild Publishing, 1980.
Briggs, Robin. *Witches and Neighbours*. London: HarpurCollins, 1996.
Brown, Allan. *Inside The Wicker Man*. London: Sidgwick and Jackson, 2000.
Burke, Edmund. *A Philosophical Enquiry Into the Origin of Our Ideas of the Sublime and the Beautiful*. Oxford: Oxford University Press, 1990.
Burne-Jones, Georgiana. *Memorials of Edward Burne-Jones* (v. 1, 1833–1867). London: Macmillan, 1906.
———. *Memorials of Edward Burne-Jones* (v. 2, 1868–1898). London: Macmillan, 1906.
Clarke, Lindsay. *Parzival and the Stone from Heaven*. London: HarpurCollins, 2001.
———. *The Chymical Wedding*. London: Pan Books, 1990.
Comyns Carr, J. *Tristram & Iseult*. London: Duckworth, 1906.
Crowley, Aleister. *Magick: Liber ABA. Book Four. Parts I–IV.* San Francisco: Weiser Books, 1997.
———. *Moonchild*. London: Sphere, 1972.
———. *The Simon Iff Stories & Other Works*. Ware: Wordsworth Editions, 2012.
Delaney, Frank. *The Celts*. London: BBC/Hodder and Stoughton, 1986.
Dickens, Charles. *A Tale of Two Cities* and *A Christmas Carol*. London: Hazel, Watson & Viney. n.d.
Dunsany, Lord. *The Blessing of Pan*. Holicong: Wildside Press, 2003.
Eaton, Evelyn. *The King is a Witch*. London: Sphere, 1976.
Eliot, T. S. *Collected Poems 1909–1962*. London: Faber and Faber, 1974.
Ellmann, Richard. *Yeats—The Man and the Masks*. London: Penguin, 1987.
Evans-Wentz, W. Y. *The Fairy Faith in Celtic Countries*. Oxford: Henry Frowde, 1911.
Forster, E. M. *The Longest Journey*. Harmondsworth: Penguin, 1978.
Forster, Leonard. *The Penguin Book of German Verse*. Harmondsworth: Penguin, 1961.
Fortune, Dion. *The Goat-Foot God*. Wellingborough: Aquarian Press, 1989.

Frazer, Sir James. *The Golden Bough—A Study in Magic and Religion* (Abridged Edition). London: Macmillan, 1950.
Garner, Alan. *The Moon of Gomrath*. Lions/Collins, 1988.
_____. *The Owl Service*. Lions/Collins, 1987.
Gaskell, Elizabeth. *Tales of Mystery & the Macabre*. Ware: Wordsworth Editions, 2008.
Golby, John (ed.). *Culture and Society in Britain (1850–1890)*. Oxford: Oxford University Press, 1986.
Goodrick-Clarke, Nicholas. *The Occult Roots of Nazism*. Wellingborough: Aquarian, 1985.
Grahame, Kenneth. *The Golden Age*. London: Thomas Nelson & Sons, 1927.
_____. *The Wind in the Willows*. London: Methuen, 1950.
Gray, Thomas. *The Poems of Thomas Gray with a Selection of Letters & Essays*. London: J. M. Dent. n.d.
Guest, Charlotte (trans.). *The Mabinogion*. London: Bernard Quarritch, 1877.
Hardy, Thomas. *The Famous Tragedy of the the Queen of Cornwall at Tintagel in e Lyonnesse—A New Version of an Old Story, Arranged as a Play for Mummers*. London: Macmillan, 1923.
_____. *Tess of the d'Ubervilles*. London: Folio, 1988.
Harrison, Martin, and Bill Waters. *Burne-Jones*. London: Barrie and Jenkins, 1973.
Hartford, Robert (ed.). *Bayreuth—The Early Years*. London: Victor Gollancz, 1980.
Holst, Imogen. *Gustav Holst*. London: Oxford University Press, 1938.
Houseman, A. E., *A Shropshire Lad*. http://www.chiark.greenend.org.uk/~martinh/poems/housman.html#ASLxxxi.
Hughes, Thomas. *The Scouring of the White Horse*. Gloucester: Alan Sutton, 1989.
Hurd, Michael. *Rutland Boughton and the Glastonbury Festivals*. Oxford: Oxford University Press, 1993.
Irving, Laurence. *Henry Irving*. London: Faber and Faber, 1951.
James, M. R. *Collected Ghost Stories*. Ware: Wordsworth Classics, 1994.
Jones, Stephen, Newall, et al. *Frederic Leighton 1830–1896*. London: Royal Academy of Arts/Harry N. Abrams, 1996.
Jung, Carl G. (ed.). *Man and His Symbols*. London: Aldus Books, 1964.
_____. *Memories, Dreams, Reflections*. Fontana, 1989.
Keats, John. *Poetical Works*, Edited by H.W. Garrod. London: Oxford University Press, 1973.
Keightley, Thomas. *The Fairy Mythology*. London: G. Bell, 1878.
Kemplay, John. *The Paintings of John Duncan—A Scottish Symbolist*. San Francisco: Pomegranate Books, 1994.
Kingsley, Charles. *The Heroes, or Greek Fairy Tales for My Children*. London: Macmillan, 1898.
Kipling, Rudyard. "Merrow Down," http://www.kiplingsociety.co.uk/poems_merrow.htm.
Lawrence, D. H. *Studies in Classic American Literature/Fantasia of the Unconscious/Psychoanalysis and the Unconscious*. London: Heron, 1969.
_____. *Studies in Classic Literature/Fantasia of the Unconsciousness/Psychoanalysis and the Unconscious*. Geneva: Edito-Service S.A., 1968.
_____. *Women in Love*. London: Book Club Associates, 1980.
Lee, Christopher. *Lord of Misrule—The Autobiography of Christopher Lee*. London: Orion, 2003.
Le Fanu, Sheridan. *The Wyvern Mystery*. Thrupp: Alan Sutton, 2000.
Loomis, Roger Sherman. *The Development of Arthurian Romance*. New York: Dover, 2000.
Maas, Jeremy and others. *Victorian Fairy Painting*. London: Royal Academy of Arts/ Merrell Holberton, 1997.
Macbain, Alexander. *Celtic Mythology and Religion*. Sterling: Eneas Mackay, 1917.

MacDonald, George. *Phantastes—A Faerie Romance*. London: J. M. Dent, 1940.
Machen, Arthur. *The Hill of Dreams*. New York: Dover, 1986.
_____. *The London Adventure—or The Art of Wandering*. London: Village Press, 1974.
Macleod, Fiona. *Pharais and The Mountain Lovers*. London: William Heinemann, 1927.
_____. *Poems and Dramas*. London: William Heinemann, 1927.
_____. *The Dominion of Dreams/Under the Dark Star*. London: William Heinemann, 1927.
_____. *The Silence of Amor/Where the Forest Murmurs*. London: William *Heinemann*, 1927.
Making History—Antiquaries in Britain 1707–2007. London: Royal Academy of Art, 2007.
Marsden, Simon. *The Haunted Realm*. London: Little Brown, 1998.
Marx, Karl. *Capital*, Edited by David McLellan. Oxford: Oxford University Press, 1995.
Masefield, John. *Tristan and Isolt*. London: William Heinemann, 1927.
Matthews, John. *The Grail—Quest for the Eternal*. London: Thames and Hudson, 1981.
Maugham, W. Somerset. *The Magician*. Geneva: Edito-Service S.A., 1968.
Mirbeau, Octave (trans. Alvah C. Bessie). *Torture Garden*. New York: Juno Books, 2000.
Moore, George. *Avowals*. London: William Heinemann, 1924.
Morris, William. *Prose and Poetry*. Oxford: Oxford University Press, 1913.
McGavock, Karen. *J. M. Barrie's Peter Pan In and Out of Time*. London: Rowman and Littlefield, 2006.
Ossian, *Fingal*. http://www.sacred-texts.com/neu/ossian/oss24.htm.
Ovid (trans. David Raeburn). *Metamorphoses*. London: Penguin, 2004.
Pater, Walter. *Marius the Epicurian—His Sensations and Ideas*. London: Macmillan, 1924.
Poe, Edgar Allan. *The Complete Illustrated Stories and Poems of Edgar Allan Poe*. London: Chancellor Press, 1988.
Pope, Alexander. *The Poetical Works of Alexander Pope*. London: Macmillan, 1927.
Powys, John Cowper. *A Glastonbury Romance*. London: Pan Books, 1975.
Reade, Charles. *It's Never Too Late to Mend*. http://www.gutenberg.org/files/4606/4606.txt.
Renault, Mary. *The King Must Die*. London: Longmans, 1958.
Russell, A. E. George. *Collected Poems*. London: Macmillan, 1935.
Saki (H. H. Munro). *The Short Stories of Saki*. London: John Lane/The Bodley Head, 1942.
Shakespeare, William. *Shakespeare Complete Works*, Edited by W.J. Craig. Oxford: Oxford University Press, 1974.
Shaw, George Bernard. *Major Critical Essays*. London: Constable, 1932.
_____. *Our Theatres in the Nineties* (3 vols.). London: Constable, 1932.
Sinclair, Iain. *Lud Heat*. Cheltenham: Skylight Press, 2012.
Spencer, Stewart (ed.). "Wagner." *Journal of the Wagner Society, London* Vol. 11, no. 3 (August 1990).
_____. "Wagner." *Journal of the Wagner Society, London* Vol. 12, no. 1 (January 1991).
Stoker, Bram. *Personal Reminiscences of Henry Irving*. London: William Heinemann, 1907.
_____. *The Lair of the White Worm*. London: Arrow Books, 1975.
Strunk, Oliver (ed.). *Source Readings in Music History* (5 vols.). London: Faber and Faber, 1981.
Summers, Montague. *The Galanty Show*. London: Cecil Woolf, 1980.
_____. *The Geography of Witchcraft*. London: Routledge & Kegan Paul, 1978.
_____. *The History of Witchcraft and Demonology*. London: Routledge & Kegan Paul, 1973.
Swinburne, Algernon Charles. *Tristram of Lyonesse*. London: William Heinemann, 1917.
Symons, Arthur. *Tristan and Iseult*. London: William Heinemann, 1917.
Tarasti, Eero. *Myth and Music*. Helsinki: Suomen Musiikkitieteellinen Seura, 1978.
Tennyson, Alfred Lord. *Poetical Works of Alfred Lord Tennyson, Poet Laureate*. London: Macmillan, 1911.

Tennyson, Hallam. *Alfred Lord Tennyson—A Memoirs by His Son* (2 vols.). London: Macmillan, 1897.
Thomas, Donald. *Swinburne—The Poet in His World*. London: Weidenfeld & Nicolson, 1979.
Tickell, Thomas. "Kensington Gardens," http://spenserians.cath.vt.edu/TextRecord.php?action=GET&textsid=33946.
Tolkien, J. R. R. *The Lord of the Rings* (3 vols.). London: George Allen & Unwin, 1974.
Wagner, Cosima (trans. Geoffrey Skelton) Diaries (2 vols.), 1878–1883, London: Collins, 1980.
Wagner, Richard (trans. Lionel Salter), CD booklet for *Götterdämmerung*, Hamburg: Deutsche Grammophon. 1998.
_____ (trans. Stewart Spencer). *Selected Letters of Richard Wagner*. London: Dent, 1987.
Wheatley, Dennis. *The Devil Rides Out*. London: Heron, 1972.
_____ (ed.). *Uncanny Tales 2*. London: Sphere 1974.
Wilde, Oscar. *Complete Works of Oscar Wilde*. London: Collins, 1977.
Williams, Charles. *War in Heaven*. London: Sphere, 1976.
Wischhusen, Stephen (ed.). *The Hour of One—Six Gothic Melodramas*. London: Gordon Frazer, 1975.
Wyndham, John. *The Day of the Triffids*. London: Book Club Associates, 1981.
Yeats, W. B. *Collected Poems of W. B. Yeats*. London: Macmillan, 1950.
_____. *The Green Helmet and Other Poems*. London: Macmillan, 1912.
_____. *The Trembling of the Veil*. London: privately printed by T. W. Laurie, 1922.

Index

Numbers in *bold italics* indicate pages with illustrations

Ace of Wands (TV series) 111, 113
Ackroyd, Peter 98
"A.E." *see* Russell, George
Against the Crowd (TV series) 160
Akenfield (Ronald Blythe) 158, 161
Albéniz, Isaac 36
Albert, Prince 23, 27
Alfred, King 191
Alma-Tadema, Sir Laurence 140
Amis, Kingsley 68
Anderson, William 68
Andrews, Barry 121
Andrews, Dana *181*
Angus Og (John Duncan) 93
Antonioni, Michelangelo 71
Apollon musagète (Stravinsky) 133
Appia, Adolphe 18, 78
The Arcadians (Lionel Monckton) 104, 129
Arminius 11
Arnold, Matthew 34–35, 45, 76, 81, 109, 117, 121, 123, 129
Arrighi, Nike 117
Artemis '81 (David Rudkin) 193
As You Like It (Shakespeare) 13
The Ash Tree (dir. Laurence Gordon Clarke 1975) 167
"The Ash Tree" (M.R. James) 9, 167
Atwood, Margaret 55–56, 57
Avalon (Rutland Boughton) 37, 39

Baigent, Michael 58
Baker, Phil 118, 173
Baker, Roy Ward 111
"Balder Dead" (Matthew Arnold) 34–35, 45, 81
Bamford, Freda 150
Bandel, Ernst von 11
Banfield, Stephen 134
Banks, Spencer 191, *194*
Bantock, Sir Granville 129–131
The Bard (John Martin) 31
"The Bard" (Thomas Gray) 30
Barrie, Sir James M. 89, 107–111, 118
Bates, Alan 72, *73*
Baudelaire, Charles 98
Bava, Mario 178

Bax, Sir Arnold 71, 87, 90
Beardsley, Aubrey 106, *112*
Beerbohm, Max 48
Benson, E.F. 21, 73, 115, 123–126, 171
Bergman, Ingmar 42, 65, 143
Berlioz, Hector 84
The Birds (dir. Alfred Hitchcock 1963) 102
The Birds of Rhiannon (Joseph Holbrooke) 97
The Birth of Arthur (Rutland Boughton) 37, 38
Birtwhistle, Harrison 66
Blackwood, Algernon 5, 69–70, 119–120
Blair, Janet 162
Blake, William 17, 193
Blavatsky, H.P. 83
The Blessing of Pan (Lord Dunsany) 1, 120–123
Blood on Satan's Claw (dir. Piers Haggard 1971) 1, 6, 60, 120, 121, *122*, 123, 171, 185
Blow Up (dir. Michelangelo Antonioni 1966) 71
Blunt, Wilfrid 27
Blyth, Edmund 16
Blythe, Ronald 158, 160, 161
Böcklin, Arnold 21, 104, 141
Book Four (Aleister Crolwey) 118
Book of Armagh 89
The Book of the Dun Cow 35, 90
Boorman, John 1, 28, 34, 41, 42, *43*, 44, 45, 47, 51
Boorman, Katrine 42
Botticelli, Sandro 40
Boughton, Rutland 36–39, 79, 90, 92, 94, 95
Bradford, Andrew 150
Brahms, Johannes 39
Brandon-Jones, Una 160
Brayton, Lily 77
Brewster, Laurie 102, 103
Briggs, Robin 159, 173, 175
Britten, Benjamin 134
Broadstone of Honour, or Rules for the Gentlemen of England (Kenelm Henry Digby) 25
Brontë, Charlotte 71
Brown, Allen 101
Brückner, Gotthold, and Max 18

211

Buckley, Reginald 37
Bulwer Lytton, Edward 125
"The Burden of Itys" (Oscar Wilde) 137–138
Burke, Edmund 181–182
Burne-Jones, Sir Edward 39–40, 41, 47, 49–50
Burne-Jones, Georgiana 49–50
Burns, Robert 154

Caesar, Julius 100
"Call of the Sidhe" ("A.E.") 90
The Canterbury Tales (Chaucer) 28
Capaldi, Peter 60
Captain Kronos—Vampire Hunter (dir. Brian Clemens 1974) 7
Carlyle, Thomas 39
Caroline, Queen 110
Carr, J. Comyns 40–41, 77
"Casting the Runes" (M.R. James) 180
Celtic Symphony (Granville Bantock) 130
The Celtic Twilight (W.B. Yeats) 86
Chaffey, Don 138
Chambers, Robert 24
Chaney, Lon 164
The Changes (Peter Dickinson) 20, 121
Charles II, King 8
"Charmides" (Oscar Wilde) 136–137, 143
Chaucer, Geoffrey 28
Chausson, Ernest 36
"Children of Lir" ("A.E.") 90
Children of Lir (John Duncan) 93
Children of the Stones (dir. Peter Graham Scott 1977) 1, 183
Chopin, Frédéric 17
Christensen, Benjamin 178
The Chymical Wedding (Lindsay Clarke) 56–60, 66, 68
Cilento, Diane 98
The City of the Dead (dir. John Llewellyn Moxey 1960) 1, **163**, 164, 169
Clarke, Alan 3, 57, 191, 192, 193, **194**
Clarke, Laurence Gordon 96, 167
Clarke, Lindsay 56–60, 66, 68
Clash of the Titans (dir. Desmond Davis 1981) 2, 138, **139**, 140–143
Clash of the Titans (dir. Louis Leterrier 2010) 141
Clay, Nicholas 43
Cleese, John 41–42
Clemens, Brian 7
Clytie (Lord Leighton) 134, 140
Cohen, Abraham 97
Cold Comfort Farm (Stella Gibbons) 158
Compendium Maleficarum (Francesco Maria Guazzo) **173**, 174
Conan Doyle, Sir Arthur 88
Conjure Wife (Fritz Leiber) 162
Connery, Sean 65
Connolly, Ella **102**
Constable, John 182
"Coole Park and Ballylea" (W.B. Yeats) 85
Cooper, John 1

Corman, Roger 180
Countess Cathleen (W.B. Yeats) 86
"Countess Cathleen in Paradise" (W.B. Yeats) 87
Cowell, Henry 186
Crane, Walter 39
Craven, Hawes 40, 176
Cropper, Anna 150
Cross, Beverley 141
Cross, Cyril 152
Crowley, Aleister 21, 22, 114, 118, 119, 146–150
Cuchulainn (John Duncan) 93
"Cuchulain's Fight with the Sea" (W.B. Yeats) 86
"Cuchullan's Lament" (Granville Bantok) 130
The Curse of Frankenstein (dir. Terence Fisher 1957) 7
Cushing, Peter 7, 65, 143, 144
Cuthberson, Iain 183
The Cyprian Goddess (Granville Bantock) 131

Dadd, Richard 88
Dad's Army TV series 80
Daedalus and Icarus (Lord Leighton) 138
D'Annunzio, Gabrielle 78
Dante Alighieri **14**
Darwin, Sir Charles 23, 24
Davies, Rupert 166
Davis, Desmond 2, 138, **139**
The Day of the Triffids (dir. Ken Hannam) 72
The Day of the Triffids (dir. Steve Sekely 1963) 72
The Day of the Triffids (John Wyndham) 71–72, 120
Debussy, Claude 39, 87, 104
"Defence of Guinevere" (William Morris) 39
Deidrie of the Sorrows (John Duncan) 94
De Keyser, David 51
Delaney, Frank 83
Demonolatry (Nicolas Remy) 174
Depp, Johnny 98
The Devil Rides Out (Dennis Wheatley) **115**, 117–118, 145, 174, 175
The Devil Rides Out (dir. Terence Fisher 1968) 90, 115, **115**
The Devils (dir. Ken Russell 1971) 171
The Devils of Loudon (Aldous Huxley) 171
Diana, Princess of Wales 22
Dickens, Charles 65
Dickinson, Peter 20, 121
Dido and Aeneas (Henry Purcell) 175
Digby, Kenelm Henry 25
Dillaine, Richard 81
Disney, Walt 60, 89
The Divine Adventure ("Fiona Macleod") 91
The Divine Comedy (Dante) 14–15
Dog Soldiers (dir. Neil Marshall 2002) 103
"The Domain of Arnheim" (Edgar Allan Poe) 96

The Dominion of Dreams ("Fiona Macleod") 91
Donohoe, Amanda 60
Doré, Gustav *14*, 20, 28, *29*, *31*, 32, 33, 34
Dotrice, Michelle 160
Doyle, Charles 88
Doyle, Richard 88, *190*
Dracula (Bram Stoker) 60, 100, 176
Dracula Has Risen From the Grave (dir. Freddie Francis 1968) *7*, 167
Dracula—Prince of Darkness (dir. Terence Fisher 1966) 7
The Draughtsman's Contract (dir. Peter Greenaway 1982) 71
Dresser, Christopher 60
Driberg, Tom 118
Duncan, John 93–94
Dunsany, Lord 1, 120
Duse, Eleonora 78
Dwyer, Hilary 166

Eaton, Evelyn 24, 146
Eclogue (Gerald Finzi) 134
Edward III, King 24, 146
Elgar (dir. Ken Russell 1962) 194
Elgar, Sir Edward 38, 57, 129, 192, 193
Eliot, George 49
Eliot, T.S. 21, 79, 145
Elizabeth I, Queen 146, 175
Escape into Night TV series 185–186
Eschenbach, Wolfram von 46, 47, 55
Evans-Wentz, Walter 25, 35, 89, 90
The Evergreen (ed. William, Sharp) 93
Ewing, Barbara *7*, 167
Excalibur (dir. John Boorman 1981) 1, 28, 34, 41, 42, *43*, 47, 51
Eye of the Devil (dir. J. Lee Thompson 1967) 1, *2*, 6, 120, 156–157, 158, 162

"Faery Song" (W.B. Yeats) 87
Fairy Enthroned (John Duncan) 93
The Fairy Faith in Celtic Countries (Walter Evans-Wentz) 25
Fairy Mythology (Thomas Keightley) 28, 151–152
The Famous Tragedy of the Queen of Cornwall (Thomas Hardy) 79–80
Farjeon, Sir Harry 109–100, 133
Faust (Goethe) 17
Faust (W.G. Wills) 176
Die Feen (Richard Wagner) 88
Fellowship of the Rosy Cross 55
Ferris, Paul 165
Ffrangcon-Davies, Gwen 90, 160
Finlandia (Jean Sibelius) 17
Finzi, Gerald 134
First Hundred Years of Wagner's Tristan, The (Elliot Zuckerman) 74
First Knight (dir. Jerry Zucker 1995) 44, 81
Fisher, Allen 97
Fisher, Terence 2, 7, 90, 98, *115*, 143
Fitzball, Edward 176

Fitzgerald, John Anster 88
"Flame on the Wind" ("Fiona Macleod") 95
Fleming, Victor 178
Flynn, Errol 67
Fonteyn, Joan 58, 158
Foreman, Lewis 131, 133
Först, Johannes Otto *67*
Forster, E.M. 114, 124
Fortune, Dion 21, 35, 51–52, 126–128
Francis, Freddie *7*, 167
Franco, James 1
Frankel Cyril 1, 160
Frankenstein and the Monster from Hell (dir. Terence Fisher 1974) 98
Franks, Chloe 164
Frazer, Sir James 6, 8, 10–11, 21, 67, 99, 127, 134, 145–156
Der Freischütz (Carl Maria von Weber) 10, 11, 15
From Hell (dir. Allen and Albert Hughes) 98
Fuqua, Antoine 45

Galahad (Rutland Boughton) 37
Gallu, Sam 1, 176, *176*
"The Garden of Eros" (Oscar Wilde) 137
The Garden of Fand (Arnold Bax) 87
Gardiner, Philip 58
Garner, Alan 60, 62, 63, 102, 187
Gaskell, Elizabeth 167–171, *168*
Gawain (Harrison Birtwhistle) 66
Gawain and the Green Knight (dir. Stephen Weeks 1973) 1, 65
Gawayne and the Green Knyghte 64
Geddes, Patrick 93
Geoffrey Paul 43
The Geography of Witchcraft (Montague Summers) 174–175
George I, King 110
George II, King 110
Gere, Richard 45
German, Sir Edward 187–188
Gibbons, Stella 158
Gilliam, Terry 1, 41, 42, 143
A Glastonbury Romance (John Cowper Powys) 51–54
Glover, Julian 178
The Goat-Foot God (Dion Fortune) 21, 35, 52, 126–128
"The God of Ibreez" (Aleister Crowley) 149–150
"God's Funeral" (Thomas Hardy) 23
Goethe, Johann Wolfgang von 8, 41, 84
The Golden Age (Kenneth Grahame) 19
The Golden Bough (Sir James Frazer) 6, 21, 67, 99, 127, 145–149, 151, 153–156
Golden Twigs (Aleister Crowley) 21, 146–150
Gonne, Maud 90
Goodrich-Clarke, Nicholas 189
Goodwin, Ron 65
The Gorgon (dir. Terence Fisher 1964) 2, 143–144

Gosse, Sir Edmund 76
Götterdämmerung (Richard Wagner) 17, 33, 42, 43, 44, 92
Grahame, Kenneth 19, 21, 115, *116*, 119
Graves, Robert 21, 135
Gray, Charles 117
Gray, Thomas 30
The Great God Pan (Arthur Machen) 21, *112*, 113–114
Green, Nigel 65
The Green Helmet (W.B. Yeats) 65
The Green Man (Kingsley Amis) 68
Greenaway, Peter 71
Guazzo, Francesco Maria *173*, 174
Guest, Val 193

Haggard, Piers 1, 6, *122*, 123, 171, 185
Hallam, Arthur 24
Hamlin, Harry 140
Hardy, Robin 1, 8, 98, *99*, *155*, *182*
Hardy, Thomas 23, 79–80, 180
Harker, Joseph 40, 176
Harryhausen, Ray 2, 138, 140, 141, 142, 163
Hathaway, Henry 41
Hawksmoor, Nicholas 97
Häxen (dir. Benjamin Christensen 1921) 178
Hayden, Linda 121, *122*
Hayers, Sidney 1, 162–163, *162*
Head, Murray 65
Head of a Celtic God (John Duncan) 93
"Heart O' Beauty ("Fiona Macleod") 94
Hebridean Symphony (Granville Bantock) 130
Hedley, Jack 164
Hemmings, David 71
Henry VIII, King 12
Henson, Nicky 185
Hepton, Bernard 150
Hermann 11
The Heroes (Charles Kingsley) 141
Herschel, William 132
Hesseltine, Philip 19
The Hill of Dreams (Arthur Machen) 188–189
The History of Witchcraft and Demonology (Montague Summers) 172, 174, 175
Hitchcock, Alfred 102
Hitler, Adolf 164
Hoffmann, Joseph *12*, 18
Hogg, Ian 192
Holbrooke, Jospeh 51, 96
Holst, Gustav 131–132
The Holy Blood and the Holy Grail (Michael Baigent et al) 58
"The Holy Grail" (Tennyson) 46, 49–50
Hopkins, Matthew 166, 169, 175
Horace 130, 131
"The Hosting of the Sidhe" (W.B. Yeats) 88
The House That Dripped Blood (dir. Peter Duffell 1971) 164–165
Housman, A.E. 188
Houston, Donald 142

Hughes, Allen, and Albert 98
Hughes, Thomas 27, 189, *190*
Hurd, Michael 38, 79
Hutchinson, Bishop Francis 175
Huxley, Aldous 171
Huysmans, J.-K. 126
Hyman, Prudence 143
"Hymn to Pan" (Aleister Crowley) 118

I Am Half Sick of Shadows (Sidney Harold Meteyard) 39
I, Claudius (Robert Graves) 135
I, Monster (dir. Stephen Weeks 1971) 65
I Walked with a Zombie (dir. Jacques Tourneur 1943) 70–71
Idylls of the King (Tennyson) 20, 25, 26, 28, *29*, *31*, 46, 108
The Immortal Hour ("Fiona Macleod") 90–93
The Immortal Hour (Rutland Boughton) 90, 92–93, 95
"In Connemara" ("A.E.") 90
In Memoriam (Tennyson) 24
In the Faëry Hills (Arnold Bax) 87
Inchbold, John William 183
Ingres, Jean Auguste Dominique 84
The Inheritor (E.F. Benson) 21, 115, 123–126
Irving, Sir Henry 17, 40–41, 77, 176
Irving, Laurence 40
Isle of the Dead (Arnold Böcklin) 141
It's Never Too Late to Mend (Charles Reade) 2

Jack the Ripper 97, 100
James, M.R. 9, 68, 96–97, 180
Jane Eyre (Charlotte Brontë) 71
Jason and the Argonauts (dir. Don Chaffey 1963) 138
"Jerusalem" (William Blake) 17, 20, 193
Jessel, Patricia 169
"John Barleycorn" (Robert Burns) 154
Johnston, Margaret 162
Jones, Darby 71
Jones, Terry 1, 41, 42, 143
Jowett, Benjamin 48
Jung, Carl Gustav 36, 55–56, 164, 186
The Jungle Book (dir. Wolfgang Reitherman 1968) 60
Just-So Songbook (Rudyard Kipling and Edward German) 187–188

The Kalevala 87
Karloff, Boris 23
Keating, David 1, *102*
Keats, John 116–117
Keightley, Thomas 28, 151
Kemplay, John 93
Kennedy, Michael 134
Kennedy-Fraser, Marjory 130
"Kensington Gardens" (Thomas Tickell) 110–111
Kerr, Deborah 156

Khnopff, Fernand 36
King Arthur (dir. Antoine Fuqua 2004) 45
King Arthur (J. Comyns Carr) 40–41, 77
King Arthur—Legend of the Sword (dir. Guy Ritchie 2014) 45
"King Arthur's Tomb" (William Morris) 39
The King Is a Witch (Evelyn Eaton) 24, 146
The King Must Die (Mary Renault) 134–135
"The King of the Wood" (Aleister Crowley) 147–148
Kingsley, Charles 141, 143
Kipling, Rudyard 187
Kneale, Nigel 1, 111, 158, 160–161, 183
Knights of the Round Table (dir. Richard Thorpe 1954) 41
Kramer, Heinrich 174
Kullervo Symphony (Jean Sibelius) 87
"Das Kunstwerk der Zukunft" (Richard Wagner) 81–82

Lacey, Ronald 65
Lady Chatterley's Lover (D.H. Lawrence) 106, 114
"The Lady of Shalott" (Tennyson) 39
The Lair of the White Worm (Bram Stoker) 58–60
The Lair of the White Worm (Ken Russell 1988) 60
"The Lake Isle of Innisfree" (W.B. Yeats) 87
Lamont, Duncan 160
A Lancashire Witches, A Romance of Pendle Forest (Edward Fitzball) 176
The Lancashire Witches and Teague o Divelly, the Irish Priest (Thomas Shadwell) 175
The Land of Heart's Desire (W.B. Yeats) 86
"Landor's Cottage" (Edgar Allan Poe) 96
Lang, Fritz 43
Lang, Matheson 77
The Lark Ascending (Ralph Vaughan Williams) 19
Larkin, Mary 185
The Last Sleep of Arthur in Avalon (Sir Edward Burne-Jones) 40
Laurie, John 80
Lawrence, D.H. 72–73, 106, 146–147
Lee, Bernard 160
Lee, Sir Christopher 7, *99*, 143, 164, 165, 176, 178
Le Fanu, Sheridan 9, 10
Leiber, Fritz 162
Leigh, Richard 58
Leighton Frederic, Lord 134, 138, 143
Le Sueur, Jean-François 84
Leterrier, Louis 141
Lévi, Éliphas 117
Lewis, C.S. 13, 54
"Ligeia" (Edgar Allan Poe) 102
The Lily Maid (Rutland Boughton) 37
Lincoln, Henry 58
"Lines Written in Kensington Gardens" (Matthew Arnold) 109

The Lion, the Witch and the Wardrobe (C.S. Lewis) 13
List, Guido von 189
Liszt, Franz 49
The Little White Bird (J.M. Barrie) 107
Llewelyn Davies, Arthur 110
Llewelyn Davies, Peter 110
Lohengrin (Richard Wagner) 36, 50
Lois the Witch (Elizabeth Gaskell) 167–171, **168**
The London Adventure—or The Art of Wandering (Arthur Machen) 98, 190
The Longest Journey (E.M. Forster) 114
Loomis, Roger Sherman 48
Lord of Tears (dir. Laurie Brewster 2013) 102–103
The Lord of the Rings (J.R.R. Tolkien) 13, 68, 92
"The Lotus Eaters" (Tennyson) 132–133
Lotus Land (Cyril Scott) 132
Lowes, John 175
Loyola 127
Lud Heat (Iain Sinclair) 97, 98
Ludwig II, King 32, 38, 45, 83

Maas, Jeremy 88
Mabinogion 61
Macbain, Alexander 16, 97, 101
Macbeth (Shakespeare) 77, 176
MacDonald, George 8, 13
MacGinnis, Niall 150
Machen, Arthur 21, 98, **112**, 118, 119, 188, 190
Mackenzie, Michael 113
"Macleod, Fiona," 20, 90, 91, 92, 94–96, 103, 104–105
Maclise, Daniel 39, 88
MacPherson, James 84, 85
MacTaggart, James 1, 150, 151, **152**, 161
Madden, Ciaran 65
Maeterlinck, Maurice 91
The Magician (dir. Rex Ingram 1926) 115
The Magician (W. Somerset Maugham) 114–115
Magick in Theory and Practice (Aleister Crowley) 118
Malleus Maleficarum (Heinrich Kramer and Jacob Sprenger) 174
Malory, Sir Thomas 44, 47
"The Man Who Dreamed of Faeryland" (W.B. Yeats) 87
"The Man Whom the Trees Loved" (Algernon Blackwood) 5, 69, 120
Mann, Thomas 104
Marianne Dreams (Catherine Storr) 69, 185–186
Marius the Epicurean (Walter Pater) 135, 140
Marsden, Simon 184
Marshall, Neil 103
Martin, Jennifer 98
Martin, John 31
Marx, Karl 48

216 Index

Maschera del Demonio (dir. Mario Bava 1960) 178
Masefield, John 80
"The Mass of Saint Sécaire" (Aleister Crowley) 148
Maugham, W. Somerset 104, 114
Maurice (E.M. Forster) 124
McCowen, Alec 58, 159
"The Meddlers" (dir. John Russell 1972) 111, 113
Melancholia (dir. Lars von Trier 2011) 74
La Mer (Debussy) 87
Merlin (Isaac Albéniz) 37
Merlin and the Fairy Queen (John Duncan) 93
"Merrow Down" (Rudyard Kipling) 187
The Merry Wives of Windsor (Shakespeare) 13
Metamorphoses (Ovid) 140, 141
Meteyard, Sidney Harold 39
Meyerbeer, Giacomo 176
A Midsummer Night's Dream (Shakespeare) 67, 88, 89, 151
Mills, John 183
Mirbeau, Octave 19
Mirren, Dame Helen 44
Monckton, Lionel 104
Money-Coutts, Francis Burdett 37
Montgomery, Archibald 25
Monty Python and the Holy Grail (dir. Terry Jones and Terry Gilliam 1975) 1, 41–42, 65, 143
The Moon of Gomrath (Alan Garner) 187
Moonchild (Aleister Crowley) 118
Moore, George 135
Morienus, Romanus 47, 56
Morris, William 39, 48, 49, 50
"Morte d'Arthur" (Tennyson) 25–26
Morte d'Arthur (Sir Thomas Malory) 47
Mortimer, Roger, Earl of March 146
The Mountain Lovers ("Fiona Macleod") 95
Mower, Patrick 117
Moxey, John Llewellyn 1, *163*
Munro, H.H. 119
Murrain (dir. John Cooper 1975) 1, 160–161
"Music on the Hill" (H.H. Munro) 119
Myles, Sophie 1, *75*
Mystic Dance of the Grail (Rutland Boughton) 38

Neptune (Cyril Scott) 133
Die Nibelungen (dir. Fritz Lang 1924) 43
Nibelungenlied 36
Nicholls, Mary Ann 97
Nietzsche, Friedrich 23, 25, 104
Night of the Demon (dir. Jacques Tourneur 1957) 149–150, 180, *181*
Night of the Eagle (dir. Sydney Hayers 1962) 1, 158, 162–163, *162*
Niven, David *2*, 6, 120, 156
November Woods (Arnold Bax) 87
Number Thirteen (dir. Pier Wilkie 2006) 68

"Number Thirteen" (M.R. James) 68
The Nutcracker (Tchaikovsky) 131

O'Curry, Eugene 89
"Ode to a Nightingale" (Keats) 116–117
Ogilvie, Ian 166
"The Old Man of the Peepul Tree" (Aleister Crowley) 148
Olivier, Sir Laurence 2
"On Behalf of Some Irishmen Not Followers of Tradition" ("A.E.") 91
"On Murder Considered as One of the Fine Arts" (Thomas de Quincey) 97
"The Oracle of the Corycian Cave" (Aleister Crowley) 149
The Order of the Golden Dawn 21, 83, 119
Orenburg, Catherine 60
The Origin of Species (Charles Darwin) 24
Oscar and Malvina (William Shield/William Reeve) 84
Ossian 84–85
Ossian—ou Les bardes (Jean-François Le Suer) 84
Ovid 140, 141, 142, 143
The Owl Service (Alan Garner) 60–63, 102
The Owl Service (prod. Peter Plummer 1969–1970) 1, 60–63

Padbury, Wendy *122*
Pagan Poem (Graville Bantock) 131
Pagan Symphony (Granville Bantock) 130–131
Palin, Michael 41
"Pan" (Oscar Wilde) 136
Pan's Garden (Algernon Blackwood) 120
Paperhouse (dir. Bernard Rose 1988) 186
Parry, Sir Hubert 17
Parsifal (dir. Hans Jürgen Syberberg 1982) 47
Parsifal (Richard Wagner) 36, 46, 47, 49, 50, 51, 56, 62, 68, 77
Parzival and the Stone from Heaven (Lindsay Clarke) 56
Pasco, Richard 144
"Pastoral" Symphony (Ralph Vaughan Williams) 19, 134
Pater, Walter 135–136, 140
Patton, Joseph Noel 39, 88
Pears, Peter 134
Pélleas et Mélisande (Maurice Maeterlinck) 91
Penda's Fen (dir. Alan Clarke 1974) 3, 20–21, 57, 167, 191–195, *194*
The Perfect Wagnerite (George Bernard Shaw) 38
Perseus and Andromeda (Lord Leighton) 138, 140, 143
Perseus on Pegasus Hastening to the Rescue Andromeda (Lord Leighton) 140
Peter Pan and Wendy (J.M. Barrie) 107, 108
Peter Pan in Kensington Gardens (J.M. Barrie) 108, 110, 111

Peter Pan, or the Boy Who Wouldn't Grow Up (J.M. Barrie) 107, 111
Peter Pan Sketches (Harry Farjeon) 109–110
Phantastes—A Faerie Romance (George MacDonald) 8, 13
A Philosophical Enquiry Into the Origin of Our Ideas of the Sublime and the Beautiful (Edmund Burke) 181–183
Photographing Fairies (dir. Nick Willing 1997) 3, 9, 88
Pictures from Greece (Harry Farjeon) 133
Planché, J.R. 84
The Planets (Gustav Holst) 131–132
Plummer, Peter 1
Poe, Edgar Allan 17, 96, 98, 102
Polidori, John 84
Pope, Alexander 89
Porter, Nyree Dawn 165
Powys, John Cowper 51–54
Pratt, Vic 151
Price, Vincent 166, *166*, 181
Prince Valiant (dir. Henry Hathaway 1954) 41
Psycho (dir. Alfred Hitchcock 1960) 102
Psychomania (dir. Don Sharp 1971) 184–185, *184*
Purcell, Henry 175

Quatermass and the Pit (dir. Roy Ward Baker 1967) 111
Quatermass 2 (dir. Val Guest 1957) 193
Quincey, Thomas de 97

Rackham, Arthur 108, 110
Rackham, Barbara 110
Radcliffe, Ann 9, 10, 17
The Rape of the Lock (Alexander Pope) 89
Ravel, Maurice 104
"Ravenna" (Oscar Wilde) 105–106, 136
Raven's Brood (E.F. Benson) 73, 171
Reade, Charles 1
Red Shift (Alan Garner) 187
Red Shift (TV series) 187
Redgrave, Vanessa 71
Rees, Yvette 164
Reeve, William 84
Reeves, Michael 1, 165, *165*, 167, *166*, 175
Reid, Beryl 185
Remy, Nicolas 174
Renault, Mary 21, 134–135
Reynolds, Kevin 1, 74, *75*, 81, 82
Das Rheingold (Richard Wagner) 17, 30, 33
The Riders of the Sidhe (John Duncan) 93–94
Der Ring des Nibelungen (Richard Wagner) 8, 11, 17, 18, 25, 30, 34, 36, 37, 68, 130, 146
The Rings of Saturn (W.S. Sebald) 190
Ritchie, Guy 45
The Rite of Spring (Stravinsky) 133
Robert le diable (Giacomo Meyerbeer) 176
Robertson, Gavin 103
Robin Redbreast (dir. James MacTaggart 1970) 1, 150–153, *152*, 161

Robinson, Bernard 143
Robson, Dame Flora 3, 157
Le roi d'Arthur (Ernest Chausson) 36
Romeo and Juliet (Shakespeare) 89, 164
The Rose (W.B. Yeats) 86
"The Rose of the World" (W.B. Yeats) 94
Rosenthal, Laurence 143
Rossetti, Dante Gabriel 47–48
The Round Table (Rutland Boughton) 37, 38, 39
Rousseau, Henri 13
Rowling, J.K. 13
Rudkin, David 3, 20, 57, 167, 191, 192, 193
Ruskin, John 182
Russell, George 90, 93, 94
Russell, John 111
Russell, Ken 60, 72, *73*, 171, 193
Russell, Robert 166

St. Bride (John Duncan) 93
"Saki," *see* H.H. Munro
Sanders, George 184
Sandys Frederick 39
Sangster, Thomas 81
Sapphic Poem (Granville Bantok) 131
Sappho (Granville Bantock) 131
Savile, Jimmy 22
"The Scholar Gypsy" (Matthew Arnold) 117, 121, 123
Scott, Cyril 132–133
Scott, Giles Gilbert 16
Scott, Peter Graham 1
Scott, Sir Walter 25, 84
The Scouring of the White Horse (Thomas Hughes) 189–191, *190*
Sebald, W.S. 98, 190
Second Battle of Moytura 48
The Seventh Seal (dir. Ingmar Bergman 1957) 143
Shadwell, Thomas 175
Shaffer, Anthony 98
Shakespeare, William 8, 13, 67, 77, 88, 89, 151, 164
Sharp, Don 1, 164, 184, *184*, 185
Sharp, Elizabeth 91
Sharp, William 20, 90, 91, 93, *95*
Shaw, George Bernard 37–38, 41, 142
Shelley, Barbara 143
Shelley, Percy Bysshe 23
Shepherd, Elizabeth 181
Shield, William 84
Shishkin, Ivan 16
A Shropshire Lad (A.E. Housman) 188
Sibelius, Jean 17, 71, 86–87, 131
Siegfried (Richard Wagner) 11, *12*, 15, 17, 43
Simeon, David 161
Sinclair, Iain 97, 98, 110
"Sir Galahad, a Christmas Mystery" (William Morris) 48
Six Metamorphoses After Ovid (Benjamin Britten) 134

Smith, Dame Maggie 2, 142
"Song of Wandering Aengus" (W.B. Yeats) 87
Songs of the Hebrides (Marjory Kennedy-Fraser) 130
The Sorrows of Werther (Goethe) 84
Spall, Timothy 101
Sprenger, Jacob 174
Spring Fire (Arnold Bax) 87
Staines, Geoffrey *194*
Star Wars (dir. George Lucas 1977) 45
Steiner, George 101
Stoker, Bram 58–60, 100, 176
"The Stolen Child" (W.B. Yeats) 108
"The Stone of Cybele" (Aleister Crowley) 149
Storr, Catherine 69
A Strange Story (Edward Bulwer Lytton) 125
Strauss, Richard 129, 130, 143
Stravinsky, Igor 133
Stuck, Franz von 21, 104, *107*
A Suggestive Enquiry into the Hermetic Mystery (Margaret Atwood) 55–56
Sullivan, Sir Arthur 40–41
Summers, Montague 172–176, *173*
Sunters, Irene 98
Survivors (TV series) 121
Swift, Jonathan 110
Swinburne, Algernon Charles 76
Sword of the Valiant (dir. Stephen Weeks 1984) 65
Symons, Arthur 78

The Taking of Excalibur (John Duncan) 94
The Tale the Pine-Trees Knew (Arnold Bax) 71
Tallis, Thomas 19
Tapiola (Jean Sibelius) 71
Tarasti, Eero 130
Tchaikovsky, Pyotr 131
Tennyson, Alfred, Lord 20, 24–36, *29*, 39, 44, 46, 47, 48, 50, 92, 108, 183
Terry, Ellen 77
Terry, Nigel 43
Tess of the d'Ubervilles (Thomas Hardy) 180
Theatre of Death (dir. Sam Gallu 1967) 1, 176–178, *176*
Theosophical Society 83
Third Symphony (Cyril Scott) 133
Thompson, J. Lee 1, *2*, 120
Thorpe, Richard 41
Tickell, Thomas 110
Tingwell, Charles 7
Tintagel (Arnold Bax) 87
"To Ireland in the Coming Times" (W.B. Yeats) 94
To the Devil a Daughter (Dennis Wheatley) 172
Tolkien, J.R.R. 5, 13, 54, 68, 92
Tom Brown's Schooldays (Thomas Hughes) 27, 189

The Tomb of Ligeia (dir. Roger Corman 1964) 180–181
Torture Garden (dir. Freddie Francis 1968) 167
Torture Garden (Octave Mirbeau) 19
"The Touch of Pan" (Algernon Blackwood) 119–120
Tourneur, Jacques 70, 150, 180, *181*
Tragic Landscapes ("Fiona Macleod") 95
Trier, Lars von 74
Tristan and Iseult (Arthur Symons) 78–79
Tristan and Isolde (dir. Kevin Reynolds 2006) 1, 74, *75*, 81–82
Tristan and Isolde (John Duncan) 93
Tristan and Isolt (John Masefield) 80
Tristan und Isolde (Richard Wagner) 36, 74, 76, 77, 79, 80, 81
Tristram and Iseult (J. Comyns Carr) 77–78
"Tristram and Iseult" (Matthew Arnold) 76
Tristram of Lyonesse (Algernon Charles Swinburne) 76–77
Turner, J.M.W. 182, 183

The Vampire (J.R. Planché) 84
Vampire Circus (dir. Robert Young 1972) 7
"The Vampyre" (John Polidori) 84
Varius 11
Vaughan Williams, Ralph 19, 134, 188
Venus and Tannhäuser (Aubrey Beardsley) 106
Vestiges of the Natural History of Creation (Robert Chambers) 24
Victoria, Queen 23, 28
Virgil 134

Wagner, Cosima 18, 27–28, 49–50
Wagner, Richard 1, 8, 11, *12*, 15, 17–18, 25, 27–28, 30, 33, 34, 36, 37, 38, 43, 46, 47, 49–50, 56, 62, 68, 74, 76, 77, 79, 80, 81, 82, 83, 88, 92, 129, 130, 142, 146, 148
Waite, A.E. 55
Wakewood (dir. David Keating 2010) 1, 21, 101–102
Die Walküre (Richard Wagner) 17, 33, 34, 149
Wallasvaara, Markus 100
Walsh, Kay 159
"Wanderings of Oisin" (W.B. Yeats) 85–86
War in Heaven (Charles Williams) 54–55
A Warning to the Curious (dir. Laurence Gordon Clarke 1972) 96
"A Warning to the Curious" (M.R. James) 96–97
The Wasteland (T.S. Eliot) 21, 79, 145, 146
Watts, G.F. 27
Weber, Carl Maria von 10, 11
Weeks, Stephen 1, 65–66
Wegener, Paul 115
Wesendonck, Mathilde 74
Wheatley, Dennis *115*, 117–118, 145, 172, 174, 178
Where the Forests Murmer ("Fiona Macleod") 91, 95–96

Whitaker, David 184
The Wicker Man (dir. Robin Hardy 1973) 1, 8, 20, 21, 28, 34, 44, 50, 68, 85–86, 98–101, *99*, 102, 123, 142, 153–156, *155*, 158, 161, 171, *182*, 183, 185, 194
Wilde, Oscar 84, 105, 136–138, 143
Wilkie, Pier 68
Williams, Charles 54–55
Williamson, Nicol 42
Willing, Nick 3, 88
"The Willows" (Algernon Blackwood) 68, 70
Wills, W.G. 176
The Wind Among the Reeds (W.B. Yeats) 87
The Wind in the Willows (Kenneth Grahame) 21, 115–117, *116*, 118, 124, 128, 133
Winstone, Ray 45
Witchcraft (dir. Don Sharp 1964) 1, 164
The Witches (dir. Cyril Frankel 1966) 1, 21, 58, 90, 120, 150, 158–160, 161, 162, 164
Witches and Neighbours (Robin Briggs) 173

Witchfinder General (dir. Michael Reeves 1968) 1, 165–167, *165*, *166*, 175
Wizard of Oz (dir. Victor Fleming 1939) 178
Women in Love (D.H. Lawrence) 72
Women in Love (dir. Ken Russell 1969) 72, *73*
Woodwood, Edward 86, *155*, 156
Worth, John 184
Wymark, Patrick 123
Wyndham, John 71–72, 120
Wyngarde, Peter 162, *162*
The Wyvern Mystery (Sheridan Le Fanu) 9

Yeats, W.B. 20, 65, 83, 85–88, 90, 91, 93, 94, 108
Young, Robert 7
Young Apollo (Benjamin Britten) 134

Zucker, Jerry 45, 81
Zuckerman, Elliot 74

www.ingramcontent.com/pod-product-compliance
Ingram Content Group UK Ltd.
Pitfield, Milton Keynes, MK11 3LW, UK
UKHW041954140426
5217IPUK00015B/788